FACING THE FUTURE

John I. Goodlad

FACING THE FUTURE

Issues in Education and Schooling

Introduction by Ralph W. Tyler
Papers selected and edited
by Judith S. Golub

McGraw-Hill Book Company

New York   St. Louis   San Francisco
Auckland Bogota Düsseldorf London Madrid Mexico Montreal
New Delhi Panama Paris São Paulo Singapore Sydney Tokyo Toronto

Library of Congress Cataloging in Publication Data
Goodlad, John I

    Facing the future.

    Bibliography: p.
    Includes index.
    CONTENTS: Schooling today.—The challenge.—Setting goals for education programs. [etc.]
    1. Educational innovations—United States.
I. Title.
LA217.G65   370'.973   76-25985

ISBN 0-07-023764-6
ISBN 0-07-023766-2 pbk.

1 2 3 4 5 6 7 8 9 BPBP 7 0 9 8 7 6

This book was set in Laurel by Rumford Press, Inc.
It was printed and bound by Book Press. The editors
were Thomas Quinn and Michael Hennelly. The designer
was Marcy J. Katz. Audre Hanneman edited the index.
Milton J. Heiberg supervised the production.

Contents

Editor's Preface

The papers collected in this volume represent the approximately ten years of John I. Goodlad's thought and research since the appearance of his previous collection of papers, *School, Curriculum, and the Individual* (Wiley, 1966). I have tried to select papers to show the range of interests of the multi-faceted mind of a man playing many roles. Dean of a Graduate School of Education at a major university, director of research for an institute devoted to studying and promoting change in education, and participant in many commissions and study groups, his attention has focused on topics ranging from the curriculum of the elementary school, to teacher education, to schooling for mankind.

In spite of this wide range of interests, a central concern with change and preparation for the future has unified and directed his work. That is why I selected the title for this book and arranged the papers under the rubric of issues, for these are issues that are of concern to all those who would improve our schools and make them and the students who attend them better equipped to face an uncertain and sometimes threatening future.

In the last ten years, Goodlad has published nearly 100 books, chapters, and articles, as well as given numerous speeches. It was obviously very difficult to make a selection for this book. Therefore, I proceeded by first determining the issues that had interested him over this time period and then looking for the best discussions of those issues that he had produced. In some cases, this meant including certain papers virtually as they were published originally, in others it meant combining parts of various papers which had discussed the same theme, and in still others it meant including a chapter from a book he had written, even though the book is readily available.

Because most papers included here were originally meant to stand on their own, the same thoughts, ideas, and examples were often repeated in several. For the most part, I have deleted repetition between chapters, but in some cases I felt that the thought or example was important enough to the argument being developed within a chapter that it should be retained, even though it was included elsewhere. All chapters have been revised by Goodlad and/or edited by me to bring them up to date and make them appropriate for inclusion in this book.

I would like to thank Elisabeth Tietz for her efficient and accurate work in preparing the manuscript, and I would like to thank John Goodlad for the opportunity to work on these papers and the learning experience they provided.

Judith S. Golub

Introduction

By assembling and skillfully editing more than a score of the pieces John Goodlad has written in the past ten years, this fascinating book of major importance for educators and parents has been created. It deals with most of the educational problems of our time—overoptimism and disillusionment, rapid expansion and restrictive accountability, unexamined openness and rigid structuring, provincial curriculum outlook and undefined global scope, preoccupation with cognitive learning and unreflective emotional expression, narrowly prescriptive teacher training and aimlessness in programs of teacher education, and the continuing problem of developing public understanding and support for schools and colleges.

I am impressed not only with the scope of Goodlad's knowledge and experience, but even more with the effective way in which he operates in three related but different roles. He demonstrates competence in the role of researcher; collecting, examining, and interpreting information about the realities of education—what goes on in schools and in the educational situations provided by the home and the larger community. Most writers on education have very little information about these realities and mistake their own limited experience and impressions gained from others for the facts about educational activities and outcomes.

Goodlad also presents a view of what education and schooling ought to be that is very attractive, actually inspiring. His utopia seems both sound and comprehensive, and possible of eventual attainment. In this sense, he is authentically prophetic.

Goodlad's knowledge of the realities of education and schooling and his conception of the ideal are joined by his design for progressive improvement and strategy for action. This is shown in his accomplishments as Director of the Research Division of the Institute for the Development of Educational Activities, Inc. (|I|D|E|A|) and his work with the League of Cooperating Schools. He has clearly demonstrated competence as a leader in the practice of education. The combination in one person of the three roles— researcher, prophet, and mover—is very rare indeed.

John Goodlad was born in British Columbia in 1920. He taught and served as principal in elementary schools of the Province before coming to the United States for graduate work, receiving his Ph.D. at the University of Chicago. He served as curriculum coordinator for the Atlanta Area Teacher Education Service, and professor at Emory University, Agnes Scott College, and the University of Chicago before going to the University of California, Los Angeles in 1960 as professor of education and Director of the University Elementary School. He was appointed Dean of the Graduate School of Education in 1967. Concurrently with these positions he has been active in a number of other important educational projects and programs, such as Chairman of the Council on Cooperation in Teacher Education of the American Council on Education, associate of James Conant in his study of the education of teachers, and Director of Research for |I|D|E|A|.

All these activities have given Goodlad opportunities for thought and action; they have not been passively experienced. As a result, his statements reflect wisdom rather than conventional clichés. From these experiences have come the substance of this book and its timeliness and authenticity.

This brief outline of his professional career does not indicate what his friends all know—that John Goodlad is a vital, vigorous, sensitive, and attractive human being. His development as a person has accompanied his continuing evolution as a professional. I have known him for thirty years, and in every contact I have been invariably impressed with his human characteristics. He cares about others, easily senses their feelings as well as their ideas, and responds warmly. There are no barriers in communicating with him, no need to spend extra time in getting his attention, nor apologizing for one's own awkwardness of expression. These human qualities contribute greatly to his quick understanding of the needs, interests, and concerns of the people with whom he comes in contact. His writing reveals his deep apprehension of the covert factors in human institutions and associations. His comments on them are not superficial.

The range of subjects with which this book deals is indicated by the following examples: Bringing about significant changes in schools; What educational decisions must be made and by whom?; Curriculum reform; Program development; Equality of educational opportunity; Desegregating integrated schools; Alternatives in schooling; Nongrading, team teaching, and continuous progress; Early childhood education; Reconstruction of teacher education; Perspective on accountability; and The school I'd like to see. These topics cover important issues of concern both to educators and to responsible citizens. They are treated thoughtfully and wisely. My reading of the book was amply rewarded by the wealth of significant ideas I gained.

Ralph W. Tyler
Senior Consultant
Science Research Associates, Inc.

Restructuring the School for Our Society

The four chapters of Part I set out some of Goodlad's assumptions about schooling and raise important basic issues about our educational institutions. Chapters 1 and 2 place these assumptions and issues in historical perspective, first looking at the recent past with its frenetic reform movements and resulting disillusionment, and then placing the contemporary scene within the context of the more than 200 years of development of the American system.

Chapters 3 and 4 discuss two basic issues. Chapter 3 deals with setting goals for schooling and Chapter 4 discusses levels of decision making and who should properly make what decisions. The papers on which these chapters are based were written either during or shortly after the completion of a project Goodlad directed, called the Study of Educational Change and School Improvement which involved interacting with eighteen schools in their day-to-day activities. The ideas expressed thus reflect contact with the real world of schools and the everyday lives of those involved in them.

Schooling Today

Before beginning a discussion of present realities or a projection of future probabilities, it is useful to make known first the assumptions and values that the writer carries with him. My views about the present condition of our schools and what should be done to improve them are influenced by four basic assumptions.

First, it is extremely difficult to predict the kinds of behavior that will be most useful for shaping and living in tomorrow's world and which, therefore, should be cultivated today in boys and girls. We know that the problems of the four P's—poverty, population, pollution, and attaining peace—will be with us to 1990 and far beyond.[1] But we know little about their implications for educational ends and means. The futility of preparing people to fill predetermined slots in our society is becoming increasingly clear, however. We can be reasonably confident, too, that the significance of jobs as such will decline in relation to the significance of important human work and

SOURCE: John I. Goodlad (with others), "Instruction," in *Citizens for the 21st Century: Long-Range Considerations for California Elementary and Secondary Education*, a report from the State Committee on Public Education of the California State Board of Education, Sacramento, 1969, pp. 443–485; John I. Goodlad, "Schooling and Education," in Otto Bird (ed.), *The Great Ideas Today*, Encyclopaedia Britannica, Chicago, 1969, pp. 101–145; and John I. Goodlad, "Catalyst Schools," ninth annual Grady Gammage Lecture, Arizona State University, February 9, 1970.

that education as an end in itself will steadily increase in signifi-cance.[2] The implication here appears to be that individual human talent must be developed as an end in itself through processes of life-long learning.

Second, the self-renewing individual probably will require profi-ciency in a talent developed for its own rather than any overtly utilitarian sake and the breadth to cope with the vast array of diverse problems and pressures inherent in modern life.[3] The school must counter the twin evils of perpetuating a narrow range of approved expectancies and of encapsulating the individual within the narrow confines of specialization.[4] To be effective, then, the curriculum must encompass a broad range of human pursuits and provide an appropriate interplay between general and special education.

Third, if we value mankind at all, we always must be preoccupied with developing individuals who possess a sense of being, identity, and worth. Self-doubt and alienation from others are perennial human ills that show no sign of lessening in modern society. Change, automation, and rapid obsolescence of values and things compound the search for identity. Clearly, from the beginning, boys and girls in our schools must assume (and this means have the opportunity to assume) responsibility for their own education. Certainly no one else can, although many other persons seem to think that they can. School must not be a struggle or even a dialogue between those who know (teachers) and those who don't (students).

Fourth, it is no longer simply difficult to select and package for instruction those few most important bits and pieces of knowledge; it is impossible.[5] There is now too much knowledge. Coverage of a few specified topics from September to June is futile. Teaching as telling must rate low in any hierarchy of instructional significance. The school program must emphasize fundamental concepts and modes of inquiry; in effect, it must promote learning how to learn. It must provide many opportunities to explore, to try, to test, to inquire, and to discover for one's self.[6]

For me, any proposals for the future of schooling must be weighed in light of these assumptions. We have reached a major turning point in our history, and the schools must change as society does. This chapter attempts to set the stage for discussion of possible directions for change by tracing a history of the recent past and sketching briefly a picture of schools as they exist today.

THE RECENT PAST

For the United States, the years from 1957–1967 constituted the Education Decade. There may be education decades again, but it is unlikely that there will be another quite like this one. It began with Sputnik and the charge to education to win the Cold War. It ended with a hot war and the growing realization that education is a long-term answer to mankind's problems and must not be confused with social engineering. The danger now is that we are becoming disillusioned with education, without realizing that we are only beginning to try it.

The years from 1957–1967 could be described more accurately, perhaps, as the Schooling Decade. The school years were extended upward and downward. The school curriculum was revised from top to bottom; the school was poked and probed at all levels and from every possible perspective; the Elementary and Secondary Education Act of 1965 brought the federal government into schooling as never before; dropout and alienation from school became prime topics for social science research; the schools became both a focal point for social protest and a vehicle for social reform; schooling joined politics and world affairs as leading topics of social discourse. "Innovation" and "revolution" were used interchangeably and indiscriminately in discussing the changes proposed for or taking place in the schools.

The years following the Education Decade witnessed a settling down from the reform ferment of the 1957–1967 period. War drained off funds needed to finance early educational commitments of the Great Society and denied funds to the later commitments. But at the same time, educational problems of the cities had never been so glaringly apparent nor seemed so far from solution. The specter of teacher militancy and the potentially explosive issue of decentralization of control joined the ferment. And the words desegregation, integration, and busing polarized society. The schools are in the middle.

Perhaps the most disquieting element of all today is uncertainty about the place of education and the role of the schools in a society that can put men on the moon but cannot solve the problems of poverty, pollution, and war. In launching his administration, President Johnson pointed out that, if one probes deeply enough, one finds education at the heart of every problem. In a sense he was right, for in the long run, no doubt, education is the answer to mankind's problems. For the short haul, however, social engineering is the more likely answer to overpopulation, hunger, joblessness, and human misery. This is especially true in times of revolution—and we are in a great revolution of the human spirit. Enlightened social engineering is the answer to men's problems; the times demand it. Enlightened education is the answer to mankind's problems; the future depends on it.

Education is a never-ending process of developing characteristic ways of thinking and behaving on the part of individuals, nations, and, in fact, mankind. Each generation has access to a long heritage from which to derive perspective. Its thinking is shaped by current books, magazines, and newspapers; by movies and television; and by a kaleidoscopic array of events and stimuli which are part of everyday life. Schooling—elementary, secondary, and higher— constitutes the most planned and ordered but not necessarily the most influential part of the process.

The Education Decade: A Brief Overview

World War II and its aftermath brought visible disillusionment with the two preceding decades of American schooling. During these decades, the leaders of so-called Progressive Education had proposed a much broader role for the schools than the teaching of reading, writing, and arithmetic. They decried narrow formalism, proposing that the schools "teach the whole child" and that the pressing social issues of the time become the subject matter of instruction. Two books of the late twenties and early thirties probably represent the characteristic progressive statement of the period. The first (1928) emphasized self-expression[7]; the second (1933) called for a school close to life, a school program which had "definite reference to the needs and issues which mark and divide our domestic, economic, and political life in the generation of which we are a part."[8]

But, as Lawrence Cremin so insightfully points out, "there are [in these books] pitifully few specific leads regarding curriculum, methods, and organization, the day-by-day concerns that so condition the life of any school."[9] The teachers, imbued with heady ideas of the power of education, somehow were to reform the schools. There were no new intensive pedagogical retraining programs for these teachers, no packages of new teaching materials, only a handful of experimental schools to provide models and precious little educational science. Progressive Education was more of the mind than of the classroom.

Reading, writing, and arithmetic went on in the schools, much as they had gone on traditionally. This was part of the trouble. Their content and their teaching needed to be updated, and other subjects needed fresh attention. By the beginning of World War II, the teaching of foreign languages had virtually disappeared from most schools. Military testing programs revealed widespread academic deficiencies among high school graduates, particularly in mathematics and the sciences. By the early 1950s, the varied voices of criticism were in full cry: Schools are neglecting the fundamentals; life adjustment education has been too long in the saddle; Johnny can't read; and—how aging progressivists must have squirmed—the schools repress creativity and individuality.

The period from 1949 to 1955 marks the end of one era and the beginning of another. Telling criticisms of contemporary American education by Bernard Iddings Bell and Mortimer Smith in 1949[10] were followed by those of Albert Lynd, Arthur Bestor, Robert Hutchins, and Paul Woodring in 1953.[11] All were penetratingly critical of progressive education. In 1955, Rudolf Flesch blistered the approach to reading in the schools that had predominated for three decades.[12] Quietly, in 1955, the Progressive Education Association closed its doors.

If I were to pick just one pivotal year to mark the close of what had been and the emergence of what was to be, this year would be 1951. In 1951, Willard Goslin, the widely respected progressive school superintendent, was forced out of Pasadena, a showplace of modern pedagogy, by a coalition of citizens opposed to school taxes and progressive education.[13] In 1951, the First Commission on Life Adjustment Education for Youth reiterated most of the well-known phrases of the progressive education movement in its report and brought down a torrent of criticism.[14] In 1951, the University of Illinois Committee on School Mathematics launched the first of what were to be several nationwide projects in "the new math," a restructuring of school mathematics which seems to have had its genesis at the University of Chicago in the mid-1940s.[15] The subject disciplines were soon to return to center stage in a sweeping reform of the school curriculum.

Change, by definition, is away from what exists. The conservative period in American education following World War II was *against* what was perceived to have existed before and *for* what progressive education had eschewed. But this conservatism was not very relevant to the 1950s; nor was it very understandable or salient to a mobile generation of young, ambitious parents looking to a new future. The world had changed—changed profoundly.

Sputnik was symbolic and catalytic. It was symbolic of the fact that an explosion of knowledge was rivaled only by an explosion of the human spirit. It was catalytic in that the instant orgy of condemnation of the schools and of self-condemnation by educators was followed quickly by plans for action on a broken front of educational reform. Education and the schools became linked with integration of the races, the eradication of crime and poverty, health, prosperity, and peace for all mankind. We narrowed our educational expectations for a few years, back there in the early 1950s. But in the Education Decade that followed the demise of progressive education, we outdid that optimistic movement in our expectations for what education—and by that we meant the schools—could and, indeed, should do.

Because Sputnik was so catalytic—and its impact must not be underestimated—this awesome triumph of man often is viewed as marking the death of progressive education and the birth of a new educational era. Preceding paragraphs reveal, however, that progressive education already had been laid to rest and that fresh educational thrusts already were well begun. The orbiting man-made satellite vastly accelerated these thrusts. Education became a national and federal concern. The National Science Foundation (created in 1950) served as the agency for financing large-scale curricular revisions in mathematics and the natural sciences, beginning in the high schools and soon extending downward into the elementary schools. Education in the nation's interest became the name of the game.

Though the guiding slogan became, "Education is too important to be left to the educators," this is misleading. Power merely shifted from one group of educators to another. Scientists, especially physicists, suddenly were revered. A physicist at Massachusetts Institute of Technology, Jerrold Zacharias, brought together scientists and selected classroom teachers in a new pattern of curriculum building. Other scientists, generously financed by the National

Science Foundation, followed the pattern, adding their own variations. Soon, there was a new alphabet soup of American schooling and versions for export: the products of the Physical Sciences Study Committee (PSSC), the School Mathematics Study Group (SMSG), the Biological Sciences Curriculum Study (BSCS), the Chemical Bond Approach Project (CBA), the Chemical Education Materials Study (CHEM), and more.

This first round of school curriculum reform in the Education Decade, extending from the late 1950s into the 1960s, was a middle- and upper-middle-class affair, primarily embracing college-bound students. The anticipated economic collapse, predicted ominously and frequently, had not materialized. An expanding, prosperous middle class of ambitious young men and women saw education as the means to even better things for their children. They turned to their schools—often new schools in new communities, staffed by young teachers and young administrators—with great expectations. These educators responded, reaching out eagerly to become co- workers in the trial use of materials prepared or backed by illustrious scholars in prestigious universities, an association that was not lost on college-conscious parents. The cry of the disadvantaged was as yet only a whisper.

While new communities were springing up, old values were crumbling. Job opportunities took young couples away from familiar haunts to challenges they had not faced before. A new kind of unemployment appeared: unemployment in the midst of plenty because of job obsolescence. Very little was "for sure." People were beginning to realize that a fast-changing culture demanded both adaptability and a rational approach to new problems. The old ways of keeping school would not suffice.

Federal leadership in Washington viewed rapid advances in mathematics, science, and foreign-language teaching, sponsored by the National Science Foundation, as essential to the nation's ulti- mate strength and status in world affairs. But publication of James B. Conant's *Slums and Suburbs* in 1961[16] focused attention on what we should have realized all along: Our inner cities were in dire trouble. To cope with our domestic problems through education, the United States Office of Education came more vigorously into the picture, adding the social sciences and English to the curriculum reform movement and laying plans for across-the-board federal involve- ment in educational change.

The effort for curriculum change in elementary and secondary schools received its momentum from forces and interests lying largely outside the state and local school systems charged legally with responsibility for determining what to teach. The pervasive nature of these forces and interests as well as their financial support make it easy to see why this movement frequently has been labeled "national" and why it was accompanied by the fear of a national curriculum. The total curriculum was influenced by the federal government in that funds were made available more generously for some subjects than for others, resulting in a curricular imbalance. But federal grantors were careful to maintain a "hands off" policy when it came to the production of learning materials. Curriculum makers were free to follow their predilections and produced curricular alternatives at a bewildering rate. If there were similarities in approach from project to project, they were the consequences of imitation and lack of imagination rather than the imposition of restrictions by funding agencies.

But the course of curricular change—and, in fact, educational change in general—was vigorously directed from within, too, by emerging thoughts about and research into knowledge, learning, teaching, and the individual. The book which influenced the new breed of curriculum reformers the most was Bruner's *The Process of Education*.[17] "Structure" (of the disciplines) and "intuition" (in learning) became as central to the jargon of the new era as "the whole child" and "life adjustment" had been to the progressive era. Bruner's phrase, ". . . any subject can be taught effectively in some intellectually honest form to any child at any stage of development,"[18] became an often-quoted justification for "solid fare" in the curriculum to be extended downward to the early years.

Bruner's ideas of "spiraling" in the curriculum go back to Whitehead, who spoke of enriched repetition in successively new contexts, as do his ideas on structure and discovery. But he links up with Dewey, too, in his concern for humanizing knowledge for popularization. Cremin reminds us, however, that Bruner did not take us back to first questions and that it is time to ask Spencerian questions more insistently than ever: What knowledge is of most worth? What priorities in education?[19]

In 1966, my colleagues and I wrote about the extant current curriculum scene.[20] A generation of American youth has now grown up with a diet of what we described then as the new alphabet soup:

BSCS, CBA, ESS, PSSC, SMSG, and so on. From the beginning the movement was directed at teachers and students in the classroom. It did not seek to change the basic structure of American education or the thinking of administrators, although the present curriculum reform wave had profound implications for both. Thousands of teachers attended year-long or summer institutes designed to update their understanding and teaching of academic disciplines. Millions of children and youths brought home assignments in mathematics, for example, that were incomprehensible to their parents. High school students approached biology, chemistry, and physics in ways and with assumptions that appear different from our own experiences as we recall them. The degree and kind of change varied from subject to subject, from school system to school system, and even from school to school within a single system. Although the movement was nationwide, it was by no means national in the sense of being uniformly prescribed from state to state or from school district to school district.

Unfortunately, much of what went on in the Education Decade was more sound and fury than substance. Our studies and observations suggest that this decade of reform has had little impact on the day-to-day life in our schools. The barrage of "new" curricula and "new" methods aimed at the schools made hardly more than surface dents.

THE SCHOOLS TODAY

During the Education Decade, I had the good fortune to participate in several studies which took me into schools and classrooms across the United States.[21] Remember, this was a period of considerable zest and turbulence in education. Reform was in the air. On visiting schools, however, I came to the tentative conclusion that reform might be described better as "in the clouds"—great clouds of educational reform rolling back and forth across the country. It appeared increasingly that very little revitalizing moisture was getting to the parched educational fields below.

In order to test this disturbing hypothesis, I decided to visit a relatively large sample of schools and classrooms in order to document what went on in them. Thanks to a grant from the Ford Foundation, I was able to recruit a staff for these observations. I chose a dozen teachers from University Elementary School at UCLA because I believed that they would be astute observers of the classroom scene and would identify quickly with the procedures and problems of fellow teachers in the schools visited. This team of observers visited 185 classrooms in seventy-nine schools located in thirty-three school districts of seventeen states and the District of Columbia. The results of their observations (recorded in anecdotal form) and of their conversations with teachers and principals were analyzed by a small research staff.[22]

Observations were restricted to the first four years of schooling—kindergarten through the third grade. However, in a subsequent study, we visited seventy-five classrooms in thirty-one school districts, these visits being spread across the full continuum of elementary and secondary education. This additional study was useful in corroborating evidence gathered from the first.

The observation instrument, used by all observers, was designed to make sure both that there would be reasonably consistent kinds of data and that there would be ample opportunity for additional comments pertaining to schools and classroom settings. The research team hoped to be able to draw conclusions regarding the extent to which widely recommended educational reforms actually had been or were being implemented in the schools. We were guided by the question, "If the most frequently discussed and recommended practices for schooling were now implemented, what might constitute a reasonable checklist of expectations?" The following list appeared to us to be reasonable.

First, classroom practices would relate to rather clearly discernible educational objectives which, in turn, would reflect larger schoolwide and systemwide agreement on school function. Second, instruction would be guided by considerable emphasis on "learning how to learn." Third, much of the subject matter employed to teach children how to learn would hold intrinsic appeal for the students. Fourth, "the golden age of instructional materials" would have clearly arrived in classrooms as evidenced by the kind and variety of materials in use. Fifth, the schools would be giving extensive attention to individual differences among students. Sixth, in view of the fact that educational psychology courses are standard in all teacher preparation programs, there would be substantial use of basic principles of learning and instruction. Seventh, there would be a good deal of human interaction in the classroom characterized particularly by free exchange among pupils in small working groups.

Eighth, the classroom framework would be flexible, providing a nongraded type of approach in selecting learning activities and in evaluating pupil progress. Ninth, rich resources from outside the classroom would be brought into the instructional process and classes increasingly would be going outside the school in order to enhance the learning process. Finally, we anticipated that there would be balance in the curriculum, with attention to mathematics, the natural and social sciences, and the arts holding strong positions beside the traditional reading and listening activities of the primary years.

Subsequent analysis of the data revealed that these were anything but reasonable expectations for the schools. In fact, they proved to be quite unreasonable. There was an enormous gap between this set of expectations and actual practices under way in the classrooms. That there was a gap did not surprise us; that it was so large startled us.

Let me briefly summarize our findings. It proved to be exceedingly difficult to determine what teachers were endeavoring to accomplish at any time or in any segment of the program under way. Even in subsequent conversations, the teachers were unable to be explicit about what any lesson or any part of a lesson was designed to do. Conversations with principals did not clarify a set of priorities for the school. Principals simply were unable to identify a sense of direction, to be explicit about changes under way, or to suggest what they would like to do if given the freedom and resources to push toward preferred ends. Neither in schools nor in classrooms were we able to find a set of functions or objectives agreed upon by the staff.

Not "how" but "what" to learn dominated consistently. Teachers and children were busy "covering" what was set forth in textbooks and workbooks. Children, either as individuals or in groups, were not seeking solutions to problems identified by them as important and meaningful. Instead, they were moderately busy on assignments predetermined by teachers.

In general, the subject matter studied appeared to be remote from the daily concerns and interests of the children. The topics were academic in character; most of the activity pertaining to them consisted of responding to teachers' questions, reading, or completing workbooks. While the children were not bubbling with enthusiasm, they appeared not to be completely bored either.

Rather, they went about their business in somewhat dutiful fashion, appearing to us to be more involved than the subject matter deserved.

The textbook predominated throughout as the medium of instruction, except in the kindergarten. With each advance in grade level, dependence on the textbook increased. Even when pupils shifted from the regular lesson to supplementary activities, textbooks still prevailed, sometimes with a different series being introduced. Rarely were the children using primary materials; rarely were films, filmstrips, record players, tape recorders, and so on in use either as instructional or learning tools, though there was evidence that the equipment was available. As other studies have documented, the textbook was the dominant instructional medium.

Given such enormous recent interest in individuality and individual differences, we were surprised to find so little provision for either. The bulk of instruction was of the total group variety, with children responding to teachers' questions. Classes were, indeed, divided into groups—usually three—for reading and language activities. But the slower children simply took longer to get to the material which the faster children had covered previously. Thus, such individualization as was provided sought to make minor provisions for differing rates of speed rather than differing kinds of learner needs.

Learning principles such as motivation, reinforcement, transfer of training, and goal setting were not clearly in use in the classrooms we visited. We found very few instances where teachers were identifying the behavior sought, reinforcing pupil responses related to such behaviors, extinguishing irrelevant responses, and the like. In brief, there was a lack of precision in guiding the learning process, suggesting either inadequate understanding or inability to use pedagogical tools.

As suggested in the findings summarized above, there were few instances of children working productively in small groups on problems of mutual interest or concern. Instead, classroom interaction was almost entirely teacher to child, child to teacher, teacher to child, child to teacher, on and on. Occasionally, children raised unique questions, whether or not relevant, but discussion seldom moved to a child-to-child interaction pattern.

Rather than finding flexibility in the selection of learning activities and in standards of evaluation, we found rather strict adherence to grade levels and group norms. Most classes though all the children were, indeed, in first grade, and not widely varying in all aspects of e used—except for those prepared by the teachers th the standardized, norm-based variety. Teachers' work laid out for a segment of the grade. The standard of comparison was the grade or group, not some identifiable criterion of performance by means of which pupil progress could be diagnosed. There were very few signs of pupil diagnosis being a factor in selecting learning activities or in evaluating.

The classrooms were largely self-contained. Children sometimes went to classes taught by specialists and specialists sometimes came into regular classrooms, but specialists rarely joined teaching teams. Some of the schools claimed to be team taught but most of these smacked more of departmentalization, with teachers taking over from each other at various times in the instructional day. We could find little evidence of clusters of teachers coming together to plan for the studies of an identifiable group of students. There was a paucity of teacher aides and of special resource personnel actually used in classrooms. Groups seldom went out into the community to extend the learning environment from confined class cells to a larger world of fields, ponds, museums, and zoos. Almost all the instruction was carried on by a teacher identified as responsible for an entire class at a specific grade level.

Several other observations of the study can be briefly summarized. The curriculum, especially at the K–4 level, was dominated by the language arts: writing, spelling, and reading, with heavy emphasis on phonics. Mathematics ranked second in emphasis. The relatively low position of science, social studies, and the fine arts suggests imbalance in the curriculum. The teaching and learning observed clearly emphasized lower cognitive processes. The higher levels of cognition involve processes of application, synthesis, and evaluation in students. But these intellectual skills were not being stressed; the emphasis was primarily on recall or recognition of specific facts and generalizations. The use of inductive or discovery approaches, stressed in the new curriculum projects, was extremely rare in the classrooms visited.

The practice of children sitting at tables in the first grades increasingly was replaced in the upper grades by children sitting in desks arranged in rows. Is this increasing immobility the cause or a

...tion of an increasing academic emphasis and a decreasing involvement of children in planning and discussing their work? There also appeared to be some other interesting increases and decreases in practices with upward progression through the grades. Evidence of globes and audiovisual equipment increased with the grade level. Variety of art supplies decreased in the upper grades, as did availability of pianos, rhythm instruments, and flannel or magnetic boards. Chalkboard space increased above the kindergarten. The relation between bulletin board displays and the ongoing program seemed to increase with the grade level.

Our observation was that teachers were generally warm toward and supportive of their students. They sought to create a positive atmosphere for children. Our findings support the conclusion that most teachers like children and that instances of sadistic teacher behavior probably are relatively isolated and overplayed. We observed that teaching and learning proceeded at what appeared to be a reasonably relaxed and comfortable pace. One did not get an impression of pressure and tension. This evidence adds to the data regarding the positive, supportive atmosphere of the classroom, though on the other hand, it increases uneasiness regarding provision for individual differences. This relaxed pace may be too quick for some and too slow for others. In addition, we found that classroom practices for supposedly disadvantaged children were not markedly different from classroom practices generally. Clearly, the school emphases deemed desirable by experts were not visible in our study.

One bright light did appear. The kindergarten rooms, more than any others, provided a variety of activities and achieved greater involvement on the part of children. Children often worked independently, in pairs, or in small groups. They moved rather freely about the room, varying their activities according to preference and with little teacher direction. Toys, blocks, and manipulative materials were in evidence, and the children frequently participated in both planning and evaluating the learning enterprise.

Before the reader blames school teachers and principals for the nonimplementation of reforms, some additional observations are in order. The elementary schools we visited were anything but the "palaces" of an affluent society. In fact, they looked more like the artifacts of a society that did not really care about its schools, a society that expressed its disregard by creating schools less suited to human habitation than its prisons. These artifacts reflect the strange notion that learning proceeds best in groups of thirty, that teachers are not to converse with each other, that learning should be conducted under rather uncomfortable circumstances, and that schools proceed best with their tasks when there is little or no traffic with the outside world.

We had hoped to conduct sustained interviews with the teachers we observed. But there were rarely quiet, attractive places to confer; we held our interviews on the run or, more favorably, when we were able to have breakfast or dinner together. These teachers wanted to talk about education: what "good" things had we observed elsewhere; would we comment on the virtues of current innovations; did we have suggestions for improving the teaching we had just observed; and on and on.

Just as teachers and principals appear to be uncertain as to what their schools are for, the communities they serve provide no clear sense of direction or guidelines. There is some evidence to suggest that parents are somewhat more favorably disposed toward educational change than are those who administer the schools or teach in them, but legions of educators who push at the forefront of innovative practice stand ready to show their community-inflicted scars.[23] Many parents are more interested in changes in the abstract or for someone else than in changes involving their own children. Social change is a formidable enterprise under the best of circumstances. Schooling too often presents only the worst of circumstances, with resistance built into both the setting and internal structure.

REFLECTIONS ON THE STATE OF THE SCHOOLS

Simply to learn that there is a significant gap between expectations for schooling and what actually goes on in schools is useful. However, certain other findings coming out of our study are much more useful in that they suggest both powerful explanatory hypotheses and some potentially productive ways to close the gap between expectations and reality. Most of these additional findings came from interviews and discussions with teachers and principals and were not directly related to the central goals of the study.

One very interesting finding pertained to the discrepancy between observations of our staff and self-perceptions of teachers with respect to their programs. Although we found the range of instructional materials to be limited, instruction to be didactic rather than inductive and oriented to the group rather than the individual, most of the teachers believed that they were using a wide range of instructional materials, were employing inquiry techniques in their teaching, and were making extensive provision for individual differences among pupils. Increasingly, we realized that most of the teachers had very limited insight into such practices. It began to dawn on us that they had not seen a wide range of instructional materials employed in classrooms; that there had been no opportunity for them to observe or participate in so-called discovery approaches to learning; and that the individualization of instruction had been more a slogan than a reality in their preparation to teach. Beyond listening to speeches, attending workshops, or reading about such ideas, they were not and had not been involved in them.

Further reflection brings the realization that very few redesigned models of schools exist. I realized the truth of this on contemplating the fact that thousands of visitors have come to the University Elementary School at UCLA each year to see nongrading, team teaching, and the individualization of instruction simply because models of such practices are not readily available elsewhere. Although these practices are talked about, there has been little movement from conceptualization to implementation so as to provide models for observation and analysis.

Many of the teachers were involved in various in-service education activities, such as taking college courses, participating in projects sponsored by universities, and serving as members of districtwide committees and task forces. But almost all this activity was individual in character; seldom were two or three teachers from the same school participating together. And there was no subsequent provision for benefits to be realized by more teachers in any given school. In effect, ideas from these in-service activities were not being channeled effectively so as to stimulate a critical mass of teachers to make constructive changes in their own schools.

A third set of findings pertained to school problems identified by principals and teachers and what they were—or, better, were not—doing about them. One cluster included broken homes, poor nutrition, transiency, lack of parental interest in schooling, and so on. Rarely, however, was there comment to the effect that these are problems over which the school has little or no control. Teachers should not wring their hands in the face of them but, instead, should pose the educational question, "Given these problems, what should the school do for and with the child?" It does no good simply to lament the existence of such problems. A more rational approach is to use them as data sources in planning curricula and instruction.

But there was a second set of problems about which the school could do a great deal: language development, reading deficiencies, attention span, classroom behavior problems, and the rest. These are problems which the school can and should resolve. We found, however, that only a few schools were at work on the very problems which teachers and principals identified as of prime concern. In perhaps four schools, there was a core of persons working under the leadership of their principal and endeavoring to grapple with school problems. In the others, no such efforts were identifiable. Although many teachers were very busy in their in-service education activities, they were not concentrating their efforts on the resolution of problems inherent in school and classroom environments.

It is relevant to identify here one of our most consistent observations. Very few of the schools presented a unique environmental identity. The schools were buildings with people in them, buildings very much like neighboring buildings. But there was little to suggest that human beings came here each day to pursue interesting activities together. The entry lobbies and hallways were innocuous, seldom displaying pupils' products. This is in direct contrast to the few British Infant Schools I have visited which bespeak a school emphasis even when the children are not there. Usually, there is a display in the lobby to suggest an interest in art, music, outer space, or something else. Usually, children's work spills over into hallways and into every nook and cranny of the school. But there was little in the schools we visited to suggest the character of daily living in them—unless that character is bland, indeed.

If our sample is to be at all trusted, it would appear that teachers in elementary schools have had little or no opportunity to observe school practices of the kind recently recommended; that in-service teacher education activities have little direct bearing on the schools as a place to live and work; that school staffs are not meaningfully engaged in constructive attack upon the problems which they say they have; and that schools lack individuality in character and purpose. It must be noted that the educational enterprise in the United States probably is the largest "business" that does not provide for the systematic updating of its personnel paid for by that enterprise. Teachers engage in self-improvement activities on their own time and at their own cost. Business and industry, by contrast, see to it that the workers are updated in whatever skills are needed and that new techniques are initiated systematically when deemed useful or advantageous. We are not going to bring about fundamental changes in schooling unless we regard the school as the unit for change and the faculty in that school as the prime agents for change.

Notes

[1] For the kinds of changes and problems anticipated for 1980 for which we should now be planning, see Edgar L. Morphet and Charles O. Ryan, *Prospective Changes in Society by 1980*, Designing Education for the Future, Denver, Colorado, 1966.

[2] For an arresting analysis of the labor-work dilemma in human affairs, see Hannah Arendt, *The Human Condition*, University of Chicago Press, Chicago, 1958.

[3] Two books by Gardner are particularly relevant in this regard: John W. Gardner, *Excellence*, Harper & Brothers, New York, 1961; and *Self-Renewal*, Harper & Row, New York, 1964.

[4] The nature, extent, and danger of our individual and collective encapsulation is convincingly presented in Joseph R. Royce, *The Encapsulated Man*, Van Nostrand Co., Princeton, N.J., 1964.

[5] This point was well developed by Joseph Schwab in an unpublished position paper prepared for the NEA Project on Instruction. For a summary of the Project recommendations, see *Schools for the 60's*, McGraw-Hill, New York, 1963.

[6] Jerome S. Bruner, *The Process of Education*, Harvard University Press, Cambridge, Mass., 1960.

[7] Harold O. Rugg and Ann Shumaker, *The Child-Centered School*, World Book Co., Chicago, 1928.

[8] William H. Kilpatrick (ed.), *The Educational Frontier*, The Century Co., New York, 1933, p. 71.

[9] Lawrence Cremin, *Transformation of the School*, Vintage Books, New York, 1961, p. 231.

[10] Bernard Iddings Bell, *Crisis in Education*, Whittlesey House, New York, 1949; and Mortimer Smith, *And Madly Teach*, H. Regnery Co., Chicago, 1949.

[11]Albert Lynd, *Quackery in the Public Schools*, Little, Brown and Co., Boston, 1953; Arthur Bestor, *Educational Wastelands*, University of Illinois Press, Urbana, 1953; Robert M. Hutchins, *The Conflict in Education*, Harper, New York, 1953; and Paul Woodring, *Let's Talk Sense About Our Schools*, McGraw-Hill, New York, 1953.

[12]Rudolf Flesch, *Why Johnny Can't Read*, Harper, New York, 1955.

[13]David Hulburd, *This Happened in Pasadena*, Macmillan, New York, 1951.

[14]United States Office of Education, *Vitalizing Secondary Education: Report of the First Commission on Life Adjustment Education for Youth*, Government Printing Office, Washington, D.C., 1951.

[15]John I. Goodlad, *School Curriculum Reform in the United States*, Fund for the Advancement of Education, New York, 1964.

[16]James B. Conant, *Slums and Suburbs*, McGraw-Hill, New York, 1961.

[17]Bruner, op. cit.

[18]Ibid., p. 33.

[19]Lawrence Cremin, *The Genius of American Education*, Vintage Books, New York, 1965, p. 56.

[20]John I. Goodlad, with Renata von Stoephasius and M. Frances Klein, *The Changing School Curriculum*, Fund for the Advancement of Education, New York, 1966.

[21]John I. Goodlad, *Planning and Organizing for Teaching*, a report prepared for the Project on Instruction, National Education Association, Washington, D.C., 1963; James B. Conant, *The Education of American Teachers*, McGraw-Hill, New York, 1963; Goodlad, *School Curriculum Reform*, op. cit.; and Goodlad, with von Stoephasius and Klein, op. cit.

[22]The data are reported in detail in John I. Goodlad, M. Frances Klein, and Associates, *Behind the Classroom Door*, Charles A. Jones, Worthington, Ohio, 1970, rev. 1974 and retitled *Looking Behind the Classroom Door*.

[23]See, for example, parental reactions to proposed changes for the schools as reported by George Gallup, *The Gallup Polls on Innovation*, Institute for Development of Educational Activities, Inc. (|I|D|E|A|), Melbourne, Florida, 1968.

2

The Challenge

It often is said about education, as about many other things, that nothing changes but the appearance of change. However, I recall vividly a former colleague blistering a graduate student who suggested as much. To prove his point, my colleague returned to the next class session "loaded for bear," carrying an armload of textbooks and curriculum guides used in Chicago schools during the concluding decades of the nineteenth century. Flipping through the documents, he cited instance after instance of marked differences between goals and topics they listed and those of 75 years later; for example, references to God and religion then and their virtual absence now.

One's view of change depends to considerable degree on the time perspective. Looking in the 1970s for widespread authentic implementation of the innovative ideas contained in the cant and rhetoric of reform in the 1960s suggests little movement. Only a small part of each successive wave of recommended change rubs off onto prac-

SOURCE: John I. Goodlad, "An Emphasis on Change," *American Education*, vol. 11, January–February 1975, pp. 16–21, 24–25, 28; John I. Goodlad, "The Educational Program to 1980 and Beyond," in Edgar L. Morphet and Charles O. Ryan (eds.), *Implications for Education of Prospective Changes in Society*, Designing Education for the Future, 1967, pp. 47–60; John I. Goodlad, "Innovations in Education," *The Educational Forum*, XXXI, March 1967, pp. 275–284.

tice. Perhaps this is not all bad since it protects us from the excesses
of those who make reputations by being more daring than their
contemporaries. But some features which cause schools to seem
inevitably and forever the same hang on stubbornly: telling and
questioning as the main form of teaching, daily instruction chopped
into arbitrary slices of time, long spells of student immobility,
textbooks and copy books, to name only a few.[1] Nonetheless, in the
sweep of 200 years since Independence, much of the tone and reality
of American education is conveyed accurately by the word
"change"—in aims, substance, access to schooling, and where and
how education occurs.

The saga is a captivating one, particularly the last 150 years of it,
during which schooling has advanced from the privilege of a few to
a widely accepted right of all. The whole of it often is described as
"the great American experiment in mass education." The challenge
to us is to move from experiment to reality.

THE AIMS OF EDUCATION AND SCHOOLING

Today, two central thrusts characterize most widely accepted
statements of goals for education in this country: (1) the full
development of the individual and (2) identification with an ever-
widening concept of social and cultural responsibility. A statement
emanating from the 1970 White House Conference on Children and
cast within a framework of "the right to learn" juxtaposes these two
thrusts in seeking to answer the question, "What would we have
twenty-first century man be?"

"We would have him be a man with a strong sense of himself and
his own humanness, with awareness of his thoughts and feelings,
with the capacity to feel and express love and joy and to recognize
tragedy and feel grief. We would have him be a man who, with a
strong and realistic sense of his own worth, is able to relate openly
with others, to cooperate effectively with them toward common
ends, and to view mankind as one while respecting diversity and
difference. We would want him to be a being who, even while very
young, somehow senses that he has it within himself to become more
than he now is, that he has the capacity for life-long spiritual and
intellectual growth. We would want him to cherish that vision of the
man he is capable of becoming and to cherish the development of
the same potentiality in others."[2]

Early goals for education were spare and stark in comparison with such a sweeping, almost ethereal statement. Going back to Colonial days in Massachusetts, we find little concern for individuality and much for responsibility in the admonition to town leaders that they take account of children's ". . . ability to read and understand the principles of religion and the capital laws of the country."[3] Although there was, a century later, some expression of concern for practical preparation for jobs in agriculture, navigation, shipbuilding, surveying, and trading, the commitment to moral instruction and love of country remained central. With the passage of another hundred years (bringing us well past Independence and into the middle of the nineteenth century), the emphasis still was responsibility—a degree of education to enable one to perform all social, domestic, civic, and moral duties.

Paralleling humanistic stirrings in Europe, there were, of course, expressions of concern over this pervading sense of education only for responsibility which resulted in a few innovative deviations during the second half of the nineteenth century. But it is the continued domination of the moral and nationalistic over a period of 250 years that makes John Dewey's emphasis on the meaning of the individual human experience so dramatic. Cremin interprets Dewey's definition of education—the reconstruction or reorganization of experience—as ". . . a way of saying that the aim of education is not merely to make citizens, or workers, or fathers, or mothers, but ultimately to make human beings who will live life to the fullest."[4]

There was no immediate and general acceptance of this idea. In fact, this and related ideas of Dewey were attacked for decades afterward and remain controversial today. Nonetheless, since publication of his pivotal *Democracy and Education* (1916), not a single major statement of goals for American education has omitted reference to individual prerogatives: worthy use of leisure (Commission on the Reorganization of Secondary Education, 1918); self-realization (Educational Policies Commission, 1938); knowledge of self (Commission on the Reform of Secondary Education, 1973).

The drive for redefinition of goals is not over; it never will be. Indeed, the cycles of emphasis and excess seem to come and go more quickly. Just twenty-five years ago, both Progressive Education and the Association carrying its name were in disarray. The "tender" in education—that having to do with great respect for the personality of individual children—was out; the "tough"—great respect for the facts and structures of disciplined knowledge—was in the ascendancy.[5] A dozen years later, John Dewey was being rediscovered in "open education," admittedly sometimes in ways to make purists shudder. Today, with the struggle and sacrifices of 1776 very much before us, what we can do for our country overshadows what our country can do for us, and "under God" is heard more often than in quite some time. "A degree of education to enable one to perform all social, domestic, civil and moral duties" sounds not at all anachronous to many and "right on" to more than a few. Continuing trends indicate, though, that "learning to be" could very well become the subtitle for an analysis of twentieth-century aims of American education prepared by historians in the twenty-first.

THE PRACTICE OF EDUCATION AND SCHOOLING

Myrdal has pointed out that Americans ". . . are at bottom moral optimists."[6] A sense of sin arises out of our self-recognized inability to live up to the precepts of our idealism. Cultural unity, says Myrdal, arises out of ". . . this common sharing in both the consciousness of sin and the devotion to high ideals."[7]

Perhaps it is the tension thus created that provides the drive for our educational preoccupation with curricular reform. We probably have more curriculum specialists and more curriculum activity than all the other nations of the world put together. We even have—or think we have—curriculum theory, an anathema to many in older, less self-conscious countries where curriculum construction is seen as a kind of trial-and-error process of human engineering wherein some options are chosen over others. Terms in the vocabulary of curriculum workers such as scope, sequence, continuity, and, above all, behavioral objectives were initially American creations and exports and not always well received abroad.

But this has been the case only recently. Courses on curriculum construction have been common in our universities for only a few decades, books on the subject for only a few more. Perhaps, then, exponents of "sound principles of curriculum planning" should not be too upset when publishers and teachers pay little attention to them. Until recently, publishers of educational materials concerned themselves almost exclusively with textbooks and with whether the content was acceptable and reasonably within pupil understanding.

Ramifications pertaining to children's interests, appropriate recognition of sexes and races, objectives to be achieved, readability, and the like followed some years—and usually decades—after the appearance of goals stressing the individual in education and self-realization. When social and psychological considerations were added to subject matter, it vastly complicated the curriculum-building process.

Knowledge of goals is about all one needs to guess early school programs in this country. In the second half of the seventeenth century, the school day was occupied with reading, spelling, and instruction in the Bible. The hornbook, a board with a handle, was inscribed with the alphabet and the Lord's Prayer. The first *New England Primer* (1690) contained epigrams, prayers, questions and answers about the Bible, and spelling lessons. Tidbits are frequently reproduced and include the well-known:

> In Adam's Fall
> We Sinned all
> An Eagle's flight
> Is out of sight
> The idle Fool
> Is whipt at School

Equally well-known is the "Praises to GOD for learning to Read";

1. The Praises of my Tongue
     I offer to the Lord
   That I was taught and learnt so young
     To read his holy Word:
2. That I was brought to know
     The Danger I was in.
   By Nature and by Practice too
     A Wretched slave to Sin:
3. That I was led to feel
     I can do nothing well;
   And Whither shall a Sinner flee
     To save himself from Hell.[8]

Reading this today, how can one feel comfortable with the proposition that schools do not change!

By the time of Independence, the curriculum was more crowded and planning was becoming complex. Provisions for vocational skills and more complicated arithmetic teaching had to be fitted in. And with separation and initial unification effected, the content of citizenship education and the teaching of national loyalty changed dramatically. The schools were having to change with the times, just as they have been exhorted and constrained to respond ever since.

With industrialization, urbanization, and rapid expansion in population during the second half of the nineteenth century, the schools shook themselves out of seventeenth- and eighteenth-century molds and created new structures which held with surprising firmness until past the middle of the twentieth. It is, I think, those highly visible characteristics of egg-crate buildings, graded classes, compartmentalized subjects, and rigid time units brought into being in the 1860s and 1870s that have provoked the charge of tortoiselike change in schools. But these things, too, shall pass—and are, indeed, passing, like the Dame School, circuit school, and Lancaster Plan before them.

But within these familiar rubrics, curriculum change (much but not all in the form of accretions to what already existed) went on apace. Vocational training in both skills and attitudes was needed for work in the factories; physical and health education made their common appearance early in the 1900s. The elementary-school curriculum of the 1920s and 1930s included arithmetic, spelling, reading, handwriting, grammar, composition, nature study, geography, history, singing, drawing, painting, and perhaps some shop and cooking for the upper years. Secondary schools commonly included algebra, geometry, some arithmetic; English composition, grammar, and literature; Latin, French, and sometimes a little German; civics, history, geography, health and physical education; physics, chemistry, and biology; and a clutch of electives in the arts, technical subjects, and home economics, depending largely on local resources.

Methods of teaching reading became (and continue to be) a controversial matter with the introduction of whole-word recognition approaches and "controlled vocabularies" in the late 1920s. Progressive education is blamed or credited, depending on one's point of view, with a rash of experiments with fused, integrated, or core curricula; society- or community-oriented approaches; life adjustment education; and child-centered education, all blossoming in the 1930s and fading in the war-torn years of the 1940s. As pointed out in Chapter 1, by the 1950s, there were many who believed the time was come to have done with our progressive follies and, in the light of the United States' new found status in the world, to tighten and prune, to cut the fat out of curricular accumulations, and to replace outworn content with the fast-ripening fruits of a knowledge explosion. It was time for the social and civic responsibility of academicians to bestir them from their more scholarly activities in order to jack up the ailing curricula of America's schools.

Emphasis on structure of the disciplines, supposedly both disciplining and freeing the mind simultaneously, though highly visible was not the only emphasis in the ensuing reform movement. Assumptions about the nature of learners loomed large; psychological considerations had been part of the fabric of curriculum and instruction for some time. Even very young children were credited with ability to learn basic mathematical and scientific concepts, to extrapolate from data and experiments, and to make intuitive leaps. The young child was "discovered educationally,"[9] the significance of cognitive development taking its place beside traditional concerns for emotional, social, and physical development for nursery school youngsters—at least in the view of a handful of influential leaders.[10]

Although these emphases were brewing in the 1950s, they came to a boil in the 1960s, spewing out all over the stove in 1965. Sputnik (1957) had touched that nerve of sin again. We flayed our schools as we once flayed witches. Our schools had gone soft, we said—and a few obligingly enterprising television cameramen soon "proved" it with views of secondary school boys in classes traditionally "for girls only." We were not quite ready to say that we, the American people, had gone soft, however.

Chapter 1 recounted some of the events of the "Education Decade."[11] It began with great confidence that the apparent ills of our educational enterprise could be cured, especially if the job were turned over to the right people (and, by-and-large, these were not the administrators and supervisors in the school districts, the education associations—especially not the NEA—nor the professors of education, who together made up "the education establishment"). There was considerable confidence, also, that this school-centered diagnosis was the correct one, that more general well-being would come with educational well-being.

A veritable host of long-standing traits, movements, tenets, and ideologies of American education came tumbling together in the Education Decade. The innovative character, which some observers from abroad have identified as our most notable contribution to educational advancement generally, was dominant. We innovated all over the place: with new approaches to curriculum content; with programmed and computerized instruction; with modular scheduling, modular buildings, and acoustically treated walls, ceilings, and floors; with nongrading, team teaching, and flexible grouping; with films, filmstrips, multimedia "packages," and televised instruction. It is not difficult to find the roots of organizational reforms in the St. Louis (1868) and Pueblo Plans (1888) or, in this century, the Winnetka and Dalton Plans; philosophical underpinnings of much curricular rhetoric in the teachings of Whitehead and Dewey; and psychological bases for new curricula and programmed instruction in the research of Thorndike and Pressey.

We updated our long-standing ambivalence about teachers and teaching as a profession by proposing "teacher-proof materials," while revering the newly emerging professorial jet set. Members of this new elite were much sought after: as advisors and consultants to the federal government, publishers, school systems, special projects, and foundations; and as speakers everywhere. Research became so revered that "no teaching the first year and then only a seminar in your specialty" was as significant as the unprecedented salary going with a much-publicized appointment of the time at a prestigious university.

Particularly fascinating is the side-by-side emergence of the "hard"/"tough" and "soft"/"tender" ideologies which, for at least half of the two centuries since Independence, seem so often to have occupied the same place and time and to relate to each other like gophers and gopher snakes. Usually, however, in the past—and especially in this century—one has tended to survive at the expense of the other, with perceived excesses in the temporary dominance of tender trends triggering the ascendance and accompanying perceived excesses in tough education. But the resurgence of the tough-minded had scarcely begun in the Education Decade before the neo-humanists were in full cry, condemning lockstep, irrelevance, and inhumaneness in schools as their tender-minded counterparts had done before them. Their historic foes were not intimidated. Today, the proponents of free schools (tender) and other drastic deviations from "the system" stand cheek-by-jowl with those who would tighten up the sloth in schools through more precise delineation of instructional imperatives (tough).[12]

The Elementary and Secondary Education Act of 1965, which both brought the pot of reform to a boil and spilled out the brew across this nation, ranks with those great federal acts of faith which gave us our land-grant universities and assured that we would not forget the vocational arts (Smith-Hughes Act) in our pursuit of the liberal arts and sciences. Although the Constitution implicitly left responsibility for education to the states, the federal government has served strategically in diagnoses of nationwide needs and reform transcending the states. From the beginning, the U.S. Office of Education and its Commissioner have been charged with periodic assessments and reports to Congress.

The ESEA represents not only a high—perhaps the zenith—in our history of faith in education and our ability to effect constructive change in schools but also a significant watershed in the post-Sputnik frenzy. Ironically, it also symbolizes the dangers of disillusionment inherent in expecting too much of our schools.

But it is overly simplistic to cite only unrealistic expectations as the cause of considerable, widespread criticism of schools at the beginning of the 1970s. The country was weary of war and the young bitter about it; our expanding economy appeared to be checked; an increasing imbalance of imports over exports was beginning to challenge the phrase, "as sound as a dollar"; our resources no longer seemed limitless; the alarm of conservationists over environmental rape was clanging more loudly; inflation and recession were twin devils; daily life was complex; our urban problems seemed as bad as before; ethnic minorities had come a long way but the road to further progress was not at all clear; women were men's burden of conscience; many things seemed not to go right. We had used and abused schools as the vehicle to improve or change all this, and they had been found wanting. A Ford Foundation report was interpreted to say that the much-touted reforms had not worked;[13] campus stress and tumult were near-dormant; shrinking enrollments suggested caution, not boldness; research grants were hard to get; the professorial jet set had dwindled to a few, now older. With some communities confronting the unfamiliar problem of consolidating or closing elementary schools, there were those prognosticators who solemnly declared teaching to be dead as a profession! But it is unlikely that education or educators will roll over.

PERSPECTIVE ON THE CHALLENGE TO CHANGE

Among those aspects of life celebrated on the 200th anniversary of the United States of America, schools loom large. While some hear only hollowness in the words of tribute, those who know our history best are appropriately stirred and are neither carried away nor turned off by the rhetoric. They know that our schools never have lived up to the most extravagant claims nor deserved the most scathing criticisms. Our institutions of learning have mirrored the strengths and weaknesses, successes and failures, of the surrounding society, overly praised when all seemed well in the land and overly cursed when little seemed to be going right. Perhaps this has been the greatest weakness of these institutions—that they have reflected our society too well and, consequently, not served adequately as constructively critical countervailing agencies. But this, too, we have expected of them: that they be responsive but conservative, that they reflect ongoing life around them. In so doing, we have virtually assured a succession of cycles of relative satisfaction and dissatisfaction, each in a fascinating way conducive to successive cycles of change.

It probably is healthy, therefore, that we are now between cycles, with neither the worst fears nor the most grandiose proposals of the past two decades realized. We did not deschool our society. Neither Pygmalion nor computers took over in the classroom. That new generation about which we were so excited goes no more to the polls and no less to prison (or vice versa) than its predecessor. Our schools are not nearly as good as the predictions of 1966 said they would be by now, nor as bad as many said they were in 1972. It appears that our schools are marked at least as much by stability as by change. Between cycles, then, we are at one of those stable periods when reflection might provide the needed perspective before we move again. What better opportunity than the year marking our 200th anniversary?

The long look at yesterday, today, and tomorrow suggests that extending opportunity for education has been one of the most significant areas of change, and yet it remains the area of greatest need and challenge. It has two parts: access and appropriateness.

The struggle for more general access, fulfillment of the right to learn, has been carried on under the rubric of equality of opportunity. It has taken place previously in the political arena and in the courts. The drive for appropriateness has been more person-centered, drawing upon growing knowledge about individual differences and humanistic concern for the individual.

Looking back with today's conceptions of what equality and individuality in opportunity and education provision mean, it is easy to fault all levels of schooling for lethargy and backwardness. The following notions guiding provisions for free public schooling throughout the second half of the nineteenth century and well into the twentieth were *enlightened* for their time but can easily be taken apart—as, indeed, they have been—as discriminatory by contemporary standards:

1. Providing a *free* education up to a given level which constituted the principal entry point to the labor force.
2. Providing a *common curriculum* for all children, regardless of background.
3. Partly by design and partly because of low population density, providing that children from diverse backgrounds attend the *same school.*
4. Providing equality within a given *locality*, since local taxes provided the source of support for schools.[14]

With the addition of individual development to the stated aims, free public education simply to prepare for entry into the labor force is not sufficient. Likewise, a common curriculum is regarded today as a Procrustean anachronism. Now that the courts have established unequivocally (1954) the right of all children to attend the same integrated local schools, the issue of what constitutes equality is more complex: Is bus-aided integration (or its absence) equal opportunity? Is the right to establish a tax-supported bilingual school equality? Is access to many "schools of choice"[15] equality? In regard to the fourth point, above, gross disparities in the ability of local communities to support schools have resulted in court challenges to the legality of property taxes as the prime base for financing schools.

The issues posed here are likely to be the motivation for and at the heart of the educational challenge for some time to come. The issue of who shall be educated is caught up in expressions such as "lifelong" and "recurring" education. Change will be toward extending opportunity downward to younger ages and upward to older ones. Access to the learning continuum at any age will become much easier; news stories increasingly recount the phenomenon of "housewives in their 30's" and senior citizens taking over community colleges in California.

The issue of providing for individual differences will be expressed in steady implementation of many innovations already largely accepted in concept. Witness this 1966 statement of what is not yet widespread:

". . . continuous pupil progress uninhibited by grade barriers; subject matter organized sequentially around fundamental concepts, principles, and generalizations; instructional materials gathered together for the task at hand and the varying abilities of the learners involved with it; criterion performance standards inherent in the learning task itself; alternative classroom placements for learners based on pupil diagnoses and individual expectations."[16]

What will continue to trouble us is how to provide simultaneously for individuals "to do their thing" and for all to acquire the education they need for performing "all social, domestic, civic, and moral duties." The sense of sin perceived by Myrdal and our fear of sloth, if nothing else, will protect against losing sight of one or the other of these twin, traditional goals.

The immediate road ahead will see us attempting to restore some of our old sense of community in regard to schooling and education. Breaking out of the egg-crate building and the 9:00 to 3:00 schedule into the larger community and the itinerant day will become *de rigueur* among innovative schools. There will be new partnerships among schools, museums, public health agencies, industry, and public media—especially television—for educational purposes. Community involvement will be more widespread; more people will be part-time teachers (and, of course, part-time students). But *citizen involvement*, after a cyclone of rhetoric and a short whirlwind of activity, will fall far short of today's predictions. This is but one of those short cycles which will move us, nonetheless, one step more toward that visionary goal of a learning society. Some good almost always rubs off from such cycles of enthusiasm and excess.

There will be changes in the ratio of federal, state, and local support for education, with the proportion paid by the first two increasing and that of the third declining. The courts will continue to play a significant role in the adjustments. Accompanying these changes will be tension regarding authority to make decisions. This tension will carry the controversy far beyond the issue of decentralization versus centralization into the finer nuances of what is better centralized and what decentralized. The stirring of this pond will keep it muddy—to a degree deliberately. Some of the fun is taken out, along with challenges to candidates for public office, when lines of authority and responsibility are defined too rationally. Change in our society and, therefore, in education has seldom been strongly motivated by desire to remove ambiguity, even though we tend to place rationality high on our scale of values.

And so, in education as in many other things, it is the worst of times and the best of times. The schools have not changed and do not change as quickly as some of us would like. On the other hand, they change much faster than others of us like. They will not be nearly as good by 2001 as some futurists say they will be; nor will they be nearly as bad as others predict. Our schools have problems, to be sure. But they are less the cause of despair than a challenge to act.

Chapter 1 concluded with a discussion of the realities of our schools today and reflections on some of the possible causes of their condition. I present here a summary of the basic problems of schooling. Later chapters will deal with issues these problems raise.

PROBLEMS OF SCHOOLS TODAY

First, there appears to be little relation between the earmarks of success in school and subsequent demonstration of those virtues inherent in many statements of educational aims. Marks in school subjects are virtually useless as predictors of creativity, inventiveness, leadership, good citizenship, personal and social maturity, family happiness, and honest workmanship.[17] Either we are not rewarding or we are not providing adequately (or both) for development of qualities so frequently set forth in statements of educational goals.

Second, there is an unwillingness or an inability (or both) to state at any level of responsibility or authority what education, schools, or specific programs of instruction are for. States are confused as to their freedom and responsibilities in this regard and do not define adequately the role of their departments of education, as any cursory examination of state courses of study quickly reveals. Local school boards are assiduous in their avoidance of the issues involved,[18] failing to take advantage of American pluralism. When the prospect of determining educational goals at the federal level of responsibility looms, we cry local autonomy, failing to realize that we have a vacuum here into which spill the wares of remote curriculum builders. Small wonder that most educators have little stomach for the determination of educational objectives.

Third, the common expectation and demonstrated function of our schools are coverage of tasks and materials that have been predetermined for specific grades and periods of time.[19] This condition appears not to have a sound pedagogical base. It denies our growing awareness of individual differences in learning and the probability that what children learn has more to do with the subject matter they are exposed to rather than to our genius in the grade placement of children and content.

Fourth, a substantial portion of the curriculum has not been justified on criteria other than habit or tradition. This is particularly true in the social studies where too many insignificant historical events are learned by rote, where homogenized community studies predominate in the lower years, and where a mankind approach is largely lacking.

Fifth, the separate-subject pattern of curriculum organization places profound problems of choice upon local school districts.[20] There simply cannot be thirty or more academic disciplines in the kindergarten. Further, the strengthening of subjects already in the curriculum through massive federal grants has not enhanced the status of relatively new but nonetheless important disciplines. Consequently, we have a badly segmented curriculum. Much of what is taught is out of date and not adequately representative of available choices.

Sixth, teacher education (and I refer to the whole of the program, not just the education courses), which should be the fountainhead, too often is a drainage ditch. There is no point in entering now into the problems and issues of what James B. Conant called "that can of worms." They have been well documented elsewhere.[21] Suffice to say that nothing short of a complete overhaul will bring to our teacher education programs, both pre-service and in-service, the vitality they must have if teachers are to effect the rapid educational evolution we want.

Seventh, there is an assumption abroad in the land that the task before us now is to implement a host of educational innovations which already have been amply demonstrated and proved worthy. This is to a degree accompanied by the assumption that federal intervention will provide the new forms and substances we need for the future. I am uneasy with respect to both assumptions.

Regarding the first assumption, we have had but a handful of potent, imaginative educational innovations during the past decade or so. Further, we have had precious little detailed development and demonstrations of these and very little interpretation or testing of the assumptions underlying them. Widespread dissemination of what we rather dimly perceive will occupy much time and energy, but that it will profoundly change or improve education is questionable. We do not yet grasp the significance of inner renewal and what is required to bring it about. Rhetoric to the contrary notwithstanding, we are locked into outworn, inadequate change strategies.

Regarding the second, we need in addition to our action-oriented enterprises a much greater commitment to protected, funded, and superbly staffed long-term inquiry of a sort that neither the federal government nor the private foundation is now providing. Evaluation of what we have done is important but insufficient.

Eighth, there is precious little experimentation with the school as an instrument of and for change. Polls suggest that the lay public is at least as ready for change as the educators.[22] But there always seems to be enough resistance on the part of vocal parents and entrenched professionals to cause undue caution on the part of administrators. Do we need schools whose very reason for existence is experimentation and innovation?

Ninth, innovations which in concept are designed to unshackle the restrictive, monolithic structure of schools appear often to be tacked on. Nongrading is supposed to raise the ceilings and lower the floors of expectancy for the class group, reduce the importance of age as a factor in determining the student's program, encourage greater flexibility in grouping practices, and so on. But a study of supposedly nongraded elementary schools in the United States found little movement in these directions.[23] Nongrading, team teaching, and other innovations of potential power are far from simple in concept and implementation. Are we expecting too much in attempting them apart from simulation, demonstration, and in-service teacher education?

Tenth, as pointed out in Chapter 1, the much-heralded pedagogical revolution of recent years is still largely in the clouds of educational reform that roll back and forth across this vast and varied land. These clouds have not yet enveloped the millions of teachers who make up the working force of our elementary and secondary schools. Most of these teachers will continue to serve for years to come.

The Education Gap

The problem with our schools today is not merely that they have failed to implement the innovations of the education decade. The deficiency is far more fundamental. We have at present in the United States a formidable education gap. By "education gap" I mean the gap between where a society might be and where individuals or groups within it now are, as perceived by individuals within that society and as seen by them to be subject to closure by educational means.

At its dynamic best, the education gap is the distance between man's most noble visions of what he might become and the conventional wisdom, a distance which is perceived by and is motivating to a large percentage of the people. The education gap is sterile when there are no visions for man beyond his present preoccupations, when his present preoccupations are scarcely discernible from those of the beasts, and when he cares not. Under these conditions, education is reduced to simple training.

Schooling takes on meaning and direction within this concept of the education gap, that is, this educational specification of the human condition and what to do about it. The functions of schooling are not, therefore, forever and everywhere the same but are a product of time and place—above all, a people's awareness of its time and place. Let us summarize, then, some realities of our time and place, realities which help to define the nature of the education gap with which our schools must come vigorously and imaginatively to grips.

I can scarcely begin here to formulate the range of forces and ideas that impinge upon and demand a response from our schools.[24] Therefore, I shall develop only a few which appear to me to be unusually compelling.

Formidable Realities

It is more difficult today than at any time in mankind's past to bring humans into possession of their culture; that is to say, of the world created out of the perceptions of humankind. The familiar idea, now virtually a cliché, of the explosion of knowledge is a reality. But there is much more: the idea that our culture is created by people and is not something "out there." Knowledge is created today at an accelerating rate which, not surprisingly, intimidates those of us who must transform it for the education of our people.

Knowledge is what and how man perceives. Knowledge and our beliefs change, therefore, sometimes so completely that the social dislocations are profound. Witness, for example, the work of Darwin. Almost unbelievably, there are pockets of the country where the open teaching of Darwin's theory of evolution—as a theory, mind you—is still considered to be a dangerous innovation, godless, and in defiance of Christianity. And there are individuals for whom the mere mention of Sigmund Freud brings forth responses indicative of some subtle but deep threat in the implications of certain Freudian theories.

A prime function of education and, therefore, for our schools is to bring men and women into possession of their culture. We are not likely to fulfill this function well when we view schooling as the coverage of uniformly approved bodies of material, nor when we view thinking for one's self as something that comes later, with "maturity," instead of now.

The curriculum, then, becomes a major focal point in determining the extent to which young persons are being brought into possession of their culture. It is the curriculum that is most susceptible to ossification, and it is the curriculum that must be continuously rejuvenated through innovation, now more urgently than yesterday.

A second compelling reality for our schools is that today, more than ever before, we possess a significant body of lore about individual differences. This human variability demands educational alternatives. To expect elimination of this variability through education is to expect what never has been and never will be. To expect

enhancement of this variability through education is to expect what
h-- h--n and what will—in fact, must—be. It is clear that increasing
al opportunity is itself going to accelerate cultural evolu-
of our best assurances of coping with an unpredictable
deliberate cultivation of these individual differences.
is emerge to meet the needs of identifiable groups and
.. They develop programs for this purpose. In time, these
ions often come to view their function as the maintenance of
these programs and to serve the needs only of clients who fit the
programs. That some individuals in schools cease to become clients
in any meaningful sense is illustrated by our nonpromotion practices
and rates, gross discrepancies in the distribution of passing and
failing marks, school dropouts, and social disorientation among
dropouts, virtually all of whom have talents worthy and capable of
development.

The organization of the school, then, becomes a major focal point
in determining the extent to which an adequately wide range of
traits and expectations is likely to be respected. Patterns of organizing the school are unusually susceptible to considerations of
efficient administration and, therefore, frequently tend not to reflect
what we know about individual differences and the irregularities of
individual development.

The third societal reality to which our schools must respond
grows directly out of quantitative success with our great experiment
in mass schooling. The very massiveness of our effort has been
deleterious for many individuals in that they have not developed an
adequate sense of identity and of being valuable human beings,
valued by "persons over the age of 30" who seem to be in control of
things and valued by themselves.

We are strangely unwilling or unable to come to the heart of the
matter. Even when the growing pressure was suddenly released in a
conflagration, as it was several years ago on various college
campuses and high schools, we continued to be myopic about at
least one crucial aspect of student discontent. The Muscatine
report[25] on the University of California at Berkeley, for example, did
not regard the students as mature enough for participation in
decisions pertaining to their own curriculum. At the same time,
Pace's studies reveal that students in large universities feel that the
program does not reach them in any deep and significant way, that
they do not participate in its planning, and that it is not planned
with their lives in mind.[26]

A prime function of schooling is to prepare the individual for life-long learning, for self-propelled education. We are not likely to fulfill this function when we give students no experience in planning and conducting their own education now, nor when we regard them as the passive recipients and educators as the active transmitters of all educational largesse.

America's schools must change, not only to meet the needs of the present but also to face the challenge of the future. I have sketched in this chapter some of the historical background of the present reality and some of the problems and challenges that this reality creates for the schools. We now turn to some of the issues posed by the reality of schooling which must be faced if we are to be prepared to meet the future.

Notes

[1]John I. Goodlad, M. Frances Klein, and Associates, *Looking Behind the Classroom Door*, rev. ed., Charles A. Jones, Worthington, Ohio, 1974.

[2]"The Future of Learning: Into the Twenty-First Century," Forum No. 5, *Report to the President, White House Conference on Children, 1970*, Government Printing Office, Washington, D.C., 1971, pp. 73–85.

[3]George L. Jackson, *The Development of School Support in Colonial Massachusetts*, Teachers College, Columbia University, New York, 1909, p. 8.

[4]Lawrence A. Cremin, *The Transformation of the School*, Alfred A. Knopf, New York, 1961, pp. 122–123.

[5]Philip G. Smith, "The Philosophical Context," in John I. Goodlad and Harold G. Shane (eds.), *The Elementary School in the United States*, Seventy-second Yearbook of the National Society for the Study of Education, Part II, University of Chicago Press, Chicago, 1973, pp. 115–137.

[6]Gunnar Myrdal, *An American Dilemma*, vol. 1, Harper & Brothers, New York, 1944, p. 22.

[7]Ibid.

[8]Ellwood P. Cubberly, *Public Education in the United States*, Houghton-Mifflin, Boston, Mass., 1919, p. 31.

[9]John I. Goodlad, M. Frances Klein, Jerrold M. Novotney and Associates, *Early Schooling in the United States*, McGraw-Hill, New York, 1973, pp. 3–10.

[10]Benjamin S. Bloom, *Stability and Change in Human Characteristics*, John Wiley, New York, 1964.

[11]John I. Goodlad, "Schooling and Education," *The Great Ideas Today, 1969*, Encyclopaedia Britannica, Inc., Chicago, 1969, pp. 100–145.

[12]Smith, op. cit.

[13]*A Foundation Goes to School: The Ford Foundation Comprehensive School Improvement Program*, The Ford Foundation, New York, 1972.

[14]James S. Coleman, "The Concept of Equality of Educational Opportunity," *Harvard Educational Review*, vol. 38, 1968, p. 11.

[15]Mario D. Fantini, *Public Schools of Choice*, Simon and Schuster, New York, 1973.

[16]John I. Goodlad, John F. O'Toole, Jr., and Louise L. Tyler, *Computers and Information Systems in Education*, Harcourt, Brace and Jovanovich, New York, 1966, p. 16

[17]C. Robert Pace, "The Relationships between College Grades and Adult Achievement: A Review of the Literature," in Donald P. Hoyt (ed.), ACT Research Reports, No. 7, American College Testing Program, Iowa City, Iowa, 1965.

[18]Margaret P. Ammons, "Educational Objectives: The Relation between the Process Used in Their Development and Their Quality," unpublished doctoral dissertation, University of Chicago, 1961.

[19]Goodlad, Klein, and Associates, *Looking Behind the Classroom Door*, op. cit.

[20]See John I. Goodlad, with Renata von Stoephasius and M. Frances Klein, *The Changing School Curriculum*, Fund for the Advancement of Education, New York, 1966.

[21]See, for example, James B. Conant, *The Education of American Teachers*, McGraw-Hill, New York, 1963.

[22]George Gallup, *The Gallup Polls on Innovation*, Institute for Development of Educational Activities, Inc. (|I|D|E|A|), Melbourne, Florida, 1968.

[23]Maria T. Delgado-Marcano, "The Operation of Curriculum and Instruction in Twenty Nongraded Elementary Schools," unpublished doctoral dissertation, School of Education, Indiana University, Bloomington, 1965.

[24]For a more comprehensive review, see *The Changing American School*, Sixty-fifth Yearbook of the National Society for the Study of Education, Part II, University of Chicago Press, Chicago, 1966.

[25]Charles Muscatine, Chairman, California University Academic Senate, The Northern Section, Berkeley Division, *Education at Berkeley*, Report of the Select Committee on Education, 1966.

[26]C. Robert Pace, "Perspectives on the Student and His College," in Lawrence Dennis and Joseph Kaufman (eds.), *The College and the Student*, American Council on Education, Washington, D.C., 1966.

3

Setting Goals for Educational Programs

This chapter was originally a talk prepared for a conference on program development. As usual, the topic given the speaker was only a starting point for discussion of important issues and ideas then occupying the speaker's mind. The paper has been revised to make it more generally applicable for purposes of this volume. [Editor]

The most difficult first step in improving educational programs is setting goals for schooling and for education generally. Without dialogue about goals and purposes, our efforts at reform will be piecemeal, often contradictory, and probably ineffectual. The dialogue is more important than the goals it produces at any given time.

The context or setting for my remarks is the organized public system of elementary and secondary schooling. However, much of what I have to say applies to educational institutions generally. Also, most of my remarks grow out of the assumption that the educational program constitutes the whole of what students encounter in these

SOURCE: John I. Goodlad, "Program Development: Identification and Formulation of Desirable Educational Goals," in *Program Development in Education*. Report of the International Symposium on Program Development in Education, University of British Columbia, Morriss Printing Co., Ltd., Victoria, 1974, pp. 56–70.

institutions, not merely the intended subject matter of social studies, science, language arts, humanities, and fine arts curricula.

Given this context, it is essential to remember that programs already exist and constitute part of the phenomenological reality to be encountered in any new planning activity. The prime quality, presumably, of program development is that it is activated by reason. But we cannot and must not assume that what new programs are designed to replace is activated by something other than reason. Quite the contrary; what exists already is rational in that it was designed, carefully or carelessly, to enable students to understand the world about them and to relate such knowledge to their interests and the attainment of their human ends. Perhaps even more important to program planners is that many of those responsible for financing, administering, and especially teaching what exists regard their present programs as eminently rational—frequently more rational than any other alternative suggested to them. Further, what exists is fortified by the reluctance of most persons involved with it to engage in more than mild changes.

There are, in the above, at least three caveats to program planners, all three of which have been ignored to considerable degree by educational innovators and curriculum makers; (1) there already are meals on the educational tables; (2) those in the kitchen planned them with diets and menus in mind; and (3) those who serve the meals in the dining halls have grown accustomed to their routine. The diets may be nutritionally inadequate, but this is quite another issue to which we shall soon turn. We should not assume, either, that those who partake of the food eagerly await an alternative diet, or that they would progress markedly differently under its influence. And, certainly, how consumers feel about their educational food has had, to date, little influence on the menus. In the educational market place, the consumers have not been the buyers.

THE SOURCES OF EDUCATIONAL GOALS

Goals arise out of the realization that there is a gap between some existing condition and an alternative condition reflecting interest. But this observation only helps to obscure complexities. For example, does this realization of a gap stem from some other goal? A mayor wishes to put in roads where there are none now—to change a condition of roadlessness to a condition of roads—and so his goal becomes to build roads. But his real goal is to become governor, and so building roads is not a goal at all but a means. And yet, to build roads, ostensibly, is indeed a goal. Thus, we get into an infinite regression: the source of a goal is a goal and the means to a goal is a goal.[1]

Perhaps it is only an exercise in semantics to suggest, then, that goals arise out of interests, but I find this notion rather useful here. Macdonald puts it this way, in speaking of curriculum: "My basic proposition about curriculum is that at all levels . . . the basic phenomenon which underlies all activity is the existence of human interest which precedes and channels the activity of curriculum thinking."[2] Some might wish to substitute the word "value" for "interest." Human interest of some kind intrudes wherever an educational decision is made.

At any rate, the mayor is interested in becoming governor, and so he activates a number of goal-oriented activities. But by the time the elections roll around, there is a financial recession, there has been a scandal in regard to contracts, and some of the new roads lead to housing developments that did not develop. The mayor's road-building activity is a liability he would love to bury.

Educational program development is plagued with such problems. No matter how precise our goals, we know relatively little as to which goals best sustain our interest in producing citizens who possess the virtues of compassion, honesty, happiness, good workmanship, or creativity. As we saw in the preceding chapter, there is little relation between success in schools as measured by marks and any of these virtues,[3] most of which are imbedded in national or state aims for education. Further, we are less certain as to the reasons for this discrepancy than the mayor was with respect to the shortcomings in his campaign. Were our subgoals unrelated behaviorally or substantively to the larger ones or did we simply bungle their attainment out of ignorance, ineptness, or sloth? To an old cliché, "having lost sight of our goals, we redoubled our efforts to attain them," we might add, "having lost sight of our goals, we redoubled our efforts to refine them."

Lest I appear to chant too despairing a refrain, let me return to the deceptively simple notion of goals emanating from awareness of gaps coupled with desire to close them. Gaps exist because of disparities between interests and perceptions of what exists. Our problem as citizens in a democratic society is, on one hand, to bring forward alternative interests and choose among those capable of being supported by the best reasons and, on the other, to make the best possible appraisals of what exists. I cannot here go into the staggering array of complexities surrounding these two tasks, and so I shall treat them simply as difficult but feasible, in the same way that putting men on the moon was both of these, but easier.

In regard to the first, that of choosing among alternative interests, I am placing the democratic attribute of best use of intelligence above the democratic attribute of participatory decision making. We want to keep our society open to alternatives, but not all alternatives are equally good. Some alternatives are more self-serving, shortsighted, and devoid of reason than others. Voting is a poor way to decide the properties of matter or the speed of sound. In effect, what is wanted are alternatives well supported by relevant knowledge or reasons.

The second task is somewhat easier but exceedingly difficult, nonetheless. It is that of determining existential conditions or, in the realm of relevant knowledge, common perceptions. The latter sometimes is referred to as conventional wisdom.

These tasks should be carried on continuously, as they are in economic and some other realms of human welfare. They are carried on only sporadically in the field of education, although some countries have created or are now creating curriculum development or policy centers for gathering data and both recommending and implementing curricular policies.

We do not yet have goals, however, after engaging in these tasks. Goals grow out of comparing selected alternatives with corresponding existential conditions, appraising the nature of the gaps, and then determining what is required to close them, resulting in relatively puerile statements of human possibilities. But when joined with commitment, they become goals to be promoted or achieved. The chances of their being attained are enhanced, some claim, by the precise specification of what they entail.

We begin to see that substituting reason for emotion in the setting of educational goals carries us into profound philosophical, sociological, and anthropological inquiry. The effort to attain goals, in turn, carries us into political, economic, and psychological realms as well as into strategies and the logistics of program implementation and change. The identification and formulation of desirable educational goals embrace all of these.

The function of educational program development, presumably, is to move the level of conventional wisdom toward new and better levels of funded knowledge, tested skills, and desirable attitudes. There are *ideological* problems of determining the nature of the education gap and what should be done about it. There are *political* problems of establishing sets of possible choices over competing alternatives—and that means not merely establishing the virtue of one over another but of placing certain choices within significant decision-making structures (such as, for example, those of state or provincial legislators). And there are *technical/social* problems of effecting changes or improving the discharge of existing program commitments.

Although those writing the scenarios for and acting in the dramas of program development may confine themselves to only one of these major sets of problems—the ideological or the political or the technical/social—no state or nation will advance far in closing the education gap unless all three are embraced in a comprehensive planning process. Because this process is so fully human, it will not be fully rational. But at least the component parts should be conducted with some awareness of the whole. In education, program planners tend to be myopic, eschewing basic value questions as theoretical or impractical and ignoring the fact that both ideas and programs must find their way through the civil/political system to make a difference.

Juxtaposition of ideological, practical, and technical/social considerations in a comprehensive program-planning process parallels, to some extent, I think what Schwab calls the *practical* in contrast to the *theoretic:*

> The method of the practical . . . is, then, not at all a linear affair proceeding step-by-step, but rather a complex, fluid transactional discipline aimed at identification of the desirable and at either attainment of the desired or at alteration of desires.[4]

I am concerned here with the practical, as Schwab defines it, and with the three kinds of problems and processes I have chosen to place within this frame. Before proceeding, however, I should make explicit what may be obscure. The formulation of major goals from the identification of an education gap as described does not end the matter of identifying educational goals. Far from it. The possibility and, indeed, probability of new goals emerging open up at each decision-making point and with each actor in the program-planning process. The frequency with which new interests intrude and their potency depend in part on the extent of centralization of authority and decentralization of responsibility. A highly centralized system of education tends to increase the difficulty—and sometimes even the personal risk—of intruding new interests. But a highly decentralized one complicates the problem of making more than parochial changes.

THE IDEOLOGICAL AND POLITICAL IN PROGRAM PLANNING

There is a speculative realm of program planning which sometimes is so generally engaged in as to warrant recognition as a national sport. Participants disagree as to what is wrong with society, where the society should be heading, and what educational programs should be doing to close the gap. Solutions vary with the times and frequently are couched in slogans, in recent years running the gamut from teach the whole child, to life-adjustment education, the 3 R's, the structure of the disciplines, integration of the subjects, humanization of the curriculum, and career education. All these imply goals for educational programs. All tend to get some temporary visibility, often more for their rhetoric than their substance.

There are, of course, less elegantly stated ideologies: Let the kids learn that life is tough; learning should hurt. Or, society is going soft; no better place than school for teaching discipline. Or, society exists for the individual; let the kids do their thing. These notions, too, imply educational goals.

But such speculation and gratuitous advice do little to enlighten ongoing processes of program planning for educational institutions. There is, however, an embryonic field or discipline of program planning which seeks to set some guidelines or ground rules so as to raise casual speculation to systematic inquiry. Tyler, Klein, and Michael on criteria for instructional material,[5] Bloom on taxonomical analysis of educational objectives,[6] Popham and Baker on clarification of instructional objectives,[7] Scriven on formative and summative evaluation,[8] Goodlad on authority and responsibility in curriculum decision making,[9] and Tyler on a rationale for curriculum planning[10] get no extra votes in determining what interests should prevail in the setting of educational goals. But what they have to say about program development frequently does modify what goes on in decision-making processes by providing alternatives seen as superior to the conventional wisdom. Conceivably, their impact would be greater were they to testify before Congressional Committees, as indeed most of them have.

But now we are in danger of leaving the ideological and straying into the political realm of the practical. While recognizing that ideas, to make a practical difference, must find their way through the political structure, our concern with improving the ideological base of the practical is with relevance and validity. Relevance takes us to the question of whether the idea pertains to closing the education gap. If the problem is joblessness, we probably have an engineering gap, at least in the present, and career education is an irrelevant solution. But if the problem is inability to read, a literacy program is relevant.

With relevance determined, the problem now becomes one of selecting among competing alternatives. Which is best, with validity defined as potential for closing the gap between one level of literacy and a higher one? There is a short history of systematic inquiry in regard to almost all such questions. Seldom are its cumulative results definitive, but there is enough knowledge in some areas to advance the level of intelligence in decision making. It is important to look to this knowledge, just as it is exceedingly important to provide more resources, mount more sustained research programs, and recruit better people for the pursuit of such knowledge.

In regard to validity of ideological alternatives, there is rarely a "best"; rather, there are alternative "goods." Rarely are we concerned about a single educational goal existing out of relation to others. The cost of proceeding diligently with one goal may be too great. For example, I discovered as a young elementary-school teacher that my success in motivating certain goals of achievement with ten-year-olds resulted in an upsurge of dangerously competitive behavior and a rash of cheating.

The problem of validity regarding educational ends and means is complicated further by the fact that means frequently are value-loaded quite apart from their presumed logical relation to a given end. That is, such proposals as open classrooms frequently are motivated by interest in social interaction and life-style rather than in the efficient attainment of prescribed objectives. A society open to educational alternatives runs the risk or enhances the opportunity, depending on one's viewpoint, for introducing new goals along with new means. Much of what goes on in education is activity-oriented rather than goal-oriented.

The best solution for enhancing the ideological base for program development in a democratic society has, I think, at least three components. The first is that of enhancing the theoretic. The second is the creation of policy centers. The third is the encouragement of independent program development activity quite apart from the formal political structure. While it is appropriate for all three to proceed in an integrated whole in a single organizational and administrative structure, it is dangerous to have only one such center. Unfortunately, it requires a certain affluence to afford the luxury of alternatives and diversity—or at least, a measure of affluence seems to help.

The theoretic is the natural but not exclusive domain of universities where it is rightfully engaged in for its own sake. It is a matter of selecting the proper questions and pursuing them with complete independence. It is conclusion-oriented inquiry in contrast to decision-oriented.[11] Tyler,[12] Schwab,[13] Herrick,[14] Taba,[15] and many others have posed some of the questions. But we are still short of an agreed-upon set of commonplaces regarding program development or curriculum as a field of study, in the sense that learning theorists explore commonplaces such as motivation, transfer of training, or reinforcement. Recognizing the significance of the practical, in Schwab's terms, is not to deny the importance of the theoretic. In fact, denying the theoretic ultimately castrates the practical.

The concept of educational policy centers is new or still foreign to most states or nations. In the United States, the Syracuse University Research Center has engaged in systematic study of program-related policy questions in the field of education, some of its funds coming from government sources. The Research Division of the Kettering Foundation's Institute for Development of Educational Activities, Inc. (|I|D|E|A|), is a non-university-based agency engaged in studies to provide a research base for policy decisions. The report of the Commission on Educational Planning of Alberta, Canada, is a first-rate example of what can emerge from policy planning.[16] The conduct of such work by a private organization, as appears now to be the case in Alberta, is a viable alternative, especially if there can be several firms and sources of financial support. Policy study centers seek not only to define education gaps but also to analyze them for clues to change and to pose recommendations and strategies for carrying out recommendations. They tend not to engage in theoretic work for its own sake but to enlighten the practical.

The curriculum centers rapidly emerging in developing countries offer promise for both assisting in the formulation of national policy and developing materials-based programs. Most of them engage seriously in evaluation. They present both the strengths and weaknesses of being closely attached to or divisions of ministries of education and the limitation, commonly, of standing alone as the developers of single versions of curricula. By contrast, the highly independent curriculum projects producing such programs as SMSG, PSSC, SCIS, BSCS, CBA, and the like in the United States provided a considerable range of alternatives, especially when versions or segments are included in the products of private publishing companies.[17] Just as the government-linked centers have difficulties getting their products through the classroom door,[18] these independent projects were confronted with this problem and the additional one of gaining sufficient access to the political structure to receive authorization even to knock on classroom doors. Many of them ultimately turned over this problem to the more experienced publishing houses so that their ideological curricular formulations might be carried more effectively through the political structure. In the process, of course, these formulations lost much of their ideology.

THE TECHNICAL/SOCIAL IN PROGRAM DEVELOPMENT

There is no question that ideological program development conceived quite apart from political processes affects the programs experienced by students, whether in public, private, or so-called free schools. Curriculum packages are adopted through the political process and, in some form of adaptation, are used. Societal controlling agencies determine whether certain subjects or topics are to be considered at all—and frequently succeed in keeping some out. Nonetheless, in schools as now conducted, whatever finds its way through the political structure ultimately is subjected to the value orientation of a program gatekeeper, the teacher.

In the final analysis, the teacher, more in a democratic society than in a totalitarian one, determines many of the alternatives from which students actually choose. Indeed, subtle nuances supplied by the teacher frequently favor one over another and determine the rewards and risks for the student in making choices.

Nonetheless, this in no way detracts from the importance of rational processes of ideological program development through which alternative ends and means are posed and justified in pure forms, so to speak, quite apart from conventional wisdom, political processes, the state of instructional technology, and the interests of individual teachers. Nor does the significance of the teacher's role detract from the significance of political processes through which one set of program possibilities gains precedence over another. What occurs in both ideological and political processes constitutes data sources which in large measure determine the teacher's degree of freedom and the alternatives from which he or she chooses.

The fact that teachers are the final arbiters, however, suggests why so many curriculum reformers in the ideological realm find tantalizing the idea of "teacher proof" materials or nonhuman teachers such as computers once they make a foray or two into the political realm or seek to tamper with the social realities of schools and classrooms. It also suggests one of the reasons why some individuals and groups have sought to prescribe precise ground rules for teachers, textbooks for students, time allotments, and the like. No wonder legislators are reluctant to give up authority for prescribing instructional decisions.

Even though the stereotype of teachers in our society in literature, film, television, and cartoon has been that of an impotent, ill-defined Ichabod Crane, the power of the teacher as final arbiter in the continuing struggle for placing one value or goal above another is widely recognized. Perhaps this is why, in part, progress toward creating any other stereotype is slow—it is safer to have impotent teachers! And, if there actually were not some relation between the stereotype and the reality, perhaps teachers would dare, indeed, to build a new social order.

However, the slogan that "it all depends on the teacher" is an empty, perhaps defeatist one. Their behavior is not nearly as technically precise as it could and should be, given significant recent progress in instructional technology. There has been at least an ideological revolution here, especially in the refinement of educational goals. But it is an oversimplification because, also, ideological processes tend to set the alternatives available and, indeed, to put a fence around choices; and political processes largely determine which, if any, ideological formulations will find their way to teachers, how much time they will allocate to them, what additional alternatives may be even considered, and the inducements to maintain the status quo or to change. Educating the individual teacher is no guarantee that the ends and means so acquired by teachers will become operative in the social structure. More often than not, the culture of schools and school systems shapes teachers rather thoroughly.[19] No, indeed, it does not "all depend on the teacher." Consequently, changing educational goals and programs involves much more than the refinement of instructional logistics.

But even teachers are not the final source of educational goals, even when working behind closed doors with control of most of the operants. Students are inordinately adept at frustrating goals held by teachers. Decline in the effectiveness of many secondary schools, for example, suggests a poor interface between today's youth culture and school programs. Many young people choose not to defer to this institution, regarding it as an unwelcome intrusion into their daily lives. Many drop out while still in physical attendance.

To use children and youth genuinely as data sources in goal setting—long talked about in educational circles—would be a significant breakthrough in program planning. To create settings wherein students set and pursue their own educational goals would be a radical innovation.

CONCLUSION

Goals arise out of interests. Planners of educational programs seek to choose among human interests in specifying virtues such as citizenship, work, emotional and physical well-being, and others deemed most worthy of attainment. Statements of goals imply a gap between such virtues and existing conditions. Statements of goals cease to be puerile and become compelling when there are commitments to their attainment. The success of public schools depends heavily on large-scale agreement on and commitment to educational goals.

Educational planners seek to create rational programs in the sense that there are close logical or empirical relations between hierarchies of goals chosen for the "best" possible reasons. This is exceedingly difficult because, as yet, educational science has not drawn the necessary paths of relations. We know little about the relation between precise behavioral goals and the more remote ends usually stated for educational systems.

But, even if we possessed such knowledge, there remain staggering problems of implementing hierarchies of related goals in practice. Goals formulated from the ideological base still must find their way through the political and decision-making structure. In the process, not only are initial goals reformulated but, frequently, they are shunted aside by other interests supported for other reasons. This occurs at every decision-making point: the societal decisions of legislators and school boards, the institutional decisions of administrators and teachers, and the instructional decisions of teachers. Whether or not included formally in the process, students manage to inject their interests, too. Even in totalitarian countries, there is slippage along the way from ideological goals to the existential goals of individual classrooms.

All these processes are grist for theory and research. Likewise, all these processes together constitute the practical domain of curriculum planners. At this point in time, both the theory to guide and the technology to expedite program development are, at best, weak. There is developing a useful technology of instruction, but at the very time when there is increasing talk of decentralizing authority and responsibility, research suggests that schoolwide program planning is virtually nonexistent. Teachers and parents at the level of the local school are not at all clear on the kinds of decisions they should make and the kind they should borrow ready-made. Who should make what decisions becomes an increasingly important question in seeking to allocate and identify authority and responsibility in program development.

If increased authority and responsibility for selecting educational goals is to be decentralized to local schools, school personnel and community representatives alike will need preparation for the tasks far beyond what they now have. Further, there will need to be time allocations extending far beyond those bits and pieces now used by teachers and parents in late afternoon or evening meetings. Just as education is too important to be left to the educators alone, so is it too important to be left to those in the community who have little else to do. There will need to be hard choices regarding what to leave appropriately for the educators and what to assign to a broad-based citizens group willing to take the time—including the time required to become reasonably knowledgeable about planning processes and educational alternatives. Likewise, the real consumers, the students, must play a role far beyond any assigned to them to date.

At the beginning level of discourse about educational goals for the local school, I have found it useful to engage educators, parents, and students alike in seeking answers to three simple questions. First, what is it about our school that we like and wish to keep or strengthen? Second, what are things to be changed that could be improved in a matter of weeks? Third, what are those things to be improved that will require months or even years?

Such questions almost always lead groups into serious discussion of school functions and goals, to plans for action and to action itself. There is something much more vital and rewarding about this approach, as contrasted with the more ethereal task of formulating a set of educational goals. Goals, almost always, will result from it, nonetheless, and will be accompanied, more often than not, by commitment to close the educational gap implied by them. There comes a time in educational program planning, as in other human affairs, to act on commitment rendered compelling by insight even though not all the facts are in—for, in fact, they never will be.

Notes

[1]In fact, long before the current spate of interest in precisely defined goals (objectives), Bobbitt virtually equated educational activities and educational objectives, proposing a process of division and redivision from ten categories to an incomplete list of 821 objectives constituting ". . . the quite specific activities that are to be performed" (p. 9). But the question of the source of the original categories still stands. See Franklin Bobbitt, *How to Make a Curriculum*, Riverside Press, Cambridge, Mass., 1924.

[2]James B. Macdonald, "Curriculum and Human Interests," Virgil E. Herrick Memorial Lecture, Madison, Wisconsin, July 1972. (Mimeographed.)

[3]C. Robert Pace, "The Relationship between College Grades and Adult Achievement: A Review of the Literature," in Donald P. Hoyt (ed.), ACT Research Reports, No. 7, American College Testing Program, Iowa City, 1965.

[4]Joseph J. Schwab, *The Practical: A Language for Curriculum*, National Education Association, Washington, D.C., 1970, p. 5.

[5]Louise L. Tyler, M. Frances Klein, and William B. Michael, *Recommendations for Curriculum and Instructional Materials*, Tyl Press, Los Angeles, 1971.

[6]Benjamin S. Bloom (ed.), *Taxonomy of Educational Objectives: The Classification of Educational Goals. Handbook I. Cognitive Domain*, McKay, New York, 1956.

[7]W. James Popham and Eva L. Baker, *Establishing Instructional Goals*, Prentice-Hall, Englewood Cliffs, N. J., 1970.

[8]Michael Scriven, "The Methodology of Evaluation," in Ralph Tyler, Robert Gagné, and Michael Scriven (eds.), *Perspectives of Curriculum Evaluation*, pp. 39–83, AERA Monograph Series on Curriculum Evaluation, Rand McNally, Chicago, 1967.

[9]John I. Goodlad (with Maurice N. Richter, Jr.), *The Development of a Conceptual System for Dealing with Problems of Curriculum and Instruction*, HEW, USOE, Contract No. SAE-8024, Project No. 454, University of California, Los Angeles, 1966.

[10]Ralph W. Tyler, *Basic Principles of Curriculum and Instruction*, University of Chicago Press, Chicago, 1949.

[11]Lee J. Cronbach and Patrick Suppes (eds.), *Research for Tomorrow's Schools*, Report of the Committee on Educational Research of the National Academy of Education, Macmillan, New York, 1969.

[12]Tyler, op. cit.

[13]Joseph J. Schwab, "Structure of the Disciplines: Meanings and Significances," in G. W. Ford and Lawrence Pugno (eds.), *The Structure of Knowledge and the Curriculum*, Rand McNally, Chicago, 1964, pp. 6–30.

[14]Virgil E. Herrick, *Strategies of Curriculum Development: The Works of Virgil E. Herrick*, selected and compiled by James B. Macdonald, Dan W. Anderson, and Frank B. May, Charles E. Merrill, Columbus, Ohio, 1965.

[15]Hilda Taba, *Curriculum Development: Theory and Practice*, Harcourt, Brace, Jovanovich, New York, 1962.

[16]Commission on Educational Planning, *A Choice of Futures*, Cabinet Committee on Education, Edmonton, Alberta, 1972.

[17]John I. Goodlad, with Renata von Stoephasius and M. Frances Klein, *The Changing School Curriculum*, Fund for the Advancement of Education, New York, 1966.

[18]John I. Goodlad, M. Frances Klein, and Associates, *Behind the Classroom Door*, Charles A. Jones, Worthington, Ohio, 1970, rev. and retitled, *Looking Behind the Classroom Door*, 1974.

[19]Seymour B. Sarason, *The Culture of the School and the Problem of Change*, Allyn and Bacon, Boston, 1971.

4

Making Decisions

The realm of the political, discussed briefly in the previous chapter, is the subject matter here. I like to think of the form of this section as reflecting the ababcb form of poetry or musical composition. Ideas which are introduced in one chapter are developed more fully in the next. This has led, in some cases, to my dividing a paper—sometimes rather arbitrarily—and including parts of it in two or more chapters, even though the original paper presented a unified whole. [Editor]

The conduct of schooling is largely a political enterprise. The schools must be organized, financed, managed, and conducted for the welfare of children and youth through those legislative, executive, and judicial processes characterizing our public affairs generally. Schooling, then, is conducted within a framework of power and struggle for power. It is no more protected from abuse of power than are other political enterprises.

SOURCE: John I. Goodlad, "What Educational Decisions by Whom?" *The Science Teacher*, May 1971, pp. 16–19, 80–81; John I. Goodlad, "Program Development: Identification and Formulation of Desirable Educational Goals," in *Program Development in Education*, Report of the International Symposium on Program Development in Education, University of British Columbia, Morriss Printing Co., Ltd., Victoria, 1974, pp. 56–70; and John I. Goodlad, "Curriculum Planning for the Revolutionary Age," address delivered at the Edgar Dale Education Communication Conference, Columbus, Ohio, May 9, 1970.

Educators, in particular, like to link education and ideas. They frequently forget that ideas, to make a difference, must find their way through and into the political structure. Ideas, then, are grist for the political mill. Once generated, they will be used, abused, quoted, misquoted, twisted, and warped for political purposes good or bad, individual or collective. To ignore this is to ignore what is real.

Various groups are willing to subordinate the virtue of this or that educational idea to the matter of whose authority will prevail in decision-making situations employing ideas. Individuals, no matter how good their ideas on substantive grounds, frequently are trampled under by all groups other than those who share their group goals. This always has been a characteristic of Western civilization. It simply becomes more harshly apparent during periods of sharp questioning and restructuring of power. Such is our present condition. But, somehow, we must find a way for authority and responsibility in educational decision making to be exchanged without impeding the flow of good ideas into the schools.

The educational stage is thus set for a fascinating drama to be unfolded. The play might well be entitled, "What Decisions by Whom?" Or, somewhat facetiously, it could be entitled, "Button, Button, Who's Got the Button?"

I shall endeavor to lay out the play in three acts. In act one, "The Schools Are in Trouble," we see that whether or not there is something wrong with the schools is not the question. The question is, *what* is wrong with them? The nature of the diagnosis will suggest the prescription, who or what will be best able to fill it, and, therefore, who will be the schools' doctors and pharmacists. Act two, "A Piece of the Action," seeks to sort out who is making what decisions and whether or not they should. Act three, "Lest the Children Be Forgotten," focuses on the school as a locus for educational improvement.

THE SCHOOLS ARE IN TROUBLE

The voices of school criticism are many and disparate, but two major choruses may be differentiated. Neo-humanists such as Goodman, Friedenberg, and Holt[1] appealed to a generation of college students with their charge that the school is an inhumane institution, warping the child's personality and sensitivity. Silberman's[2] accusations regarding mindless pursuit of obscure ends reached a diversified audience of laymen, school board members, and educators. On the other side of the ideological coin is the widespread charge that schools are inefficient and wasteful and that those operating them must be held accountable for greater efficiency and for improved learning on the part of students.

At first, the "romantic" critics sought only to go outside the system in the creation of "free schools." But then there were growing signs of their wanting to work inside the system in order to have their beliefs more widely implemented. Somewhat to their surprise, the neo-humanists are finding that not all administrators are bad or misled and that not all teachers are sadists, although "they" must be out there someplace. In time, these critics will discover that independent pupil planning and self-selection, curricula based on students' interests and needs, child study programs, sensitivity training, group therapy, and the like are not unfamiliar breezes but are winds that have blown across the school scene before. Perhaps this discovery will lead to a fresh round of outraged disaffection for the system that does not quickly enough assimilate new ideas. Or, hopefully, it will perhaps lead to the realization that there are no special villains to be singled out and to more serious efforts to understand and change the system.

On the other hand, neo-behaviorism brings with it the sound of machines, especially the hum of computers, surely and efficiently ordering the disarrayed affairs of people. There is little despair or pessimism in these quarters. Planning, programming, budgeting systems will set things right. Some of today's most ardent advocates, fully aware of the need to inject their ideas into the political process, belie the cool rationality and empirical research that have characterized Skinner and lesser-known behavioristic scholars and decision makers. The extravagant nature of their claims can lead only to further disillusionment—and that we need not at all.

In fact, when one observes and listens to some of the more ludicrous activities and pronouncements of extremists in both camps, one is inclined to say, "A plague upon both your houses." But further reflection suggests the enormous advantages of being able to play the central tenets of these two movements one against the other. Further, one comes to realize that it is to the degree that both are blended and woven into the fabric of American education that there will be a measure of order to our planning for tomorrow and increasing realization of and attention to the fact that schooling and education are human processes. We will change and improve them only to the degree that the humans involved are changed. Their change, in turn, requires responsibility, authority, and accountability for those decisions that are proper for them to make. We must strive toward decision-making processes that assure inclusion of the best ideas from these two movements, humanism and behaviorism, that have so profoundly influenced educational thinking.

A PIECE OF THE ACTION

The major question, then, becomes: "Who should make what decisions?" But first it would be well to find out something about the extant decision-making process. Elsewhere, I have conceptualized three decision-making levels according to the actors and, to a lesser degree, the nature of the decisions.[3] These levels I have labelled societal, institutional, and instructional, somewhat following Parson's analysis of social systems.[4]

Briefly, societal decisions are those made for classes of learners, such as adolescents, by some controlling agency, such as the legislature or a school board, usually at a level in the structure remote from those for whom the decisions are intended. Institutional decisions are those made for specific students now in the programs, or soon to be enrolled, by those directly responsible for the education of these students. Instructional decisions are those bringing intended learnings to specific students who are then required to make some sort of adaptation to them.

All three types can be simulated ideologically—that is, outside of the political structure—and this is an appropriate activity for theorists. In free schools, the levels tend to be collapsed, and this is a very attractive feature for free spirits wishing to escape the bureaucracy of public education. But they soon find that they cannot escape the decisions. The burdens and complexities of dealing with them frequently douse the spirits of even the most doughty.

Experience in using this three-level analysis of reality shows that it holds up in developing as well as developed countries. However, this experience, together with Griffin's study[5] and the studies my colleagues and I have conducted regarding educational change,[6] suggests that the least active of the three levels is the institutional. Few schools have goals or thought-through programs to which they are committed; few schools engage seriously in translating state, provincial, or national educational aims into statements of local relevance. Perhaps this is because the task is so difficult and time-consuming, as McClure's study reveals.[7] At the same time, school staffs engaging in it seriously and in sustained fashion extoll the values of the process[8] and frequently insist on the right to engage in it.

Recent stress on local accountability and some movement toward decentralization of decision-making authority may be changing this vacuum in institution-based goal setting, but there is as yet little evidence to suggest that schools, "free" or not, are playing a significant role in determining educational goals for or with the students enrolled. I am not necessarily suggesting that local schools or even school systems are the proper setting for the *initial* formulation of goals. But, given the generality of state or national aims, when they are stated at all, I am suggesting that there is a need to translate societal goals into operational institutional ones and to rearrange priorities or even to choose among alternatives in the light of community and pupil needs and realities. Perhaps, in so doing, the fragile link between what teachers do and our idealized ends for education and schooling would be strengthened.

This trend in my analysis turns me back to the troublesome question of who should make what decisions. The situation as it now exists is chaotic. Griffin had little difficulty getting satisfactory agreement among independent judges regarding decisions thought to be appropriate for a societal body such as legislators, as discrete from those considered appropriate for teachers at the instructional level.[9] But Hill's study of legislators revealed both their readiness to intrude into the instructional process and their general ignorance of past legislation applying to their current interests.[10] Some saw little need to be informed, and few recognized the implicit issue of authority and responsibility and its importance.

Thus, at the very time when we desperately need clarity, the matter of who should make what educational decisions is exceedingly confused. State legislators pass laws which, as often as not, restrict teachers in their efforts to adapt method and content to the needs of learners. State and local boards of education frequently duplicate each other and, at times, assume authority presumably delegated to administrators. Superintendents, principals, and teachers are not at all clear on their realms of jurisdiction. Likewise, the lay citizen knows not how to influence the schools or to participate meaningfully in their improvement. The forces which must collaborate if the schools are to be improved rarely work together, let alone communicate.

It is not at all uncommon, in the midst of complex problems and social disarray, for simple answers couched in slogans to emerge. One of many current slogans is "accountability." Clearly, in the eyes of many, teachers are responsible for children's learning and must be held accountable for improvement. Ironically, the call for accountability often is accompanied by restrictions on the very freedoms teachers need if they are to be held accountable. It should not surprise us, then, to find that increasing teacher militancy is accompanied not only by demands for higher salaries but also by requests for improved working conditions, including a larger say in educational decisions.

One cannot legitimately quarrel with legislators who seek to improve education through the passage of better legislation; with school board members who enter zealously into their responsibilities; with citizens who desire to act for better schools; and with teachers who want freedom to teach. But all these groups, in their zeal or in their less commendable drive for power, tend to reach beyond the land that is rightfully theirs to plow and to neglect their own ill-kept furrows. Schools and the children in them are, as a consequence, the losers.

Confusion in Action

If each school staff is to be held accountable for developing and implementing institutional plans, then each must possess the authority necessary to make decisions unencumbered by inappropriate restrictions. Most schools possess more authority than they think they have. Nonetheless, most also are restricted by pressures, negotiated agreements, or even legislative acts that interfere with the decisions for which they are to be held accountable. All those groups seeking a piece of the educational action must become more acutely aware than they appear to be now that the decisions they make ultimately affect the individual school and the people connected with it. These groups, too, must be held accountable— accountable for the ways their actions affect school and classroom.

Unfortunately, who makes what decisions and how decisions made at one level in the educational enterprise affect decisions at other levels are relatively unexamined questions.[11] Consequently, in the game of power that accompanies education as a political process, the drive of organized groups—including professional ones— is to influence or to make the decisions and to ignore the question of who should make them. Since no organized pressure group speaks for the school as a unit, the struggle for power could seriously curtail the freedom of the school to make decisions affecting it and perhaps, make a mock of current drives to hold it accountable.

Let me offer a few examples of what I am talking about. The education code in a large state specifies that no child below the fourth grade may be enrolled in a class of more than thirty pupils. No doubt, this regulation was passed with the good intention of maintaining low enrollments at the primary level. But forward-looking schools have been moving into a variety of nongraded, multigraded, and multiaged practices that mix children of various ages. In such schools in that state, however, these practices run into obstacles when children of eight or nine and grades below the third are mixed with older children or higher grades where the pupil-teacher ratio may be greater than 30:1. The state acts properly when it acts to provide resources for quality schooling. It acts improperly, however, when it goes beyond such societal decisions to make institutional decisions limiting the way in which school staffs group children for learning.

Sometimes, local school boards, in their zeal, make decisions that infringe directly on the prerogatives of the teacher in the classroom. In one such instance, the superintendent, without consulting the teachers, recommended that a phonetic-alphabet approach to the teaching of reading be used exclusively in the primary grades. The board was delighted. It approved the recommendation but added that tests be given semiannually and that the teachers be held accountable for improvement in reading scores over each semester. Usually, in cases of this kind, which are frequent in one form or another, teachers focus their distress on what is required, in this case the method of teaching reading. But this is the wrong focus of attention. The right question to ask is whether or not a board and a superintendent should make such decisions. In my judgment, restricting the pedagogical procedures of teachers in this way is a direct infringement on their right to make instructional decisions. When persons outside of the classroom—whether they be legislators, school board members, or administrators—make such decisions, they and not the teachers must be held accountable for the resulting success or failure of the pupils.

In one state, a parent brought suit against a nongraded school on the grounds that his child suffered mental anguish through being placed with younger children for instructional purposes. The judge ruled against the plaintiff but ordered an end to nongrading on the grounds that the state was required by law to provide a K–12 system of instruction. This implied to him the necessity of there being 13 clearly defined "grades."

The decision was challenged by the state education association and the National Association of Elementary School Principals (see Chapter 8). These segments of the organized education profession saw the decision as dangerous to the decision-making authority of the school to provide education in the light of current, forward-looking thinking.

Meanwhile, however, a somewhat similar type of storm was brewing in another state, with the organized profession taking a rather different stand. For some years, a local board of education had been looking into the pros and cons of merit-pay plans. Apparently, it began to link up the possibilities with team teaching accompanied by differentiated staffing. The local teachers association viewed this linkage, in turn, as a threat to salary negotiations for fully certified personnel. Its thrust increasingly became tied up with the notion of a certified teacher in every classroom and this, in turn, with a fixed pupil-teacher ratio. There was the possibility that the teachers group would include "no differential staffing" as a clause in the bargaining agreement.

Here, the professional group, in its zeal to protect teacher welfare, was in danger of bargaining away the rights of the local schools to make appropriate decisions for children. The substantive was sacrificed to the political. (Ironically, the day may come when a complete reversal of position will be necessary in order to protect teacher welfare.) A profession is established, maintained, and respected on the basis of the substantiated body of knowledge and skills required for its practice. Professional standing and recognition come under public scrutiny when concern for such knowledge is traded for power in the political arena.

In the shifts of power likely to occur in the future, the organized profession must be exceedingly careful not to argue out of both sides of its mouth, even though other groups will do so. Regarding the first instance involving nongrading, I was asked by the professional groups to present a brief for the courts, and I argued, in part, against restrictive legislation. The anachronistic code should be struck from the books, leaving better methods to be found through research and experimentation, not court rulings. Also, I presented the substantive case for nongrading, even though I realized that this was not the basic issue at stake. In the second instance, team teaching was again not the basic issue, but a brief favoring differentiated staffing on substantive grounds would somewhat embarrass the teachers association in its political role.

One could cite thousands of instances to illustrate the confusion—nay chaos—with respect to authority and responsibility for decision making in education. But just a few additional examples will suffice. They are *not* fictitious:

1. The board of a fast-growing school district approved construction of a modern, open-space school. The superintendent then picked a principal to design and implement the program for which the building presumably was designed. Within a year after the school was opened, several parents complained to the board about undue noise and freedom in the large open spaces being used for team teaching. The board reacted by instructing the superintendent to order the principal and his staff to revert to the more orderly procedures presumed to characterize traditional school buildings. The principal resisted, requesting and being granted the opportunity to conduct a survey of parental opinion regarding the school. The returns were highly favorable. Soon after, the superintendent moved on to bigger things and the board selected this principal as the new superintendent. Cases of this kind seldom turn out so happily.

2. A state legislature, unhappy over the results of reading tests in the schools, proposed that at least half of all time devoted to the teaching of reading in the state should stress oral reading. As can be imagined, this proposal caused no small outcry on the part of primary teachers in the state.

3. For years, the sixth-grade class of an elementary school had studied the United Nations. Teachers, parents, and children came to expect this as standard fare for the first semester. On one occasion, just before school was to open, the regular teacher became seriously ill and was granted a year's sick leave. The substitute who was hired had her own ideas about what should be taught in the sixth grade and proceeded to teach, during the first semester, a social studies

unit dealing with exploring and governing outer space. Many parents and several of the teachers became quite upset and exerted pressure to discontinue the unit, attacking the new teacher in the process. The teacher soon came to the principal in desperation, wondering whether it would be advisable for her to resign.

4. A state board of education decreed that, henceforth, persons would be certified to teach in the state only if they held an undergraduate major, an undergraduate minor, and certain specified courses in education. The teacher-preparing institutions found that compliance with the new regulations virtually eliminated all courses in education other than those specified and began to release or reassign, wherever possible, the surplus faculty members, most of whom taught certain specialized courses often lumped together as "methods courses." Preparation in the teaching of reading was seriously cut. Within a few years of this succession of decisions, there was a growing outcry against the quality of teaching reading in the schools of the state, and it was proposed, therefore, that teachers be held accountable for improvement in the teaching of reading. Testing of children was to occur at regular intervals.

These anecdotes reveal many significant decisions by groups of persons who should be held responsible and accountable for various aspects of the educational process. Were the right decisions being made by the right people?

The education of a child in school is much more than the relatively simple matter of his interacting with the teacher and the learning fare selected by that teacher. His school education is a product of many decisions by many people, not all of whom know him, his talents, his interests, and his needs. Many of the persons making these decisions have never questioned whether or not they should. Most have never met the others whose decisions affect the learner at the end of the line. Most are quite unaware of the ultimate impact of the decisions they make.

One result of this situation is duplication, overlap, and confusion in the bundle of decisions which are made for education. The laws passed by state legislatures often hit their mark, but not always with beneficial consequences. Further, even the most permissive and helpful legislation frequently is confused and confounded by directives laid down by state departments of education. Local boards of education vacillate between assuming too much authority and responsibility for some spheres of involvement while completely neglecting others. Some superintendents virtually neglect their principals. Others require that principals appear in person before the school board to request permission on matters which should fall within the superintendent's scope of independent judgment and authority.

Lack of clarity in matters of educational decision making can and does create conflict. Teachers are instructed to use a phonics approach in teaching reading but, obviously, must risk violating such directives in dealing with children whose hearing is impaired. Principals and teachers in many schools violate the existing education code in order to exercise their own best judgment in dealing with educationally handicapped children. In some states and school districts, it is almost impossible to teach without violating some requirement enacted at remote levels of decision making.

Perhaps the most serious consequence of this confusion is that some of the most important educational decisions go by default. For example, state boards of education frequently hassle over how reading should be taught—a matter for which they have no competence—while neglecting to give attention to the inadequate, outdated system of financing the schools which exists in most states. Many local boards stoutly resist any educational guidance from federal levels of education, especially in the area of determining what is to be accomplished in their schools. However, very few school boards give systematic attention to this question. Consequently, the ends and means they seek to protect are determined largely by those commercial publishing houses whose textbooks are adopted for their schools. Principals and teachers are quite capable of identifying a host of complex problems faced by their schools at any given time. But only a handful of school faculties is at work on the problems which they themselves identify as pressing.

I have done little more here than to identify a problem of grave importance. The determination of decision-making roles within the political structure governing education probably is the most urgent problem now facing us. I conclude this topic by suggesting (1) that who should make a decision bears a relationship to who has the data (e.g., teachers should work with children in setting specific reading goals for individuals and should not be handicapped by restraining regulations in the education code); (2) that there needs to be much more stress on school-by-school planning; (3) that the planning at levels getting increasingly close to specific students must use as one data source the corresponding decisions already made at more remote levels; and (4) that increasingly, students must become both data sources and more intimately involved in determining their own goals and programs.

To come back to where I began, I am fully aware of the fact that the conduct of schooling is largely a political process. But it also is a substantive one, depending on the infusion of knowledge over conventional wisdom. I am arguing only for somewhat greater rationality in the decision-making process. Two essential criteria in judging rationality are, first, whether the persons or groups most likely to have the relevant knowledge are making the decisions and, second, whether or not they are the persons to be held accountable for the decisions. The question is only temporarily one of who has the authority to make the decision, because authority often is not rationally allocated and is subject to challenge by and transfer to other groups. The opening question to raise before plunging into the decision-making arena is whether this is the realm or level of decisions in which I should be involved and for which I am likely to be held responsible.

Legislatures are properly involved in the educational decision-making process when they make and fulfill commitments to educate the young or the handicapped at public expense; to alleviate restrictions on opportunities for disadvantaged groups to gain access to schools; to maintain an equitable tax structure for the support of education; to determine priorities in the light of knowledge pertaining to statewide conditions, national needs, neglected fields for human development, and the like. State boards of education behave appropriately when they translate priorities into broad aims or goals to guide local boards and their schools. But both groups behave inappropriately when they rule on the way in which the curriculum or classes of local schools should be organized, pupils grouped, or reading taught. Not being professionals, they lack the framework of knowledge required; and, being far removed from the scene, they do not possess the specific data needed for such decisions. Not only do they behave irrationally when they become so involved, but, in addition, they consume the time and energy so badly needed for putting their state responsibilities in order. Legislators and school board members must be held accountable for such misplaced attention and for its impact on our children.

Local boards of education parallel state boards of education in regard to the nature of their responsibilities, with national and state goals as data sources but with priorities reflecting concerns of the immediate community. Since these board members are much closer to schools and children, there is an enormous temptation to become experts on curriculum, school organization, classroom practices, and evaluation procedures; to pronounce quality judgments on the basis of casual visits to classrooms; and to generalize from scattered complaints or accusations regarding the schools' effectiveness.

Again, teachers tend to focus primarily on whether or not they agree with the decisions of the board on specific educational practices rather than on the more important question of whether or not the decisions are properly those of the board to make. Generally, they do not object to such board decisions if they are reasonably compatible with teachers' views on the same topics. Instead, however, they should strenuously object to transgressions of this kind. Democracy depends upon it.

Teachers are responsible and accountable for instructional decisions—those decisions made just prior to or at the point of contact with students. For their judgment in selecting this or that topic or method of instruction to be impeded by laws or regulations enacted by people at places remote from this instructional level is to jeopardize the quality of learning. Teachers must not be held accountable and must not accept accountability for learning when their degrees of freedom to make instructional decisions are significantly limited by inappropriate laws, rules, or regulations.

Left with freedom to make instructional decisions, teachers will make stupid as well as wise ones. Such is the nature of democratic processes. But occasional mistakes are no excuse for removing authority from all those at this level now exercising it. This merely creates a higher level of incompetence. No, the solution is to provide opportunity for those responsible to learn the behavior required. This not succeeding, the subsequent step is the removal of incompetent personnel. As the teaching profession seeks increased authority in the decision-making process, it must accompany this drive with a process for dealing with its own incompetents.

LEST THE CHILDREN BE FORGOTTEN

To be true to one's calling is to argue for it in the marketplace. In education, there are many competing persuasions. The physicists want more and better physics; the biologists, more and better biology; the coaches, more athletics. The anthropologists, economists, and psychologists would like to see their disciplines firmly established in the precollegiate curriculum. And then there are legislators and assorted groups wanting drug abuse education, sex education, ethnic studies, instruction in religion, sensitivity training, essay contests, cinematography, and on and on.

But schools deal with finite time. There are only so many hours in a day, days in a week, weeks in a year. Out there in the ideological world are hundreds of callings, each seeking time and identification in the programs of real schools and real students. In order to have their interests represented, most educators understand something of the games of power and politics which they must play to advance their interests through the political structure to the schools. Without considering the full range of alternate persuasions available and the stringent nature of time restraints in schools, they join the power games people play in promoting their views. Winning becomes increasingly attractive and absorbing. Frequently, purposes beyond winning are lost to view. Children invariably are the losers.

Each group ultimately gets around to accusing the others of having forgotten the children. If children were to sit in on the games of their elders, they would shake their heads in dismay.

Legislators may pass laws, boards may set goals of citizenship for the schools, and superintendents may see to it that new courses of study are written. Ultimately, however, all this must be translated into the programs of local schools if it is to affect students. Much of it, as we have seen, is blunted on school and classroom doors. Teachers do not keep up to date with the plethora of new laws introduced to the education code each year; good citizenship cannot be wished into being; and courses of study are singularly lacking in charisma. A turned-on or turned-off school faculty determines whether the institution is a vital place that engages students, an irrelevant place intruding on students' time, or a fenced, temporary prison conducted in the name of education. Clearly, the individual school, with its students, teachers, parents, and community, is the truly organic unit for educational vitality and change. And yet, ironically, the single school probably is the weakest link politically in the entire structure of the decision-making process.

This could be a good thing, provided we come to recognize more than we do now the fact that all the groups competing for a piece of the action share the school. The school is the place where the excesses of competing interests must be washed out for the welfare of those to be educated.

Too often, however, the school is the victim in the power struggle and is torn apart by selfish motivations or hamstrung by rules and by pressure groups preying upon it. The school, as a living social entity of human beings, must become more self-consciously aware of the fact that this is where ideologies both begin and end so far as what happens to students is concerned. School faculties must begin to work together as they have not done before in hammering out the kind of environment its residents are to enjoy. Students, parents, supervisors, administrators, and the larger community must be brought into a continuing dialogue about what school is for. The professional/technical staff must make decisions regarding the design of the curriculum and the ways in which classes are to be organized and conducted and must evaluate the effects of actions in relation to school goals.

But the school often is an isolated, lonely entity that grows in upon itself. Therefore, it should be linked to other schools in new social systems sharing ideas, talent, and concern for improved schooling. In the process, we must define the decisions which school groups should make as contrasted to those to be made more remotely and to those to be left to the discretion of individual teachers.

It follows, then, that the school must be regarded as a testing ground for ideas. Before we conclude that behavioral objectives are beacons beckoning us to the new learning paradise, let us see what schools can make of them. Before blindly adopting the "open school" as the ultimate solution for all that is wrong in schooling, let us have schools give it a try. Perhaps we will find that there are several roads to the good life, not all of them yet discovered. As Bruce Joyce suggests, it is both possible and desirable to conduct several alternative models of schools simultaneously.[12] There is an appropriate role for the self-directed model of the humanists, for the goal-directed model of the behaviorists, for problem-solving approaches, and for discipline-oriented curricula.

Current deficiencies in American education lie less with teachers who are ill-prepared in their subjects or who are lazy and indifferent than with our *collective* failure to make the school a vital place that grips lawmaker, taxpayer, and educator alike in a common commitment to its welfare.

In the struggle for power and influence that characterizes the educational enterprise, we will continue to fight the cause of teacher welfare, promote our fields with unbridled enthusiasm, pass laws that appear to provide a better day for this group of children or that, and formulate better overarching aims for education. But let us also strive to avoid those many seemingly attractive actions that, in the long run, will hinder local schools in dealing effectively with the overwhelming problems confronting them. Lest the children be forgotten.

Notes

[1] Paul Goodman, *Compulsory Mis-Education*, Horizon Press, New York, 1964; Edgar Z. Friedenberg, *The Vanishing Adolescent*, Dell Publishing Co., New York, 1959; John Holt, *How Children Fail*, Pitman Publishing Co., New York, 1969. This is only a small sample of authors who have written on similar themes.

[2] Charles E. Silberman, *Crisis in the Classroom: The Remaking of American Education*, Random House, New York, 1970.

[3] John I. Goodlad (with Maurice N. Richter, Jr.), *The Development of a Conceptual System for Dealing with Problems of Curriculum and Instruction*, HEW, USOE, Contract No. SAE 8024, Project No. 454, University of California, Los Angeles, 1966.

[4] Talcott Parsons, *The Social System*, Free Press, New York, 1951.

[5] Gary A. Griffin, "Curricular Decision Making in Selected School Systems," unpublished doctoral dissertation, University of California, Los Angeles, 1970.

[6] These studies are reported in the six volumes of the |I|D|E|A| *Reports on Schooling*, Series on Educational Change, McGraw-Hill, New York, 1973–1975. Also see film reports, *The League*, available from |I|D|E|A|, P. O. Box 446, Melbourne, Florida.

[7] Robert M. McClure, "Procedures, Processes, and Products in Curriculum Development," unpublished doctoral dissertation, University of California, Los Angeles, 1965.

[8] John I. Goodlad, "Staff Development: The League Model," *Theory Into Practice*, vol. 11, no. 4, October 1972.

[9] Griffin, op. cit.

[10] Henry W. Hill, "Curriculum Legislation and Decision-Making for the Instructional Level," unpublished doctoral dissertation, University of California, Los Angeles, 1970.

[11] For an excellent analysis of accountability in relation to levels of decision making, see Kenneth A. Tye, "Educational Accountability in an Era of Change," *Metropolitan St. Louis Conference on New Dimensions of Teaching*, St. Louis White House Conference on Education, St. Louis, 1970.

[12] Bruce Joyce, *Alternative Models of Elementary Education*, Ginn and Company, Waltham, Mass., 1969.

Issues For Today...

We now turn to a set of issues that are currently exercising the minds of educators, educational researchers, and concerned citizens. Goodlad first discusses curriculum as a field of study and analyzes the cycles of excess and reaction that have characterized curriculum movements. He proposes directions for the next cycle and offers a model for looking at curriculum that could well make the process more rational.

Chapter 6 addresses the issue of equality of educational opportunity, not only as a social issue but as an *educational* issue. Outworn practices within the school have mirrored and perpetuated the injustices of the larger society, so that opportunity can not be equalized only by court decree and methods such as busing. Traditional educational practices need to be reformed in order to promote equal educational opportunity within the school. Chapter 7 extends the argument to propose educational means to overcome inequality. Thus, nongrading, team teaching, and differentiated staffing are proposed not merely as "innovations" or avant-garde practices but as practical means of combatting inequities and dealing with the very real individual differences that exist in any group of students.

The concept of nongrading is defended in Chapter 9—defended literally, since this paper resulted from a commission by the National Association of Elementary School Principals to prepare a brief for a court case challenging the right of a Michigan school district to establish a nongraded school.

Chapters 9 and 10 deal with two issues occupying the center ring in the political circus. "Early Schooling: The Young Discovered" offers an analysis of the current state of the field of early childhood education which should provide some perspective in current discussions about extending public-supported schooling downward. "Perspective on Accountability" cautions those who assume that demands for accountability in education will solve our problems.

5

Curriculum: *A Janus Look*

An old god is invoked in a discussion of a young field of study. This paper has been considerably updated for inclusion in this volume. [Editor]

On three counts the Roman god, Janus, is relevant to what I am about to say. First, Janus has been represented as having two faces, one looking forward and the other backward. I look from the present into the recent past and from the present into the imminent future. Second, Janus was the animistic spirit of doorways and archways. I speak to the problems of cutting doorways between and building archways over different levels of curriculum decision making. Third, Janus, in Roman mythology, was guardian of the gate of heaven (the "opener" and the "shutter") and god of all beginnings. Those of us who work in curriculum might be expected, then, to invoke Janus in making our beginnings and to reckon with Janus at the ending believed by some to be still another beginning.

RECENT CURRICULUM EMPHASES

Curriculum, in theory and practice, is now ready for the tenets of progressive education. In fact, a large part of progressive education

SOURCE: John I. Goodlad, "Curriculum: A Janus Look," *Teachers College Record*, vol. 70, November 1968, pp. 95–107.

that once was embodied in the conventional wisdom—if not the professional practice—of educators is now embodied in the conventional wisdom of a new generation of educators. But they did not learn it from their history books. They acquired it, in part, from the discipline-centered curriculum reform movement and its accompanying psychological baggage that moved in behind the dying propaganda thrusts of life-adjustment education. Then, what they had acquired was humanized by the alternative education movement that followed.

The first (1951) and last (1954) reports of the two Commissions on Life Adjustment Education for Youth almost coincide with the creation of the National Science Foundation (1950), which came to finance many curriculum reform projects in subsequent years, and the appearance of products from the University of Illinois Committee on School Mathematics (1951), perhaps the earliest of the organized interdisciplinary groups.[1] And the death of the Progressive Education Association (1955) and of its journal (1957) coincide in time with the early efforts of Jerrold Zacharias to organize his fellow scientists for school curriculum reform,[2] and with Sputnik (1957). The decade of the fifties marks the ending of one era and the beginning of another.

My statement that a new generation of educators is learning the conventional wisdom of one era from the conventional wisdom of another appears, at first glance, to be enigmatic if not in error. The beginning of the new era certainly did not take its rhetoric from the dying gasps of life-adjustment education. Progressive education already had lost its intellectual vigor before the life-adjustment movement fell victim to the fusillade of attacks ultimately intended for the larger, longer parent movement.[3] What is now referred to as the discipline-centered curriculum reform movement[4] had no orthodoxy throughout most of the decade of the 1950s. It simply was against what appeared to be excesses as expressed in earlier pedagogical cant: "the whole child," "persistent life situations," "intrinsic motivation," and particularly "teaching children, not subjects" and for what appeared to be neglected—subject matter as perceived by specialists in the disciplines. In 1938, Boyd Bode had predicted, ". . . if [progressive education] persists in a one-sided absorption in the individual pupil, it will be circumvented and left behind."[5]

Change, by definition, is away from what exists or appears to exist. And change is likely to be excessive or give the appearance of excess when what it seeks to replace is or appears to be excessive. Perhaps this is why the discipline-centered curriculum reform movement acquired an orthodoxy so soon. In the 1960s, its own central tenets became cant: "discovery method," "intuition," "structure of the disciplines," and even "learning by doing." If lineal credit is given at all, it is to Whitehead, and appropriately so, but there are shades here of both John Dewey and William Heard Kilpatrick.

It is no small irony that, as the movement grew from its suburban, middle-class beginnings to encompass concern for students in harsh urban environments, it sounded some notes that echoed reports of the Commission on Life Adjustment Education for Youth. It is an even greater irony that it was Jerrold Zacharias, a key figure in vitalizing curriculum content, who spoke passionately from the floor of the 1965 White House Conference on Education urging greater consideration for children in the deliberations and recommendations. The content of instruction must not for long remain cloistered; it had to be humanized for learning. Clearly, we did not apply in the fifties and sixties what we might have learned from the thirties and forties.

Jerome Bruner, who shares credit for concepts (particularly "intuition" and "structure") underlying curriculum reform in the 1960s, likewise shares blame for our failure to draw concepts from the more remote past to balance excesses in the recent past. By not referring (in his highly personalized report of the 1959 Woods Hole Conference,[6]) to two generations of curriculum inquirers and inquiries, some of which included thinking very much like his own (although rarely so well stated), Bruner's contribution was not cumulative. Indeed, neither the links to nor the differences from John Dewey, Charles H. Judd, and Franklin Bobbitt, to name only a few, were stated. And since most of Bruner's readers were not readers of these earlier men, it is not surprising that, for example, the concept of inquiry was born anew.

But linkages to the past might not have changed anything anyway. A new generation of curriculum makers was ready for the proposition ". . . that any subject can be taught effectively in some intellectually honest form to any child at any stage of development."[7] Others among Bruner's observations fell on deaf ears: "Is it worthwhile to train the young inductively so that they may discover the basic order of knowledge before they can appreciate its formalism?"[8] "But the danger of such early training may be that it has the effect of training out original but deviant ideas."[9] "There is a surprising lack of research on how one most wisely devises adequate learning episodes for children at different ages and in different subject matters."[10] And, ". . . it may well be that *intrinsic* [italics mine] rewards in the form of quickened awareness and understanding will have to be emphasized far more in the detailed design of curriculum."[11]

Two sentences in particular take us back to the thirties: "We might ask, as a criterion for any subject taught in primary school, whether, when fully developed, it is worth an adult's knowing, and whether having known it as a child makes a person a better adult."[12] ". . . a curriculum ought to be built around the great issues, principles and values that a society deems worthy of the continued concern of its members."[13] Could we be reading George S. Counts? If we add to this last quotation what Bruner does not quite say—that the students themselves should choose from among these great issues in determining their curriculum, we could be reading Harold Alberty. And Bruner comes close: "Perhaps anything that holds the child's attention is justified on the ground that eventually the child will develop a taste for more self-controlled attention. . . ."[14] Imagine Bruner, twenty years younger, fashioning with Alberty the core curriculum!

Unfortunately, the 1960 breed of curriculum makers no more heard this side of Bruner than they heard the disclaimer in the 1951 report of the Commission on Life Adjustment Education for Youth: life adjustment education ". . . emphasizes active and creative achievements as well as an adjustment to existing conditions; it places a high premium upon learning to make wise choices. . . ."[15] Had the several statements I have lifted from Bruner and more like them constituted the essence of his book, Bruner would have been a less significant figure in the curriculum reform movement now recently behind us and certainly would not have contributed to its orthodoxy. His several bold hypotheses, clearly countercyclical to the perceived excesses and deficiencies of the progressive education era, made the difference and contributed significantly to the innovative thrust of the 1960s.

It is quite possible, however, that a much older Bruner, witnessing but perhaps not contributing to a new curriculum reform, will prefer to remind us of his secondary rather than his primary propositions. In these lie something of the shape of what might be expected of curriculum innovation in the 1980s. An older Dewey, too, viewing in dismay what he was charged with having wrought, sought to remind us of the full breadth of his argument. In the parts of Dewey we chose to forget lay the seeds of at least part of what happened in the fifties and sixties.

There is tragedy in the distorted emphases of an era, no doubt of that. Personal tragedy and societal tragedy. Curriculum planning, like other human phenomena, suffers at any given time because of preoccupations that obscure other relevant emphases. But it is these overemphases, too, that give societies their innovative spurts and the individuals who spawn them their raison d'être. Perhaps the poet Yeats was thinking of tragedy in this dual sense when he said: "We begin to live when we have conceived of life as tragedy."

But excesses can become neuroses, and neuroses, in turn, interfere with rational functioning, inhibiting the power of individuals and the power of societies to right themselves. Lawrence Kubie reminds us that neuroses, rather than being inevitably correlated with the creative process, distort and corrupt it.[16] A society must seek to right itself, then, before the creative thrust of an innovative excess becomes neurotic, inhibiting the creative energy needed for the countercyclical thrust.

Undoubtedly, an innovative period in curriculum development lies ahead for the 1980s. It will be more countercyclical, I believe, to the 1950s and 1960s than to the 1930s and 1940s. The 1970s might well be forgotten. The challenge—conspicuously ignored in the past as, no doubt, it will be ignored in the future—is to capitalize on the excesses of the past while sustaining excesses into the future.

PERSPECTIVE IN CURRICULUM ANALYSIS

Curriculum planning involves at least two very different kinds of processes. First, there are political and legal considerations. Controlling agencies set forth guidelines which sometimes take on the character of law. He who would understand curriculum planning or any curriculum in all its ramifications, perforce must understand the political-legal structure within which it exists.

Second, curriculum planning is a substantive enterprise in that it has certain perennial foci of intellectual attention. Thus, there are commonplaces which can be treated from differing perspectives in the same way that commonplaces of philosophical thought—the nature of knowledge, man, and the good life, for example—can be treated from differing perspectives. To the extent that such commonplaces are, indeed, common in curriculum discourse and to the extent that this discourse is made rigorous by relevant logical-deductive inquiry and empirical research, a field of study emerges.

Viewed against these criteria, curriculum as a field of study is, at best, embryonic. There is and has been vigorous discourse about ends and means: objectives and how to derive them, whether to have them, and how to define them; content and its validation, organization, and ossification; and so on. There has been effort, too, to arrange these commonplaces so as to give some rational guidance to curriculum building. There has been little model or theory building; both have suffered from a paucity of descriptive and experimental data. And the dialogue has suffered from general omission of inclusion/exclusion criteria. As a consequence, participants rarely appear to be addressing themselves simultaneously to the same commonplaces, and so talk right past each other. The dialogue might be described better as a series of monologues.

Several colleagues and I, not to be outdone, formulated a kind of team monologue, on the assumption presumably that several persons talking as one past everyone else is better than one person talking all by himself past everyone else. Building on the work of Ralph Tyler,[17] we formulated a tentative conceptualization of some ends-means commonplaces in curriculum and superimposed a tentative conceptualization of the political structure within which curriculum planning might be conducted in a complex society.[18] We came up with a model—still in revision—which was brazenly intended for enriching curriculum discourse (even if systematically rejected) and increasing rationality in curriculum making (which, of course, it would not do if rejected, whether systematically or unsystematically!). Rationality we defined as simply the recourse to good reasons.

The details of this model serve little purpose here. But its broad outline provides a framework which, even if only glimpsed, may reduce somewhat the extent to which I talk past you. By developing a model of the substantive commonplaces of curriculum and of the political considerations in curriculum planning, we provided a backdrop for appraising ideological formulations of what curricula or a curriculum should consist. Thus, one could systematically appraise the recommendations of various reformers (for example, some years ago, those of James B. Conant for the American high school[19]) and compare them with other recommendations, keeping the same commonplaces in view throughout. Similarly, we could place the proposals of Jerome Bruner [20] in historical perspective, predict the inclusions and exclusions likely to result in practice from applying his emphases, and perhaps even formulate the proposals necessary to balance these emphases. Assuming some soundness in the model (and I further assume its improvement and the formulation of alternative models through continuing inquiry) and some use of it, we might anticipate parallel growth in the viability of ideological curriculum proposals, less blind faith in the ill-informed curricular pronouncements of political or military heroes, and less skittering about from emphasis to emphasis and fad to fad.

Such a model provides, also, a backdrop for analyzing how the political structure functions with respect to curricular decisions and even for planning how to go through it or around it in seeking to influence the curricula of schools, classrooms, and students. Ideological curricula, to affect those for whom they are intended, must penetrate or circumvent the political structure.

Our model poses three levels of decision making: societal, institutional, and instructional.[21] We do not say that all three should exist. There are no "shoulds" in our model other than the overriding implication that its categories and suggested processes are appropriate to a conceptual model of curriculum. But we do imply that curriculum decisions are likely to be made at all three levels in a complex society. (In a simple society, these levels are likely to be collapsed into two or even into one.) In the United States, local, state, and even federal authorities make curricular decisions that affect what is studied by the nation's children and youth. These are societal decisions. Teachers, acting in concert, develop curriculum guides for their schools and school systems, paying varying degrees of attention to societal decisions. These are institutional decisions. And teachers, acting alone, formulate plans for specific groups of students entrusted to them, again ignoring or paying their respects to societal and institutional decisions. These are instructional decisions.

Where among these levels the power lies varies from country to country. Consequently, the strategies most likely to bring about an appropriate balance or a temporary imbalance of power, or to augment one level and nullify another and thus to effect evolution or revolution in the curriculum, likewise vary from country to country. This is why the seminal innovation of one country is the abortion of another.

To summarize briefly what may appear to have been an airy and irrelevant digression, a conceptual model of the kind I have been discussing aids perspective on two counts. First, it provides substantive criteria for appraising current and recent curriculum planning efforts and for projecting ideological innovations for tomorrow. Second, it focuses attention on the curricular structure prior to posing innovations designed to remedy its shortcomings. Now, let me use it in continuing my Janus look.

THROUGH A GLASS NARROWLY

By using this perhaps imprecise perspective and looking at the two recent eras through smaller panes of glass, some interesting differences come into view. First, in direct contrast to the 1930s and 1940s, the decades of the 1950s and 1960s witnessed precious little dialogue about the commonplaces of curriculum among those forging the new curricula. There was some discourse at the periphery by a handful of curriculum specialists, but little of it had vitality. Contrast this, however, with the spirited exchanges of an earlier era among George S. Counts, Harold Rugg, Boyd Bode, William Heard Kilpatrick, John Childs, and H. Gordon Hullfish. Paralleling the work of this group and particularly seminal in the 1920s were the contributions of Henry C. Morrison, Franklin Bobbitt, and Charles H. Judd.

The differences between these groups are somewhat akin to the differences between the younger and the older Dewey who provided a bridge between the two. Admittedly, it was a bridge which from time to time suffered the fate of the bridge on the River Kwai. The latter group had certain natural roots in Dewey (circa 1900) and Edward L. Thorndike. There are some present-day extensions in the work of those behavioral scientists who concern themselves with education. The links to a curriculum past and present are weak, but the pulse still beats and will beat stronger. The beat would be weaker if it were not for the personal bridge provided by Ralph W. Tyler whose roots in curriculum and in the behavioral sciences go back to Charters and Judd, in particular.

The former group—the Teachers College, Columbia, group in

contrast to the Chicago group—began with and in many ways ended with Dewey whose death roughly coincided with the ending of one era and the beginning of another. One looks in vain today for powerful carriers of this great past. The group was philosophical rather than psychological in orientation, but, by now, philosophy was turning in upon itself and away from its traditional preoccupation with the nature of man and the good life. Its thrusts have had no impelling resurgence, but, thankfully, they are preserved and interpreted in the historical inquiry of Lawrence A. Cremin.

Whatever the differences between the Chicago and the Columbia groups—and they were at times monumental—they possessed in common one important characteristic: their deliberations took in a wide range of educational and, therefore, curricular commonplaces. What is education for? How are its ends to be achieved? What are the relevancies of society, learners, and subject matter as data sources for curriculum decisions? How are learning opportunities to be put together for most effective learning? The questions are still being asked but rhetorically and not in the right places.

This observation brings me to a recommendation for tomorrow. It is more of a plea than a recommendation because I have no specific target audience for it and little to suggest as means for bringing it about. *The curriculum planning process, at all levels of decision making, must be enriched by a lively continuing dialogue, addressing itself systematically to defining the commonplaces of curriculum and alternative stances toward them.* The problems of education and of mankind broadly are now so raw and bare that our energies are almost wholly devoted to treating them.

A second significant difference between the present and recent eras is in political orientation. The Teachers College Group (with Counts as leader in this instance) saw need for the schools to reform society itself.[22] Rugg, for example, viewed the schools as physical forums in the debate and educators as its leaders.[23] The change strategy was loose, perhaps even naive, but it was true unto the movement. It depended on ideas, in keeping with Dewey's doctrine that the most unsettling thing is a new idea. The movement sought to change the thinking of people—teachers, principals, superintendents, and the lay public—in the idealistic expectation that they in turn would change the schools. And improving the schools, for many progressives, was the means to improving education and society as a whole.

The discipline-centered curriculum reform movement had no

such broad and idealistic goals. It was as pragmatic as its times. And it was politically savvy. Its leaders went immediately to a source of enormous funds (enormous, at least, in contrast to those available in previous decades)—the National Science Foundation. They influenced that source directly. Then, the movement bypassed the societal and institutional levels of curriculum decision making to go directly to the instructional. Curriculum reformers did not seek to influence school boards or administrators. Teachers, not superintendents, were invited to summer institutes. And new textbooks—the most potent influencers of what boys and girls learn—were put into the hands of these teachers.[24]

A third difference between the two eras is a corollary of the second. In the progressive era, the components of curriculum were put together predominantly at an ideological level. The influence on real schools and classrooms was indirect and pervasive and often was diluted until the original colors were washed away. Furthermore, the concepts were complex, frequently obtuse, interrelated, and enormously difficult to implement. Theoretically oriented interpreters and innovators were required; these always are in desperately short supply. The names of Carleton Washburne, Helen Parkhurst, and Corinne Seeds immediately come to mind. They depended, necessarily, on charisma; scientific tools of leadership were not available. Only a few of the mechanics of what they did are transferable. Meanwhile, most of the ideas remained in the minds of the devoted and entranced—probably fuzzily conceived there—and did not provide in the classroom the kind of expression that facilitated experimental comparisons or even filial identification.

In the discipline-centered era, by contrast, the components of curriculum were put together at the instructional level in the form of materials. Some of the instructional packages were designed to be so complete as to be "teacher free." But teachers intervene between students and materials, nonetheless. The limited conceptual and theoretical baggage is diverted; there is slippage from conception to implementation. To the extent that teachers do not understand or cannot implement the concepts of structure and inquiry to be acquired by the students, the goals of the curriculum projects are thwarted. Teachers brought up on deductive methods of teaching and learning do not take readily to the inductive requirements of materials with an orientation to "discovery" learning.

A fourth difference between the two eras pertains to their

significant omissions. Progressive education virtually eschewed text-books. Its comprehensive view of the educational enterprise simply defied packaging. But teachers have always depended heavily on textbooks. They depended heavily on them during the progressive era, often being required by education authorities to use specific textbooks. Teachers were faced with an almost irreconcilable dilemma. They sat at the feet of Kilpatrick and lesser exponents of progressivism, participating in discussions of some rather loosely defined concepts of project and activity methods for which there were few explicit models. Then they returned to the realities of their classrooms where the specifics of curriculum guides and textbooks won out. Progressive education remained virginal. One is tempted to say "almost virginal," since there was, indeed, an occasional breakthrough.

Whereas progressive education sought to shape the whole length and breadth of the school program, the discipline-centered movement sought to shape only subject matter for learning and teaching. It neglected the institutional level of planning. We were not shown what model schools would look like if total curricula were developed so as to use a week's or a year's time to best advantage. We lost sight of the fact that organizing a subject for learning and teaching and organizing the child's curriculum, to say nothing of his total education, are two different things.

Finally, both the progressive and the discipline-centered eras were deficient in the learning opportunities actually prepared for or with students. Progressive education, seeking topics which were meaningful in the life of the child or to his larger world, stretched across many disciplines, often paying little attention to their structure or method. Mathematics, or art, or science, more often than not, was applied. In the graphic arts part of his social studies lesson, the child learned something about the shape of a pyramid but little about the shape of art. Progressive education needed the rigor of the subject-centered era that replaced it. But the time was not yet; progressive education was circumvented and passed by.

The discipline-centered movement, by contrast, in seeking topics to develop the structure and methods of the various fields, too often overlooked the burgeoning interests of the child, many of which might have been picked up and used spontaneously. The child was to discover the basic order of knowledge, but probably before he could appreciate its formalism. We used as a criterion in determining what the child *should* learn what he *could* learn. Such a criterion is necessary but insufficient. The discipline-centered curriculum era needed the leavening of the era it so rudely thrust aside. It needed the contextual virility of first questions. Preoccupied with updating and ordering content, curriculum reformers ignored questions of first purposes, of what kinds of human beings we seek to produce, and of what knowledge is of most worth.[25]

I said at the outset of this paper that the curriculum reform movement we inherited from the 1960s is ready for the tenets of progressive education. Let me add now that curriculum, circa 1950, was equally ready for the tenets of the discipline-centered era. Surely we are now ready for the tenets of both.

IN CONCLUSION

I conclude with a series of observations and proposals which emerge (logically and rationally, I trust!) from what has gone before. With these I conclude my Janus look.

First, the curriculum planning process, at all levels of decision making, must be enlightened by a lively, continuing dialogue, addressing itself systematically to the commonplaces of curriculum and to alternative stances toward them. The problems of education and of mankind are now so raw and so bare that almost our full energies go into treating them, rather than into long-term inquiry. There should be curriculum study centers so set up that they cannot, indeed must not, succumb to activist pressure. A first order of business should be the sustained rigorous work that will make of curriculum a field of study. The practical benefits will follow, but we must regard them as secondary for the present.

Second, the work that is to go on in such curriculum study centers must be carried at least one stage beyond verbal abstraction to a level of model building and simulation. It is possible, I think, to define and to agree upon a set of conceptual commonplaces in the field of curriculum. There are certain alternative sets, but the overlap is likely to be substantial. However, the alternative stances with respect to each commonplace and each combination of commonplaces are many. Curriculum inquirers should play conceptual games with these alternatives, holding competing sets of alternatives constant long enough to see their shape and potential worth and to formulate curricula based on them. Simulation techniques, aided by the computer, now make this possible.

Third, there must be schools specifically charged with testing those simulated patterns or models believed to be most promising. The function of such schools would be experimentation; educating children would be an extremely important human by-product but not their prime function. Schools now existing, however good, do not meet this criterion. In effect, the schools I have in mind would collapse within themselves societal, institutional, and instructional levels of decision making. They would reach out beyond themselves not for political sanction but for conceptual confirmation in the form of promising models already simulated but not refined and tested. Their commitment would be to remain true to concepts, and from concepts their authority would be derived. Proceeding systematically, they would provide the substantiating or negating feedback so necessary to the systematic refinement of conceptual models.

I recognize that we should have, also, some freewheeling experimental schools which would create their own concepts as well as develop models. The process described above would be reversed, with systematic model and theory building following rather than preceding the schools' innovative thrusts.

Fourth, one specific aspect of curriculum planning requires immediate attention if a new era of curriculum planning is to profit from the two eras that have been my targets. This is the business of assembling or integrating the learning opportunities with which students are to have their curricular romances. Progressive education suffered from an excess of learners' problems during one phase and society's problems during another.[26] The discipline-centered movement suffered throughout from subject-matter myopia and surgical slicing of learning episodes. We now need experimentation with alternative modes of assembling the relevant and possible components of curricular structure. Neither the structure of society, nor the structure of human beings, nor the structure of subject matter gives us the structure of a curriculum. It is some of all these, with the mixtures varying according to time and place.

Fifth, and perhaps most important, reform of school and classroom curricula, whether according to progressive or discipline-centered concepts or a combination of the two, is not enough. There are other curricula: of television, of work experience, of leisure-time activities central to the individual. Education is more than schools. And curriculum planning is much more than manipulating selected components until they become elegant curriculum designs. Curricula are individual and group tools that serve and, in fact, fashion human functions.

Our best hope is that all our curricula together will make it possible to maintain a state of dynamic tension between our best dreams of what each of us as individuals and mankind in general might become and where we now stand on our various paths toward the realization of these dreams. The gap between expectations and present realities must never close; good education must see to that.

The future, like the past, must have its excesses. Excesses are the creative thrusts of individuals and of society, the countercyclical reactions to yesterday's excesses. But let us temper them with our lessons from the past so as to forestall crippling neuroses. Our excesses turn this sober educational pursuit into sport and recreation. It is a tragedy that they are so often followed by painful retribution. But to have learned that life is tragedy is to begin to learn to live.

Notes

[1]However, exploratory work pertaining to "the 'new' mathematics for the schools" dates back to the 1940s, notably at the University of Chicago where a group of mathematicians and mathematics educators engaged in exploratory work in the early and mid-40s. And, of course, the mathematics they proposed was not really "new."

[2]See James D. Koerner, "EDC: General Motors of Curriculum Reform," *Saturday Review*, August 19, 1967, pp. 56–58, 70–71.

[3]See Lawrence A. Cremin, *The Transformation of the School*, Knopf, New York, 1961. I am indebted to Cremin but do not hold him responsible for these interpretative paragraphs.

[4]See John I. Goodlad, *School Curriculum Reform in the United States*, Fund for the Advancement of Education, New York, 1964; and John I. Goodlad, with Renata von Stoephasius and M. Frances Klein, *The Changing School Curriculum*, Fund for the Advancement of Education, New York, 1966.

[5]Boyd H. Bode, *Progressive Education at the Crossroads*, Newson & Co., New York, 1938, p. 44.

[6]Jerome S. Bruner, *The Process of Education*, Harvard University Press, Cambridge, Mass., 1960.

[7]Ibid., p. 33.

[8]Ibid., p. 47.

[9]Ibid., p. 48.

[10]Ibid., p. 49.

[11]Ibid., p. 50.

[12]Ibid., p. 52.

[13]Ibid.

[14]Ibid., p. 72.

[15]United States Office of Education, *Vitalizing Secondary Education: Report of the First Commission on Life Adjustment Education for Youth*, Washington, D.C., 1951, p. 1.

[16]Lawrence S. Kubie, *Neurotic Distortion of the Creative Process*, The University of Kansas Press, Lawrence, Kansas, 1958.

[17]Ralph W. Tyler, *Basic Principles of Curriculum and Instruction*, University of Chicago Press, Chicago, 1950.

[18]The group consisted of Margaret P. Ammons, Alicja Iwanska, James A. Jordan, Maurice N. Richter, Jr., and John I. Goodlad. The work is reported in John I. Goodlad (with Maurice N. Richter, Jr.), *The Development of a Conceptual System for Dealing with Problems of Curriculum and Instruction*, HEW, USOE, Contract No. SAE-8024, Project No. 454, University of California, Los Angeles, 1966.

[19]James B. Conant, *The American High School Today*, McGraw-Hill, New York, 1959; and, more recently, *The Comprehensive High School*, McGraw-Hill, New York, 1967.

[20]Bruner, op. cit.

[21]My first formulation of these levels was in 1960, when I sought to develop a framework around which to organize research in curriculum for the period 1957–1960. (See "Curriculum: The State of the Field," *Review of Educational Research*, vol. XXX, June 1960, pp. 185–198.) I used them later in writing a volume for the NEA Project on Instruction. (See *Planning and Organizing for Teaching*, National Education Association, Washington, D.C., 1963.) In preparing this paper, I encountered use of societal, institutional, and instructional levels by Derek Morell, Joint Secretary, The Schools Council, London. (See "The New Dynamic in Curriculum Development," *New Dynamics in Curriculum Development*, Ontario Curriculum Institute, Toronto, 1965, pp. 25–40.) Perhaps a dialogue has begun!

[22]George S. Counts, *Dare the Schools Build a New Societal Order?* John Day Co., New York, 1932.

[23]Harold Rugg, *American Life and the School Curriculum*, Ginn and Co., Boston, 1936.

[24]See *The Principals Look at the Schools*, National Education Association, Washington, D.C. 1962, pp. 23–24.

[25]For an engaging discussion of this need, see Lawrence A. Cremin, *The Genius of American Education*, Horace Mann Lecture, University of Pittsburgh Press, 1965, pp. 49–63.

[26]Ralph W. Tyler, "The Curriculum—Then and Now," *Elementary School Journal*, vol. 57, April 1957, pp. 364–374.

6

Educational Opportunity: The Context and the Reality

Educators have a responsibility to ensure "equal educational opportunity," whether for students who walk a few blocks to their neighborhood schools or are bused a few miles or arrive from the next town. Goodlad warns that the benefits of education will continue to be distributed unfairly until we realize that traditional school practices have made a large contribution to the problem. [Editor]

In this country, the term "educational opportunity" is almost inextricably tied up with "*equal* educational opportunity." This paper discusses both. Likewise, it deals with both education and schooling, two concepts frequently and erroneously used synonymously. Implicitly, the paper recognizes that education is the broader concept of which schooling is a part.

This is not a historical paper in any structural or, especially, chronological sense. Part I deals with the changing concept of educational opportunity. It reveals the difficulty of using any standard yardstick in appraising the status of educational oppor-

SOURCE: John I. Goodlad, "Educational Opportunity: The Context and the Reality," in *Educational Change: Implications for Measurement*, Proceedings of the 1971 Invitational Conference on Testing Problems, Educational Testing Service, Princeton, New Jersey, 1972, pp. 3–14.

tunity at one time as compared with another. Part I deals more with the context than the conduct of schooling, whereas Part II focuses on the latter.

EDUCATIONAL OPPORTUNITY: A SHIFTING CONCEPT

"Educational opportunity" is a relative concept. It takes on different meanings with the passage of time, with a shift in place, and when viewed from a socioeconomic, legal, or psychological perspective. Similarly, the concept of "equal educational opportunity" has changed over the years and will change in the future.

The meaning of educational opportunity derives in large measure from the *functions* perceived for education in the society. Where upward mobility is virtually closed by a rigid class structure, those in the upper, controlling classes view schools as serving to maintain this structure. Educational opportunity is access to that part of the educational structure designed as appropriate for one's station in life. The system usually consists of tracks or tiers; class status predetermines the appropriate track.

Where class lines are loosely differentiated, education more often is instrumental to upward mobility. The function of the schools is to provide at least the minimum core of knowledge and skills requisite to entering and moving up in the socioeconomic system. The schools seek to provide, therefore, a common educational experience for all. The criteria for judging educational opportunity are quantity and availability: how much constitutes a minimum (or, later, adequate) core and how one gains access to the system.

This last criterion provides a breeding ground for questions about *equal* educational opportunity; for example, to what extent and on what basis is access difficult for some individuals and groups? Likewise, it is an easy step from preoccupation with quantity to considerations of the quality of educational opportunity. And from input factors such as dollars, teachers, and programs, one moves to output or effects in judging quality. Here, too, the aims or functions to be served by the educational system provide the backdrop for the rhetoric defining the concept. Educational opportunity can be evaluated against the socioeconomic background of access to and retention in the labor market or against that chimerical screen of individual development.

All these functions and accompanying perceptions of educational opportunity have characterized the scene in this country. The treatment of native Americans, blacks, and other minorities provides a parallel with the closed system of other places. The expansion of elementary and secondary education has been a response primarily to socioeconomic considerations. But contributing to the GNP is now widely challenged as a criterion for judging educational opportunity.

Much of what follows derives its structure from Coleman's excellent analysis of the concept of equal educational opportunity.[1] He points out that, almost from the beginning of the rapid expansion of public education in the nineteenth century, the concept consisted of the following elements:

1. Providing a *free* education up to a given level which constituted the principal entry point to the labor force.
2. Providing a *common curriculum* for all children, regardless of background.
3. Partly by design and partly because of low population density, providing that children from diverse backgrounds attend the *same school.*
4. Providing equality within a given *locality,* since local taxes provided the source of support for schools.[2]

There was a relatively close fit between these concepts and educational opportunity as expressed by the schools during the rapid expansion of elementary education in the second half of the nineteenth century and into the early years of the twentieth. But the elements summarized by Coleman were badly strained by the events that took place between World Wars I and II, especially industrialization, urbanization, population growth, and resulting increased expectations for secondary schools. Less and less were children and youth of diverse backgrounds attending the same school. With disparities in economic support of schools among communities, states, and regions becoming more and more apparent, it became increasingly difficult to defend equality of educational opportunity on a local basis.

What became strained immediately following World War I was the concept of a common curriculum at the secondary level. The high schools were called upon to serve a new clientele for whom the academic college-preparatory curriculum appeared not to be appropriate. Only a small fraction of this new student body would go on to college. How to differentiate the curriculum for college-bound and non-college-bound youth became of nagging concern.

At the heart of the problem lay the issue of who could, would, or should go on to college. It is one thing to predict that 75 percent will not; another to predict specifically *who* will not; and quite another to reduce their options by preselection of a curricular track. Small wonder that the testing field blossomed.[3]

By World War II, the principle of comprehensive secondary education for all was well established. But the gap between the principle and reality was formidable. The fact that most youth attending high schools would not go to college had relatively little impact on the general conduct of secondary education. But, in the eyes of many, the academic curriculum was so watered down as to be inadequate preparation for college.

The problems and issues are still with us, and we still search for solutions. Meanwhile, developing countries around the world, on the brink of expanding secondary education rapidly, must make momentous decisions regarding vocational/technical schools (which cost several times more to construct, equip, and maintain), academic schools, or truly comprehensive schools. The road to enhanced educational opportunity appears to be that of transcending the schools to provide work experiences, apprenticeships, internships, and a variety of collaborations with commerce, government, industry, and the arts.

The flight to the suburbs, following World War II, sharply reduced the opportunity for children of varied backgrounds to attend the same school. One could still argue, defensively, that educational opportunity and, ultimately, access to a higher socio-economic level were open; the outward trek simply was delayed for some. But inaccessibility to the local schoolhouse on the basis of color could not be denied. The concept of "separate but equal" was ruled unequal in 1954 by the Supreme Court of the United States.

Of great significance for any current analysis of educational opportunity, the Justices considered the psychological and educational effects of segregated schooling on the child. How is the concept of "equal" to be reconciled with "separate" if segregation itself in some way limits the benefits education is supposed to provide? This query has entered consistently into subsequent court cases regarding de facto segregation in the public schools.

Coleman sharpened the implications of a concept of opportunity based on effects when he said, ". . . equality of educational opportunity is equality of results given *different* individual inputs. . . . Such a definition taken in the extreme would imply that educational equality is reached only when the results of schooling (achievement and attitudes) are the same for racial and religious minorities as for the dominant group."[4] In his monumental survey of educational opportunity, Coleman and his associates discussed possible relations between the population mix as a differential input in the educational setting and educational effects.[5]

We have opened Pandora's box. It is one thing to view educational opportunity from the perspective of traditional inputs such as length of schooling, preparation of teachers, class size, funds spent, and the like. But the prospect of matching these and more subtle input variables to predictions of effects in planning and conducting educational programs, for individuals as well as groups, requires the elevation of educational practice to an applied science. Such a prospect provides direction for educational research of a kind the field has not enjoyed. Because of the importance and urgency of the issues, however, action is not likely to await research. The needed resources are more likely to go into a good deal of trial-and-error activity, rather than into the research efforts that might well be mounted at this time.

We have, thus, come around full cycle: instead of schooling being the circuit-breaker, it has become part of the system for maintaining socioeconomic differentials. But although minority groups make up a vastly disproportionate part of our most economically disadvantaged, poverty is not confined within racial or ethnic boundaries. The costs of schooling relative to the property tax base reveal part of the problem. Berke points out, "Variations in property tax base per pupil are immense. Ratios of four or five to one among areas in the amount of property per pupil are not at all unusual. The local property tax, therefore, makes it four or five times easier for some districts to raise a given amount of money from their own resources than it is for others."[6]

But the cost of schooling goes up, regardless of disparities in ability to pay. James and his colleagues pointed out that between 1930 and 1960 the national average cost per pupil rose 331 percent, but the per capita value of taxable property in large cities rose only 97 percent.[7] Further, it costs more to provide less in the cities.

Recognizing these problems, the Supreme Court of California in 1971 ruled on the illegality of the current system of property taxation in financing the public schools. This case and the United States Supreme Court case of 1954 together tell a significant story about the changing concept of educational opportunity in this country.

We have come a long way since Horace Mann. One is inclined to wonder where we would be today had we followed the path proposed by the Workingmen's Party of New York rather than that of the several fathers of the common school. In the late 1820s and early 1830s, the Party called for state-financed and controlled compulsory boarding schools and urged that each child be sent to such schools *as a means of creating a common environment* so that the education of all would be, indeed, equal.[8] Today, of course, we would be required to add genetic manipulation to assure equality of readiness to profit from that environment and, following this, carefully controlled manipulation of the environment to assure equality of effects. With both kinds of interaction based on precise sciences and impeccably applied, will we have attained the ultimate in educational opportunity? And will we be beyond freedom and dignity? At any rate, I think we will be a little beyond what Horace Mann had in mind.

EDUCATIONAL OPPORTUNITY IN AND THROUGH THE SCHOOLS

The preceding has drawn primarily upon the context within which schooling has proceeded to sketch our changing perceptions of educational opportunity. It has suggested just a few of the implications for the conduct of schooling. Meanwhile, the schools have gone on about what they thought was their business.

In what follows, I have eschewed references both because of the vast literature on each of what might be termed the commonplaces of schooling and because of the difficulty in selecting just a very few definitive but comprehensive items on each one. Because of space limitations, I have chosen only some of the most readily recognizable elements of schooling and a sparse array of examples.

The schools are and have been viewed in the United States as the major vehicle for educational opportunity. The rhetoric accompanying the drive for more and better schools has emphasized two educational aims, whatever else may have been stressed at various times: (a) development of abilities to participate constructively and responsibly in the social order (to be able to read and understand the laws of the land, contribute to the GNP, and so on), and (b) development of individual potential for its own sake.

How well have the schools done in the light of these goals? In seeking to respond here to such a question, we are not concerned with whether these aims are appropriate or feasible for schooling. These are quite separate questions. We have grown up with the twin expectations, reiterated in every possible way, that the functions of the schools are to serve society and the individual. We are concerned, then, with the schooling gap—the gap between perceived expectations and perceived reality. Obviously, analysis of this gap brings into play personal interpretations of both the meaning of these educational expectations and conditions of schooling at any given time. The values are implicit.

Admissions policies throughout the hierarchy of schooling raise serious questions about individual opportunity, from definitions focusing on accessibility of schooling to definitions pertaining to effects. When a child is born determines whether he will begin school in the first grade a few days before his sixth birthday or a few days before his seventh. If the early years are as vital to subsequent development as most of the specialists in early childhood education suggest, then this delay of one-sixth of the life-span already transpired could be of serious consequences. This limitation in educational opportunity could be corrected by establishing a birthday, let us say the fifth, nationwide as the date for legal access to school. Variations because of date of birth or place of abode, which have little or nothing to do with ability to take advantage of schooling, would be wiped out.

There is a vast literature on the abuses in *testing practices* and their impact on access to educational opportunity and, subsequently, the amenities of life. Interest during the 1950s in the use of tests for selecting children for limited places in public-school kindergartens illustrates an interesting quick turnabout in prevailing conceptions of educational opportunity. High test scores were used by some school psychologists as a basis for selecting those children thought to be *most ready and most able* to profit from earlier attendance at school. In the light of current thinking about disadvantage, it now would be more appropriate to use high test scores as a basis for *excluding* children from a limited number of places in kindergarten (even though a few school districts still are mired in the former practice).

Before leaving the subject of testing, it is significant to point out that tests have been used disproportionately little as a means of providing alternative, more appropriate learning opportunities for individuals. Tests have been part of the machinery for keeping the gates closed rather than for opening windows on new possibilities. Only rarely have we used tests at the outset of a program of studies to excuse students from what they already know in order to pursue what they do not know. And so, those who do badly on tests frequently are barred from what they might profitably learn; those who do well often are provided a second opportunity to study what they already know. There is something so diabolically perverse about such a scheme that I seem to be denied the language for describing it.

It is difficult to reconcile very much of school *marking systems* with the dual aims of education cited earlier. One does not need to study Skinner's experiments to know the value of positive reinforcement in getting returns from instructional investments. And yet, 75 percent of the failing marks go to 25 percent of the pupils, most of whom are being negatively reinforced merely by attending school. And we can take little comfort from the supposed objectivity of the marking system. We know that in the humanities and the social sciences teachers' marks vary widely in judging the same pupil products. But even in mathematics, student marks frequently bear a disturbing correlation with the congruence or disparity between pupils' and teachers' values.

School marks enter heavily and sometimes strangely into decisions of the socioeconomic marketplace. The boy or girl who drops out of school carrying poor grades not only suffers the expected limitations in job and income but also, in many places, must pay more for the insurance he needs for the car he drives to work. Furthermore, such a youth who needs a job and applies for a vacancy on the evening shift will have less chance of getting it than one with good grades who has not dropped out of school and does not need the job. Society, too often, reflects on the outside the school's abuses on the inside. These examples and many more become particularly disturbing when one reflects on the observation so effectively articulated by Pace that grades seem only to predict grades, nothing else; not good work habits, not success in marriage, not dependability, not vocational success, not compassion.

Grouping practices have denied students access to stimulating peers, alternative learning opportunities, and upward mobility in the system, thus denying them some of the satisfaction they might have had while in school as well as some of the beneficial effects assumed to result from school. At the elementary level, children frequently are segregated into separate classes on the basis of some criterion of achievement, most often in reading. This practice erroneously is termed "ability grouping." The criterion used, however, is often not one of specific ability—a prediction of how the children are likely to perform—but rather a measure of how they already have performed. This is, indeed, a prediction but it is also a self-fulfilling prophecy. Although the results of research into pupil grouping are equivocal, one body of evidence stands up quite consistently: the children in the assumed-to-be-slow group do less well than their counterparts in heterogeneous classes.

Such practices often are used to give "academic" justification for racial segregation in presumably integrated schools. Consequently, it is not uncommon to find in predominantly *white* urbanized schools outside of the inner city "ability-grouped" classes comprised almost entirely of *black* children. The school, too often, faithfully reflects on the inside society's abuses on the outside.

It is necessary to distinguish sharply between grouping designed to bring students together for periods of time for achievement of specific purposes and grouping that segregates students for indefinite periods on a single criterion of assumed or apparent likeness. The former is useful and justifiable. One of the most serious and least examined limitations of the latter is that it deprives all students of the diversity in human background and personality to be derived from a truly "common" school. Further, following Coleman's analysis, such practices may very well hamper some students with respect to the academic goals of schooling. It appears, given certain extant knowledge and concepts of educational opportunity, that careful planning to assure heterogeneity rather than homogeneity in the internal structure and conduct of schooling is the more defensible policy.

The graded, lockstep structure of schooling and the *promotion practices* accompanying it play their part, too, in limiting educational opportunity. Contrary to the practices and supporting arguments of many teachers and principals, nonpromotion is not effective in enhancing pupil progress. Further, nonpromotion is not effected on the basis of rigorous criteria and hard data. Whether or not a child is promoted depends heavily on the school he happens to attend and the teachers he happens to get. And, in the elementary school, three out of five nonpromoted pupils are boys; in the first grade, the ratio of boys to girls is even higher.

Some research suggests that the elimination of grades and the substitution of nongraded plans of school organization better reflect our knowledge of individual differences and facilitate conditions conducive to maximum learning. But efforts to change are hampered by tests and textbooks geared to grades and a host of expectations and practices that have cemented in the graded school. Educational practices devised for different times continue, in spite of the evidence against them, thwarting efforts to move toward schools that would reflect more faithfully changing knowledge and beliefs.

The relation of the *curriculum* to educational opportunity is a topic so vast that it is foolhardy to pursue it here. Parents are very much preoccupied with their children's early successes in walking and talking which they frequently see as related to achieving parental goals. They pay relatively little attention to sensitivity to sound, color, and the aesthetic which are seen as at the fringes of parental goals. A pyramiding kind of reinforcement takes place, cutting off potential talents and shaping the others toward the apex. The elementary school picks up the process at a higher, narrower place on the pyramid. Science and social studies in the elementary-school curriculum are very little of either; rather, they are the language arts with somewhat different content. And art is very little of art; it is a way of depicting social studies cum language arts in pictures.

Perhaps the most damning indictment of the curriculum, eloquently and repetitiously set forth by the neo-humanists, is that it fails to grip the student in vital, meaningful ways. Here, the expectations of many citizens have changed markedly from a future orientation to a "now" orientation. If the second of the dual aims cited earlier is to be interpreted as providing for self-selected student interests and goals, with accompanying rather than, at best, delayed gratification, then the school must be viewed as deficient.

CONCLUSION

Two sets of changing conditions have thrown formidable problems before our unrelenting drive for educational opportunity. The
first is unprecedented technological and industrial growth with all
the accompanying factors of urban crowding, mobility, and social
disarray. These conditions have surrounded the schools and infused
their operation with de facto segregation, gross inequalities in
ability to support schools, and marked inequalities in what must be
coped with and often circumvented if quality education is to be
provided.

The second set consists of our expectations for educational opportunity. Have they become more enlightened? Or has the first set of
conditions merely brought our shortcomings into sharper perspective? There probably is some truth in both implications; the
relations are exceedingly difficult to unravel. Clearly, neither meaningful analysis of educational opportunity nor constructive progress
in providing it are possible if both are confined to educational
systems and schools. It is a grave error, therefore, to condemn the
schools alone for our present perceived shortcomings with respect to
the provisions of educational opportunity and equality therein.

But it is an equally grave error to absolve the schools because of
our hindsight in social, political, and economic realms or because of
our ineptness in social engineering. For example, we often have
chosen education as the scapegoat when we should have looked
elsewhere and used educational solutions when engineering was
required. Nonetheless, we simply must not ignore the fact that the
schools have too faithfully reflected inadequacies and inequalities of
the larger social order, created a good many of their own, and
succeeded in injecting some of their malfeasances into the
surrounding society.

We have reached, with respect to educational opportunity, that
dangerous and challenging time when conditions, concepts, and
practices are in such disarray that virtually complete rethinking and
reordering are called for. Tinkering and patching will continue; that
is the nature of much human endeavor. But we need a fresh
conceptualization and a new map. What do educational opportunity and equality of opportunity mean today? What should they
mean? Where are we in the world of action with respect to this
conception? Where should we be tomorrow, and what do we need
to do to get there?

Notes

[1]James S. Coleman, "The Concept of Equality of Opportunity," *Harvard Educational Review*, vol. 38, no. 1, 1968, pp. 7–22.

[2]Ibid., p. 11.

[3]It is of interest to note that the emergence of curriculum as a field of study also was vastly accelerated by the dilemmas of secondary education.

[4]Coleman, op. cit., pp. 16–17.

[5]James S. Coleman et al., *Equality of Educational Opportunity*, U.S. Government Printing Office, Washington, D.C., 1966.

[6]Joel S. Berke, "The Current Crisis in School Finance: Inadequacy and Inequity," *Phi Delta Kappan*, vol. 53, no. 1, September 1971, p. 3.

[7]H. Thomas James, James A. Kelley, and Walter I. Garms, *Determinants of Educational Expenditures in Large Cities of the United States*, Cooperative Research Project No. 2389, School of Education, Stanford University, Stanford, California, 1966.

[8]Seymour Martin Lipset, "The Ideology of Local Control," in C.A. Bowers, I. Housego, and D. Dyke (eds.), *Education and Social Policy: Local Control of Education*, Random House, New York, 1970, p. 27.

7

Desegregating
the Integrated School

**Here's a novel way of discussing and justifying the concepts
of nongrading, team teaching, and differentiated staffing. [Editor]**

Segregation is and has been the condition of America's schools.
Segregation by race, religion, or socioeconomic status is obvious and
parallels poverty as the most visible social, political, and educational
domestic issue of our time. It is the issue that makes or breaks
today's big-city school superintendent and school board members.
Nonetheless, the progress now being made toward integration of
black and white boys and girls in our schools, halting and troubled
though it may be, surpasses our most optimistic predictions of a
decade ago, especially in small school districts.

But this integration of the races is taking place in an increasingly
segregated school milieu. Most men and women over forty recall an
elementary school in which the sons and daughters of mill owners,
shop proprietors, professional men, and day laborers attended side
by side, except in the South. School boundaries, reaching out into
fields and hills to embrace the pupil population, transcended

SOURCE: John I. Goodlad, "Desegregating the Integrated School," in *Education Parks*,
Clearinghouse Publication No. 9, United States Commission on Civil Rights, Washington,
D. C., October 1967, pp. 14–28.

whatever socioeconomic clusterings existed. But population growth and urbanization, accompanied by the flight to the suburbs, has changed all that. A large proportion of the population lives today in ghettos. Race remains, indeed, a shameful criterion for separation. But the more subtle factors of class distinction separate black from black and white from white within the larger cloth of black and white demarcation.[1]

Unfortunately, certain conceptions of school function, expectations for learners, and school practices—particularly placing and grading pupils—that have long characterized our formal educational enterprise also serve to segregate and stereotype boys and girls within otherwise integrated schools. The need to eliminate discriminatory policies and practices within our schools will be with us long after the most serious de facto and de jure barriers to racial and socioeconomic integration are removed. They were with us in the village schoolhouses many adults once knew. They will be with us in new educational configurations we plan to create. Desegregating integrated schools is the most difficult challenge along the road to equalizing educational opportunity, partly because the problems are so pervasive and partly because agreement on neither goals nor methods will be easily achieved.

The central question for years to come is not whether there should be an educated elite, although that question is bound to get the star's share of the spotlight. Rather, it is how to assure equal opportunity to acquire whatever human attributes are needed by each individual for his or her pursuit of and contribution to the good life.

THE IMPACT OF THE SCHOOL

We now know that the most rapid period of development of human characteristics is in the first few years of life.[2] We know, too, that significant gains on measures of general intellectual functioning are achieved by children whose mothers are exposed to a program of cognitive stimulation and skill development in child rearing.[3] In general, gains are nonreversible. That is, the attainment in a given characteristic at age six, for example, includes what had been attained by age five plus the increment achieved between ages five and six. There is, of course, a loss of specific learnings with the passage of time.

The challenge to education—whether in the school, the home, or the larger community—is to produce the maximum increment for each interval of time. We want each child, whatever his genesis, to have optimum subsequent opportunity to achieve his potential, realizing full well that ultimate attainment depends on the circumstances of both his birth and his environment. Currently popular principles of education reject the theory of simple unfolding of the human organism, or at least support the notion that unfolding can be aided by environmental intervention.[4]

Perhaps the most dramatic instance of broad-scale environmental intervention is the provision of nursery schools in Israel for the so-called Oriental Jew. The parallel in the United States—launched hurriedly and lacking much of the theoretical underpinnings and evaluative structure of the Israeli program—was Head Start. Both were designed to produce near optimal growth, especially in cognitive and language development, during the period immediately preceding entry into formal schooling. The very name of the latter implied the intent: to get a head start on school.

The Israeli experience suggested that the children enrolled in the nursery school program did, indeed, make gains over and above those predicted for them without such exposure. On the discouraging side, however, the follow-up of these children in school suggested that they did not continue to make near-optimal growth during subsequent time intervals. There was a cumulative deficiency by the end of the second and third grades. The same phenomenon was observed for children attending Head Start programs. The concern is that Head Start will prove to have been but a palliative for the children affected.[5] Children from harsh environments, when in school, tend to lag behind their environmentally advantaged counterparts—whether or not exposed earlier to Head Start.

There is an obvious reason. The environmental circumstances inhibiting optimal cognitive and language development are not fundamentally affected by Head Start. They persist and detract from what should be the stimulating effects of school. This fact is profoundly discouraging to educators who cannot expect to have a massive impact on these home conditions within the foreseeable future.

But there is also, in my judgment, a much more subtle reason. Traditionally, schools have not been markedly countercyclical to the conditions of their surrounding environments. In fact, they have tended to reinforce the conditions brought into the schools by the pupils. This was true of the village schoolhouse. It is true of the urban or suburban ghetto school. It will be true of the new kinds of schools of the future, unless we are more aware and more imaginative than we have been in the past.

The one thing that schools are authorized to do something about is their own programs. The fact that children often come to them grossly undernourished both physically and mentally is most unfortunate. But it is a fact—a fact that cannot be rolled back and that must not be ignored. (Even if schools were to extend their scope downward to include all four-year-olds, there would still be the facts of gross differences in "readiness" for school to be reckoned with.) Similarly, the fact that the circumstances of deprivation prevail, often throughout children's school lives, also is most unfortunate. But this, too, is a fact that can be neither rolled back nor ignored. The crucial question is, "Given these facts, how should schools take account of them in *planning and conducting their programs?*"

I have said that schools are not markedly countercyclical; that they tend too much to reinforce rather than offset environmental distortions or emphases. I have said, further, that certain conceptions of school function, expectations for learners, and school practices tend to segregate and stereotype boys and girls even within otherwise integrated schools. Such statements demand clarification and documentation.

Our expectations for schooling are, in general, coverage of a predetermined body of material by all students within a specified period of time, usually a year and a grade.[6] Coverage, therefore, becomes the function of schooling. We may protest otherwise, but practices all too frequently belie our protestations.

The functions of schooling must be twofold: to enable the student to possess and shape the culture and to live effectively and satisfyingly within that culture. Efforts to fulfill such functions through coverage of content are anachronistic.

Further, common expectations for all students deny human realities. Children come to school from markedly different backgrounds, with widely varying levels of attainment, and with striking differences in their readiness to proceed. These environmental conditions tend to persist; levels of attainment tend to become more varied as pupils proceed through school;[7] and a class group at any given time reveals gross differences in the readiness of individuals within that group to proceed with a specified learning.

The grade levels and graded expectations that have characterized the conduct of American education for more than a hundred years appear to be out of phase with today's conceptions of school function and the growing body of evidence about individual differences among children.

Efforts to make the graded system work have met with continual frustration. When it was fully realized that children do not and cannot complete the same work in the same period of time, the adjustment mechanism used was and is nonpromotion. Subsequent research revealed that nonpromoted children, when compared with promoted children of equal past performance and measured intelligence, perform at a somewhat lower academic level, decline in their social relations with other children and in their self-image, and lose interest in school.[8]

Nonpromotion, then, does not advance general intellectual performance, academic attainment, or individual self-respect. In time, it results in an accumulated backlog of generally undiagnosed problems: sixth-grade academic achievement is lower in schools with high rates of nonpromotion than in schools with low rates of retention.[9] Nonpromotion—the major device employed to adjust the inadequacies of our graded school system—does more to segregate and stereotype slow-learning children (and ultimately to force them out of school) than it does to remedy their educational deficiencies.

The reverse of nonpromotion, regular promotion for the slow learning child, appears not to be a happy solution, either. Although promoted children of mediocre past performance in general fare better than their nonpromoted counterparts, many reveal the undesirable consequences of being unable to contend with expectations of the higher grade. They express concern over parental attitudes toward their schoolwork, cheat more, and give indications of self-doubt.[10] If neither promotion nor nonpromotion produces desirable effects for slow-learning children within our graded system of schooling, then perhaps we must question the basic structure itself.

The second major effort of our schools to make the graded system work is a variety of class-to-class grouping practices. Always with us are proposals to bring together in "homogeneous" classes pupils of like ability or present academic attainment. The "commonsense" argument is that gifted students, working together, will not be held back by their less able colleagues. Similarly, retarded pupils, proceeding at a more appropriate pace with others of like ability, will not be embarrassed by exposure to superior performance. Like many commonsense proposals in education, however, there appears to be little other than impassioned rhetoric to support it. In fact, practicability, research, and rhetoric argue equally strongly for the opposite position.

We have had little success in achieving anything that could reasonably be called homogeneous classes.* Ability grouping is particularly ineffective in this regard. Measures of intelligence have been markedly unsuccessful as criteria for bringing together classes that could be regarded as reasonably similar in general or specific attainment. Achievement grouping, on the other hand, which divides into smaller groups a group that is widely diversified with respect to attainment in any subject, obviously reduces the diversity in these smaller groups. But, because of the fact that each student varies so much from subject to subject in his own pattern of attainment, these more homogeneous groups remain about as heterogeneous in everything else as they were before. It takes a very large school population and constant grouping and regrouping to bring together reasonably homogeneous classes for each subject.

Even under such conditions, however, the homogeneity is more apparent than real. Balow, using eight components of reading performance, tested classes of second-grade children grouped homogeneously on the basis of two general components of reading performance. He found that the assumed homogeneity was no longer maintained; heterogeneity corresponded to that found in classes which were not ability grouped.[11] About all we can conclude about a class that appears to be homogeneous is that we have not yet looked closely enough to find the heterogeneity that really exists.

Since classes set up as alike in attainment or ability have sloppy edges, it is not at all surprising to find that studies of their effects are inconclusive. The findings simply do not lend credence to a tight argument for or against such class-to-class grouping so far as subsequent academic achievement is concerned.[12]

There appear to be at least three questionable side effects from the use of nonpromotion and interclass grouping in our elusive pursuit of grade standards and homogeneous classes. First, there is a

---

*A sharp distinction must be made between setting up homogeneous classes, discussed here, and the everyday practice of grouping children within a class for a variety of changing purposes after pupils have been assigned to classes on some basis.

steady sifting of perhaps a quarter or more of the students to slow classes, the 25 percent of the student body that receives 75 percent of the failing marks. Most instances of grade failure and repetition occur in this segment.

Second and related, teachers of classes segregated for supposed likeness of pupils assume far greater likeness than exists.[13] In effect, the gross differences among children in any group are obscured rather than revealed. It is not likely, therefore, that there will be adequate instructional provision for individuality.

Third, children's grade failure and segregation on the basis of limited ability or performance does not enhance their self-respect. Further, not much is expected of such children. In fact, we have some evidence to suggest that learning proceeds more effectively when teachers have high but realistic standards and when everything possible is done to enhance students' self-image.

In summary: (1) environmental deprivation characterizes the social milieu of a substantial segment of our pupil population throughout their school career; (2) traditional practices of nonpromotion and interclass grouping in the graded school system are likely to pile up in academically segregated classes a disproportionate number of disadvantaged children and youth; (3) experience and research to date suggest that such practices do not remedy the learning problems of pupils who are so segregated; and (4) certain side effects of nonpromotion and interclass homogeneous grouping in schools seem to aggravate the very conditions education for disadvantaged boys and girls is supposed to remedy.

Common use of the graded school system and its accompanying adjustment mechanisms of nonpromotion and homogeneous class grouping tend to create an internal school condition of academic segregation of slow-learning youngsters. Since environmental deprivation and school retardation are disproportionately the lot of blacks and other minorities, academic segregation in racially integrated schools becomes also racial segregation. Many minority-group children are thus denied the assumed advantages of integrated schools. The goals of equal educational opportunity are subverted by traditional practices deeply imbedded in schooling. Clearly, we have before us a perverse reality: the necessity of preventing and remedying segregation in the integrated school.

The fact that racial segregation accompanies academic segregation in the nominally integrated school sharply delineates the need for two positive sets of educational circumstances. First, each student should work at his optimal level of readiness in each field of endeavor without stigma and without enforced separation from his natural peers. Second, the school milieu should provide for diagnosis of the readiness and learning potential of each child. Subsequent prescription must not result in the immobilization of the child in a segregated class placement.

In regard to the first, a trap to be avoided is that of simply moving each child along with his age group regardless of accomplishments. This is a misguided educational practice of earlier eras, another poor adjustment mechanism of the graded system. The age of a child is far more useful in determining his social relationships than in determining his readiness for specified learning tasks. *A recommended way out of the dilemma of adjusting learning tasks upward or downward without destroying the age-group propinquity most boys and girls seem to seek and need is the nongraded school.*

In regard to the second, there is no evidence to suggest that homogeneous grouping either increases the likelihood of individual pupil diagnosis or provides the range of alternatives necessitated by pupil variability. This practice assumes conditions that do not really exist and encourages a monolithic approach rather than a varied approach to instruction. Pupils, varied as they are in present attainments, characteristics, and rates of progress, need to be placed in a wide and changing array of groups, groups that are reconstructed through diagnosis of and prescription for the students comprising them. *A recommended procedure for providing the essential flexibility involved is cooperative or team teaching.*

Unfortunately, both nongrading and team teaching in practice often deviate markedly from the conceptions supposedly underlying them. For example, most schools claiming to be nongraded have not adjusted learning tasks upward or downward to accompany individual differences in an age group without walling off members of that group one from another. In fact, many so-called nongraded schools are not nongraded at all; they simply employ time-worn practices of homogeneous interclass grouping under a modern label. Those responsible for educational planning must be acutely aware of this corruption and, should they move to nongrading, be sensitive to the fact that new labels do not necessarily beget new practices.

Similarly, some schools claiming to practice team teaching have brought about nothing more than a systematic sharing of subjects among teachers. The same old practices of stereotyping and segregating pupils continue under a new label. Neither diagnosis nor prescription from an increased range of alternatives is enhanced.

The vagueness and misconceptions regarding nongrading and team teaching are such that they are not likely to be clarified by general talk. Specifics are called for, in spite of the fact that specifics have inherent in them the danger of seeming to deny other alternatives. There are many ways of organizing and conducting nongraded, team-taught schools. The intent below is to illustrate conceptions that hold unusual potential for desegregating the integrated school.

Figure 1 suggests the nature of the central problem to be reckoned with. The spread in reading attainment of a second-grade class is usually from four to six years. The lower end of the scale cannot be depicted adequately because reading tests are not constructed to measure it. The spread in a fifth-grade class is eight or more years and overlaps the second grade at its lower end. *But the spread in age at each of these grade levels is only a year or a little more.*

Bar graphs for each of the other subjects would reveal somewhat smaller but, nonetheless, substantial ranges in achievement. Further, if the attainment of each child were plotted on these bars, a substantial variation in attainment from subject to subject would be demonstrated. It is impossible to provide appropriate programs of instruction for each child in these divergent patterns without ignoring present grade placements of children.

To ignore grade levels and grade placements is to take a significant step toward nongrading. Two alternative approaches suggest themselves. The first is simply to assign each teacher a class of, for example, seven-year-olds who normally would be in the second grade. There is nothing new here. But then the teacher is to ignore the grade level and is provided with a diverse array of instructional materials more realistically geared to the spread of the group. This procedure need not cost more; materials simply are distributed differently. Each teacher, in a self-contained classroom, strives to reach the floors and ceilings of the class through a variety of individual and small-group procedures. The ellipses in Figure 2 suggest the effort to encompass the full range of individuality while maintaining in one classroom a completely integrated age group. Homogeneity in age is maintained as in graded schools, but heterogeneity in present attainment is recognized and, within the capabilities of each teacher, is dealt with.

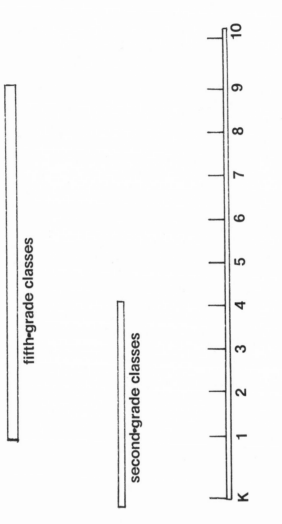

Figure 1. Common spread within and overlap of second- and fifth-grade classes in reading.

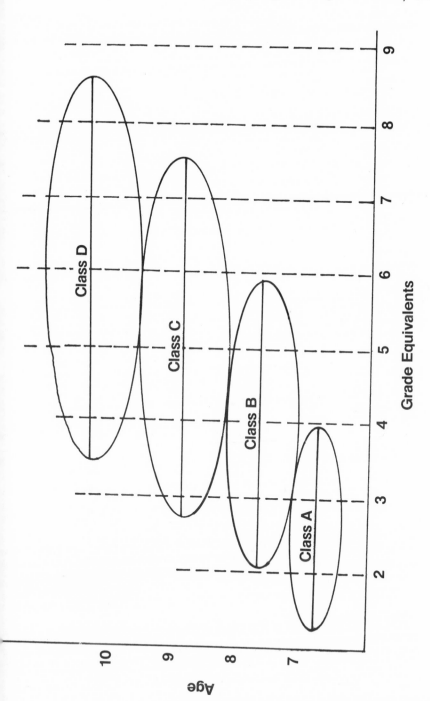

Figure 2. Spread of individual attainments provided for instructionally in nongraded, self-contained classes.

This approach places a heavy burden on the teacher. Actually, the range of individual differences to be managed is no greater than in a graded self-contained classroom, but the expectations are different. The teacher is being called upon to provide for individual differences. By contrast, the graded system obscures individuality and suggests the desirability of striving for a common denominator. Meeting the expectations of nongrading in a satisfactory manner simply is more demanding.

For this reason, some teachers are attracted to a second alternative, one in which nongrading is coupled with cooperative or team teaching. Two or more teachers of nine-year-olds, for example, bring their classes together and consider them to be just one large instructional group. Then, planning together, they subdivide this group on a day-by-day (sometimes hour-by-hour) basis, occasionally teaching a single large group but usually working with small clusters or with individuals.

There appear to be many advantages to this procedure.[14] It becomes possible, for example, for one teacher to concentrate on the particular learning problems of perhaps a dozen boys and girls while another teacher supervises the remainder. One teacher is able from time to time to stand back from bustling activity in order to observe the behavior of one child. Then, all the teachers diagnose and prescribe on the basis of these observations. More students and more teachers make possible many kinds of groupings. No child need be permanently in any one group. Hence segregation within the school is reduced to a minimum.

Once teachers manage to hurdle the physical and psychological barriers of the graded, self-contained classroom and to perceive the flexibility of nongrading and team teaching, they usually become creative in developing many variations on the themes introduced above. A particularly promising one for the avoidance of segregated class groups is the inclusion of several age levels in the nongraded, team-taught group. As nongrading becomes a way of both thinking and practicing education, age becomes less important in assigning pupils to groups. Figures 1 and 2 reveal that age is a rather poor criterion for determining what to teach or what already has been learned.

Figure 3 shows five clusters of students and teachers in a nongraded, team-taught school. Each ellipse encompasses both the ages and the grade equivalents brought together in each team. The

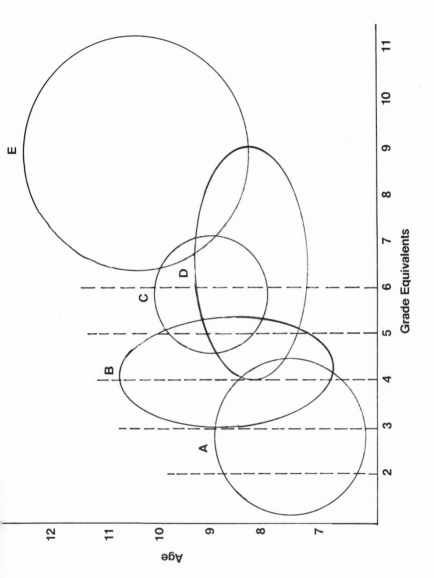

Figure 3. Clusters of teachers and pupils in a nongraded, team-taught school.

size of the ellipse, small or large, suggests that clusters include varying numbers of students and teachers. Thus C is the smallest cluster and E the largest.

Following from left to right in Figure 3, then, cluster A contains boys and girls between the ages of 6 and 9 and provides instruction across what would be four grades in a graded school. Cluster B spreads over ages 7 through nearly 11 and includes three grade levels. Cluster C includes three age levels and four grades. Cluster D takes care of children from 7 to 9 and spreads across six grades. Cluster E includes ages 8, 9, 10, 11, and 12 and five grades. Of course, grade levels are ignored, but the concept is used here to convey the departure from typical graded conventions.

Groups might well contain from 50 to 150 or more pupils and the equivalent of two or more teachers. The word "equivalent" is used here because there is no need to follow conventional staffing patterns. A group of ninety children might well be taught by two full-time teachers, two interns, two student teachers, and a community helper. For example, although the University Elementary School at UCLA is budgeted for a full-time staff of twenty-five persons, up to fifty often are on the payroll.[15]

Nongrading and team teaching of this more complex species are possible in traditional school buildings, but such patterns of class organization and the new flexible buildings go hand in glove. Any school district that is today still building compartmentalized egg-crate schools is wasting the taxpayers' money.

It takes only a little imagination to perceive not only possible variations along the lines of what is depicted in Figure 3 but also the potentiality of such patterns for dealing educationally with individual differences. There is no need to segregate slow learners in a nonpromoted or "homogeneous" class because they are unable to do the work of the grade. The norms of expectancy simply are spread out to reach them; there are no grades. It is not necessary to overlook the limited accomplishments of a child simply to keep him with his age group. By spreading out the ages in the total group, it is possible both to adapt academic work to individual needs and to provide appropriate peer associations. There is no sifting of slow learners, usually those who are environmentally disadvantaged, to academically and often racially segregated classes because youngsters of all academic levels are provided for within the nongraded, team-taught cluster.

SUMMARY

Integrated schools, enrolling children from all racial and socio-economic segments of the city, constitute a bold effort to rectify long-standing inequities in educational opportunity that have disproportionately disadvantaged minority-group boys and girls. Ironically, however, they reveal the fact that certain long-standing school practices have tended to perpetuate the very environmental disadvantages that education is supposed to overcome. Specifically, grouping practices based on measures of ability or attainment have tended to bring together in segregated class groups those children that seem to be profiting least from school. These tend to be environmentally handicapped children. In large cities especially, these children are or will be disproportionately minority-group members.

The problem lies not with integrated schools as such but with their likelihood of perpetuating those grouping and grading practices that characterize our schools generally. These practices segregate the slow-learning child. If integrated schools are to accomplish their commendable mission and avoid resegregation in ostensibly desegregated schools, they must move vigorously to certain new practices now being recommended, practices designed to overcome inequities in educational opportunity through concern for human variability and individuality.

One of these is nongrading which seeks to raise the ceilings and lower the floors of educational expectation and program to coincide with the full range of individual differences always present in an instructional group. The second is team teaching which breaks down the teacher-per-class-per-grade concept and opens up possibilities for teams of teachers, teacher aides, and others to work together in planning programs based on diagnosis of all those individuals constituting an enlarged group.

The combination of nongrading and team teaching is particularly powerful in integrated schools in our larger cities which provide an endless array of alternative ways to set up clusters of teachers and students. At the same time, each cluster takes on an identity and provides a school within a school to offset the dangers of anonymity in the large school setting. Most important of all, this pattern of school and classroom organization provides maximum flexibility with respect to the placement and re-placement of pupils for instructional purposes. Segregation of any group on any criterion for an extended period of time is so unlikely to occur through the natural operation of the system that it would have to be brought about by deliberately sabotaging the system. By contrast, such segregation is difficult to avoid in the graded school.

Nongrading, team teaching, and other flexible approaches to school organization do not in themselves remedy the educational disadvantages of harsh environments. But they do remove some of the norms and traditions that have contributed to stereotyping and segregating boys and girls who carry their environmental disadvantages into the classroom throughout their school experience. And these innovations create an expectancy for individualized approaches to learning, approaches that tend to eschew segregated groups.

Notes

[1] For one of the best analyses of this condition in print, see Bruno Bettelheim, "Segregation: New Style," *School Review*, vol. 66, Autumn, 1958, pp. 251–272.

[2] For a comprehensive summary and analysis of the research, see Benjamin S. Bloom, *Stability and Change in Human Characteristics*, John Wiley & Sons, New York, 1964.

[3] See, for example, Phyllis Levenstein, "Cognitive Growth in Preschoolers through Verbal Interaction with Mothers," *Journal of Orthopsychiatry*, vol. 40, April 1970, pp. 426–432.

[4] There is growing support for the possibilities of chemical intervention, but these are, at present, too controversial and too little supported by prolonged experimentation to enter significantly into public policy. See Barry Commoner and others, "The Elusive Code of Life," *Saturday Review*, October 1, 1966, pp. 71–79.

[5] In the long run, the significance of Head Start may prove to have been symbolic. It alerted us dramatically to our long-standing delinquency regarding the welfare of substantial numbers of our children.

[6] John I. Goodlad, M. Frances Klein, and Associates, *Looking Behind the Classroom Door*, rev. ed., Charles A. Jones, Worthington, Ohio, 1974.

[7] John I. Goodlad, "Individual Differences and Vertical Organization of the School," in *Individualizing Instruction*, Sixty-first Yearbook of the

National Society for the Study of Education, University of Chicago Press, Chicago, 1962, pp. 218–219.

[8]John I. Goodlad, "Research and Theory Regarding Promotion and Nonpromotion," *Elementary School Journal*, vol. 53, November 1952, pp. 150–155.

[9]Walter W. Cook and Theodore Clymer, "Acceleration and Retardation," in *Individualizing Instruction*, op. cit., pp. 179–208.

[10]John I. Goodlad, "Some Effects of Promotion and Nonpromotion upon the Social and Personal Adjustment of Children," *Journal of Experimental Education*, vol. 22, June 1954, pp. 34–43.

[11]I. H. Balow, "Does Homogeneous Grouping Give Homogeneous Groups?" *Elementary School Journal*, vol. 63, October 1962, pp. 28–32.

[12]For a review of the research, see Ruth B. Ekstrom, *Experimental Studies of Homogeneous Grouping*, Educational Testing Service, Princeton, N. J., 1959; and Nils-Eric Svensson, *Ability Grouping and Scholastic Achievement*, Almqvist and Wiksell, Stockholm, Sweden, 1962.

[13]John I. Goodlad and Robert H. Anderson, *The Nongraded Elementary School*, rev. ed., Harcourt, Brace & World, Inc., New York, 1963. See Chapter 1.

[14]For a comprehensive treatment of the theory and practice of team teaching, see Judson T. Shaplin and Henry F. Olds (eds.), *Team Teaching*, Harper & Row, New York, 1964.

[15]John I. Goodlad, "Meeting Children Where They Are," *Saturday Review*, March 20, 1965, pp. 57–59, 72–74.

8

The Case for
the Nongraded *School*

**The Editors of *The National Elementary Principal* speak
first . . .**

An unusual case developed in the state of Michigan regarding the
legality of nongraded schools. It began in September 1968 when
William J. Schwan and his wife, acting on behalf of their son
James, brought suit against Hazel Tribilcock, principal of the
Horsebrook School, a nongraded elementary school in the
Lansing Public School system. According to the complaint, the
child had suffered embarrassment and humiliation as a result of
his being transferred from a "third-grade" class to a class of
primarily second graders. Damages in the amount of $100,000
were claimed. Later the case against the principal was dismissed
the court holding that under the circumstances the principal had
the right to assign the student to the class in question. The Board
of Education of the Lansing School District was then added to an
amended complaint as a party defendant.

The amended complaint alleged that the Board of Education
lacked the authority to operate nongraded elementary schools. In

SOURCE: John I. Goodlad, "The Nongraded School," *The National Elementary Principal*, vol.
L, no. 1, September 1970, pp. 24–29.

addition, it alleged that the operation of these nongraded schools had impeded the education of the plaintiff, causing confusion and insecurity which had affected his mental well-being, and that unless such schools ceased operation, irreparable damage would result. At the time the complaint was filed, there were twenty-two nongraded and twenty-six graded elementary schools in the Lansing School District. The legality of these nongraded schools came into question, however, as the result of two sections of the Michigan School Code, which provide that a board of education in Michigan may establish one or more nongraded schools only for the instruction of incorrigible or truant children. Thus, the issue in the case became: Did the Lansing School Board of Education have the authority to establish nongraded schools other than for the purposes specified in the Code? In December 1969 Judge Sam Street Hughes of the Ingham Circuit Court ruled that the Board did not have such authority and that nongraded programs be eliminated by January 23, 1970. His decision was appealed by the Lansing School District to the Michigan Court of Appeals. The Michigan Association of Elementary School Principals, feeling that the decision of the Court is not in the best interests of children, requested that the National Association of Elementary School Principals ask John I. Goodlad to prepare a brief on the soundness of nongraded programs, to be entered in support of the educational issue at hand.

As a result of a motion carried at the February meeting of the NAESP Executive Committee, Dr. Goodlad was asked to write a brief and to become a party to the suit as Friend of the Court in support of the Lansing School District. Dr. Goodlad's brief, which was presented with the appeal, follows. [The Editors, *The National Elementary Principal*]

The nongraded school represents a major response on the part of educators to one of the most relevant and compelling bodies of knowledge available to them: the knowledge about individual differences among human beings. However, these data achieved the status of scientific generalizations only after the structure of schooling in the United States had become rather well established. Consequently, efforts to align schooling practices with the relevant knowledge encountered the resistance of established expectations and procedures. The fact that this situation parallels other fields of endeavor makes it no less frustrating or unfortunate.

The graded school—for which the nongraded school now is being proposed as an alternative—was rapidly becoming standard practice in most cities of the United States by the 1860s. It emerged as part of the highly successful drive to establish attendance at the common school as the right of all rather than the privilege of a few. Accompanying this principle were rapid increases in population and urbanization and, of course, in school enrollments. The casual educational procedures of earlier decades simply did not suffice. It was necessary to absorb and classify increasingly large numbers of children seeking public school enrollment. The establishment of grade 1 for six-year-olds, grade 2 for seven-year-olds, and on up through the years and grades was a logical, practical response to the problem of managing large numbers of pupils in the schools. The apparent efficiency of the system accelerated its rapid adoption.

There was, however, a basic fallacy in the system—a fallacy which led to unfortunate and unsatisfactory attempts at adjustment. The graded system was accompanied by textbooks and other guidebooks for pupils and teachers designed to prescribe an appropriate body of work for each year and grade of schooling. It was soon discovered that significant numbers of children did not cover the prescribed work for the grade, even when punished or rewarded for their efforts. The fact that some children easily accomplished these requirements also became apparent. Regrettably, the solution employed to correct these differences in pupil progress sought to adjust the child to an imperfect system rather than to make adjustments in the system. Some children were not promoted and were forced to repeat all the work of the grade; a few were accelerated so that they skipped the work of the succeeding grade.

As stated earlier, the data suggesting an alternative to this graded structure were not available at that time. Also, there were no hard data on the effects on children of these adjustment practices of nonpromotion and grade skipping. These were yet to come. Before the end of the century, however, insightful educators—including the presidents of Harvard University and the University of Chicago—expressed deep concern over what they termed the lockstep system which sought to bring the diverse abilities of students into a narrow range of expectancy set by the grade level. A few educators began to experiment with plans which encouraged more individualized rates of progress through the school.

During the early decades of the twentieth century, the secondary school was established beyond the elementary school as an accepted part of the common school. Similarly, in forward-looking states, kindergarten was proposed as the first year in a K–12 system, and the whole was protected by laws. Presumably, the intent of these laws was to assure all children the opportunity of completing high school or its equivalent. Additional provisions were made for children and youth who, for reasons of truancy, mental retardation, and the like, had fallen far behind the work of the grade to which they normally would have been assigned. Ungraded classes were created to take care of these extreme deviations. But a wide range of individuality remained to be accommodated by the graded system.

Educators sometimes have referred to this system as a Procrustean bed. The slow have been stretched and the quick have had their limbs chopped short to fit the predetermined pattern.

The nineteenth century arguments for greater flexibility in school structure were buttressed by research and inquiry in the twentieth century. Early studies pointed to the costs in dollars and cents of having children repeat grades and criticized the system for its wastefulness. Later studies raised ethical questions; they pointed to the enormous range in nonpromotion rates from school to school and school district to school district (from less than 5 percent in some primary classes to 20 percent in others, for example) and suggested that a child's progress in school depended as much on teacher whim and fancy as on individual ability and performance.

In addition, a rash of studies in the 1930s, 1940s, and 1950s raised serious questions about the effects of nonpromotion on children. It was found, for example, that repetition of a grade did not enhance pupil achievement as expected. Rather, the nonpromoted children studied tended to do less well than children of like ability and past performance who were promoted regularly. Other studies discovered negative self-concepts and undesirable social development among some nonpromoted children, but they also concluded that promoting children into work for which they were not ready resulted in some undesirable consequences.

Throughout the first half of the twentieth century, research such as this and commonsense reasoning arising out of experience raised serious questions in the minds of some educators regarding the pros and cons of retaining children for an additional year in the same grade. Nevertheless, the graded system itself was not seriously questioned until this evidence was augmented by increased insight into individual differences among children and youth.

The subject of human variability is now a major topic of inquiry among geneticists, biologists, psychologists, pediatricians, and educators. It is almost impossible to sort out the educational implications of the data on physical, biochemical, social, and psychological differences among individuals. But the salient facts on academic factors have been sorted out and are compelling. We know, for example, that by the time children complete the fourth grade, there is a four-grade spread in their average achievement. This spread increases by more than a grade per year in succeeding years. Employing a rough (and conservative) rule of thumb, the spread in average achievement, then, is about four years in the fourth grade, five in the fifth, six in the sixth, and so on. The spread in reading achievement is even greater—about six years in the fourth grade, seven or eight in the fifth, nine or ten in the sixth, and so on. To attempt to encompass these enormous differences within the educational expectations and specifications of a grade borders on futility, if not irresponsibility.

A developing child represents within himself variability and diversity comparable to that of a class of children. He does not grow and develop "all of a piece," so to speak. He spurts forward with one trait and lags with another; interests and abilities tend to foster some traits and retard the development of others. By the time he reaches the fourth grade, he may be a sixth grader in spelling, a seventh grader in reading, a fourth grader in mathematics, and a fifth grader in something else. Clearly, he is advanced in most things, but what grade should he be in? The school records classify him in the fourth grade and, unfortunately, observation reveals him to be exposed in the classroom to work that is very similar or even identical to that of his classmates, some of whom are performing at much lower levels. He and all his classmates are labeled "fourth graders" and, for the most part, do work labeled "fourth grade."

The kinds of research summarized above, together with this growing awareness of individual differences and their possible implications, undoubtedly contributed significantly to increased questioning of and dissatisfaction with the graded school. They contributed also to at least initial formulations of an alternative plan called the *non*graded school.

While writing our book, *The Nongraded Elementary School*, which first appeared in 1959, Robert H. Anderson and I searched about for prototypes and antecedents for what we had in mind as a replacement for the apparent inflexibility of the graded school. We explored a plan which had been initiated in a few schools and school districts during the 1940s and 1950s under the label, "the ungraded school." This was not what we were seeking to emulate although, to be sure, it possessed a few elements of what we wanted. For the most part, however, this plan merely provided for placement of the child in a grade level where he could find some success, with the grade label removed to avoid stigma, if at all possible. This was a step in the right direction, but it fell far short of providing for the wide range of individuality present in an age group. As a result, we chose instead the term "nongraded" and sought to spell out the characteristics of a school geared to pupil variability rather than to arbitrary grade designations of content.

Unfortunately, the nongraded school is not easily understood or developed. It is not simply the school we have known with grade labels removed. Nor is it a return to the one-room schoolhouse, as is sometimes suggested. There are no models from the past that do justice to the concepts involved. But there are some solid assumptions with which to work in seeking to create a school for maximum individual development.

One set of assumptions underlying the nongraded school pertains to individual differences among learners, an assumption solidly backed by evidence, as we have seen. Children of the same age differ widely in their readiness to learn; they move forward at different rates of speed; and they acquire quite different patterns of learning and thinking. The nongraded school is designed to widen both the expectations for a class and the actual range of learning activities in a class so as to provide appropriate, challenging learning for each child. Obviously, this is an ideal to be worked for, never to be fully attained, but an ideal which is held in truly nongraded schools.

A second set of assumptions pertains to the nature of knowledge. Knowledge is human and, therefore, subject to change. Knowledge is also structured and cumulative, not merely a miscellaneous array of conclusions. Recent changes in the curriculum proceed from such assumptions and seek to encourage not a succession of topics across a grade level but rather the specification of concepts and skills to be learned over a period of years. The child is to progress continuously forward in his acquisition of them. Graded specifications and requirements tend to break the flow of this progress; they emphasize acquisition of specific items rather than the fundamental structure of knowledge.

On the other hand, the nongraded school eschews grade-by-grade designations of content in favor of what is sometimes referred to as a spiral curriculum. Instead of studying magnets in one grade, batteries in another, combustion engines in still another, and atoms in a much higher grade, the pupil's attention is turned to the concept of energy and he studies energy in the related context of magnets, batteries, engines, and atoms. Even kindergarten children begin to understand energy in many forms, including atomic energy. But when they "spiral" up to atoms at some later point in school, they go more deeply into what they had merely been introduced to at an earlier point on the educational continuum.

A third set of assumptions underlying nongrading pertains to the nature of learning. Both the *what* and *how* of learning are unique to each individual. Each derives meaning from the opportunities to respond that come before the individual. Gifted students become sluggish and listless when the learning fare is repetitive, when they already have had ample opportunity to exhaust its meaning. Slower-learning students become confused, frustrated, and even angry when they are only rarely able to derive meaning from what they are expected to learn. In time, they tune out and become psychological dropouts while still in school. The nongraded school is designed to provide, as normal procedure, appropriate stimulation for the gifted, the slow, and everyone in between.

A fourth set of assumptions pertains to the nature of man. People develop best, we think, under conditions of trust, support, and encouragement. A characteristic of the graded school is built-in failure—failure in the form of daily inability to cope with expectations of the grade and failure in the form of nonpromotion. Some argue that failure is a good thing and, under certain conditions, we would agree. But failure begets failure. Expectations and tasks must be adjusted to facilitate a reasonable balance of success and failure. Under the traditional graded system, 25 percent of the children experience 75 percent of the built-in failure. This cannot be described, with any stretch of the imagination, as a "reasonable" balance between success and failure. By seeking to relate the tasks to children's readiness for them, the nongraded school encourages success on the assumption that success is self-motivating and tends to beget success.

Since these assumptions and more like them are suggestive rather than prescriptive, it is not at all surprising that nongraded schools differ from one another. The movement toward nongraded schools is relatively new and so, for this and other reasons, the label "nongraded" cannot be trusted.

Most teachers experience great difficulty in breaking away from long-standing practices, and thus there are schools without grade labels that are essentially graded schools. Others are so attuned to individual differences among their pupils that they devise essentially nongraded programs while still functioning under the grade labels. In their efforts to meet individual differences well-intentioned teachers frequently are frustrated by state laws and restraints which specify class size, grouping practices, materials to be used, and like matters. Textbooks, tests, report cards, and the very language employed to discuss our schools are tied to graded expectations and assumptions.

Well-developed nongraded schools—and there are, as yet, few of these—almost invariably have certain features in common. First, nongrading is schoolwide and not confined to a few classes. Consequently, teachers do not hesitate to select learning activities that normally would be confined to older or younger children in the traditional graded school. Their colleagues share the same assumptions and therefore do not resent what would be considered an intrusion on their "territory" in graded schools. Second, teachers select content, materials, and topics for instruction in the light of the class's spread of abilities, attainments, and interests. Consequently, they rarely possess in their rooms the same books for all pupils. Materials of instruction are shared throughout the school. Third, both grouping practices and instruction follow both preliminary and ongoing diagnosis of children. Thus, much of the program is tailor-made, changing in shape, size, and character as the child changes and matures. Fourth, age becomes less and less important as a criterion for conducting this tailor-made process. Increasingly, classes are made up of several age groups; children work on what is appropriate for them and not on something which is arbitrarily specified for a grade or age. At the University Elementary School, UCLA, for example, one finds three-, four-, and five-year-olds working and playing together or seven-, eight-, nine-, and ten-year-olds dispersed into several working groups. The British Infant Schools, which have attracted favorable attention in the United States, feature "family groupings" of five-, six-, and seven-year-olds.

Moreover, nongraded schools usually encourage many examples of children teaching each other, with tutors not necessarily being the oldest. Children learn a great deal from their peers outside of school. Using the power of peer teaching inside the school seems to make good sense. Visitors to multiage classrooms in the nongraded school find, to their surprise, how difficult it is to differentiate children by age and, like teachers and children, soon become unaware of age distinctions.

Because it involves so much more than the mere removal of grade levels, the nongraded school is a significantly changed school. For this reason, it tends to run afoul of well-established practices which have grown up around the graded school. The old record systems which classify teachers and classes by grades no longer suffice; inventories of supplies by grades no longer apply; report cards must be changed or, preferably, replaced by conferences on pupil progress; and standardized graded tests lose their meaning and must be replaced by new forms of assessment. As a result, there are profound implications and adjustments here for administrators, teachers, parents, test makers, and textbook publishers. (The children appear to be the only ones who take matters readily in stride.) And there is threat here, too—threat which frequently is accompanied by some resistance to change.

Attempts to measure the effects of nongraded schools have been inconclusive. This is not surprising, given the tender age of the movement toward nongrading, the assumptions underlying it, and the rather primitive character of assessment instruments and techniques. When a change is to be made in a business or industrial procedure, affected employees are trained for it, often by temporarily releasing them from their jobs or alternating them with a replacement staff. But teachers must "keep school" while seeking to change it. Usually, the special preparation they need for the new tasks is not available in the school district and must be sought elsewhere on their own time and at their own cost.

Largely for these reasons, change in education is inordinately slow, and the operational slippage from a concept or model to implementation is formidable. And so, although nongrading as an idea has been around for some years, it still must be regarded as innovative and experimental. Acceptance in theory far exceeds establishment in practice. To compare a supposedly nongraded school with a graded one is to compare a school which recently has been modified, minimally or substantially, with a school which has had many years to refine its practices.

Actually, it is somewhat surprising that nongraded schools have held their own with graded schools in the few reasonably controlled comparisons that have been made, in view of the fact that the criteria of comparison and the procedures used almost invariably are based on the assumptions of grading rather than the assumptions of nongrading. For example, achievement tests are geared closely to the way in which content is specified for the grades. A teacher in a nongraded class, however, selects content from many "grades." It would be interesting to see how graded and nongraded schools (that is, schools nongraded in more than name) would compare on tests derived from the criteria pertaining to the assumptions and programs of both types of schools. But even with the results in hand, most people would tend to base their preferences on the degree of fit between their own values and assumptions and those of graded and nongraded schools.

Dissatisfaction with our schools has currently reached monumental proportions. There is little agreement on what to do. Many people believe that the schools have changed too rapidly along permissive lines. Others believe that they have failed to respond to changing conditions, especially in our inner cities, and should be completely reconstructed or even abolished. Actually, the rate of change has been painfully slow. Our schools are characterized by textbooks, workbooks, teacher talk, and too little pleasure or excitement in learning. We desperately need new models which reflect the relevant knowledge and insights we have gained since the first truly graded school opened its doors in 1848. The nongraded school increasingly is being recognized as one such model. To make a significant difference, however, it must be combined with a host of additional, related reforms.

Additional Readings

B. Frank Brown, *The Nongraded High School*, Prentice-Hall, Englewood Cliffs, N.J., 1963.

John I. Goodlad and Robert H. Anderson, *The Nongraded Elementary School*, rev. ed., Harcourt, Brace & World, 1963.

William P. McLoughlin, *Evaluation of the Nongraded Primary School*, St. John's University Press, Jamaica, New York, 1969.

9

Early Schooling:
The Young Discovered

Since schooling for young children occupied much of
Goodlad's attention during the time covered by this collection
of papers, I decided to include this combination of two chapters
from *Early Schooling in the United States* in this volume as a
precise statement of his views on the issue. Although *Early
Schooling* is a joint authorship, the two chapters presented
here were written solely by Goodlad. [Editor]

There is today in the United States an upsurge of concern for the
education of young children. During the past dozen years or so, this
concern, with its emphasis on the crucial importance of the child's
earliest experiences for the whole of his later life, has come to the
forefront in our social, educational, and political thinking to a
degree that only recently would have seemed unlikely. Even in the
late fifties, when national concern with the processes and products
of education began to make themselves felt in new programs and
new pressures on the elementary school, preschool pupils and their
teachers were still an enclave apart. A relatively small and often

SOURCE: John I. Goodlad, M. Frances Klein, Jerrold M. Novotney, and Associates, *Early
Schooling in the United States*, McGraw-Hill, New York, 1973, Chapters 1 and 7.

select group, they busied themselves comfortably with finger paints and rhythm bands, juice and crackers and jungle gyms, well out of the mainstream of educational controversy.

Preschool had been conceived of by all except a handful of perceptive individuals as actually *ante*education—something before *real* education begins—as the very term *pre*school implies. It was still the era when play was considered the prime medium for the preschool experience. The notion of play as the context of preschool life was not a trivial one for students of early development and education. Parents and teachers were concerned with the development of young children but, following the lead of Gesell and others, they believed that formal instruction must wait for increased maturity. It would benefit a child little to push him prematurely into structured learning. Without the essential attainment of necessary maturational levels, what he was taught would in any case not stay with him and might, in the future, even interfere with later learning. What could help him was the chance to unfold—physically, emotionally, socially—in an environment that was warm, secure, and responsive. The young child coming to his first school needed space to play in, large equipment to develop muscular strength and coordination, aesthetic and dramatic experiences, and the chance to find himself as a person among peers. From these things he could benefit, and within the context of more or less supervised and structured play he would find them. And these children did indeed learn and grow. Usually, they successfully made the transition to "real" school when they turned six. They soon began to read and numerate, to do the expected academic tasks with considerable success. Their preschool experience apparently worked.

What few people failed to realize in those days, however, was that most of these children came out of comfortable homes where literate parents had talked and read to them since babyhood; where music was played and the visual world was observed and discussed; where children were taken beyond the confines of the home, whether to supermarket, playground and zoo, or long distances by plane and train. In a very real but then largely unrecognized fashion, these homes supplied cognitive elements in the children's total educational experience. They needed little additional intellectual stimulation when they got to nursery school, for they had already absorbed it at home. Home and school collaborated more, and to better purpose, than generally was recognized.

Most preschools in the fifties were privately run. Inevitably, they drew to them children whose parents could afford to pay the fees. Only a handful of public school systems offered classes below the kindergarten level, and even kindergartens generally were provided only by school systems in the affluent suburbs. Where public kindergartens existed in big-city systems, there were not enough places for all the eligible children. Those who got to go to kindergarten were the ones whose parents registered them first; by definition, they were the children of the alert, the aware—those who could read notices and act on them. The children of the very poor, the disoriented, the non-English speaking or illiterate, the immigrants from rural areas were inevitably left out. Yet these were the children who most needed the preschool experience.

Ironically, in the 1950s, one of the screens sometimes used in allocating the limited number of places in kindergarten was tests of readiness. If a child showed up well on these tests, measuring or predicting certain skills presumably related to early success in school, he was more likely to be selected.° The tests corroborated family advantage. Only a decade later, thinking had so changed that federal funds were available to seek out and provide preschool learning activities to the very children who would have been excluded by the tests in the fifties.

Prior to the 1960s in this country, then, educational experience before the first grade was restricted to the upper- and middle-class child. In this respect, the United States differed from many European countries where early schooling had begun as a response to the pressures and needs created by the Industrial Revolution. Froebel in Germany in the eighteen-thirties and forties, Montessori in Italy in the first years of the twentieth century, the McMillan sisters in England during and after World War I, all had concerned themselves with the children of factory workers, dispossessed peasants coming to the city, slum dwellers, the depressed and deprived. The thrust of preschool education had been to meet the needs of these groups. Crèches for babies and toddlers whose mothers must work, health and immunization programs for young children who suffered from rickets and malnutrition, attempts to educate little boys and girls who received no education at home—these had been the strong concerns of preschool educators in Germany, Italy, England,

°Ironically, there are recent signs of a return of this practice as part of the "back-to-basics" movement.

France, and Scandinavia. And certainly in Russia after the Revolution, preschool classes had been seen as a means for building the new society, even as they freed mothers to work in field or factory. But in the United States the chance to go to nursery school was the prerogative of the relatively well-to-do. Geographical setting played a role as well. For the child on ranch or farm, the child in the country village or the small city, as well as for the poor child, school began with the first grade.

Of course, there were some nursery classes run by settlement houses, church groups, or other philanthropic organizations in the central areas of the big cities. Some limited preschool education for children of the poor has had a long and honorable history in the United States. It was on the early education of poor children, during the era of intense influx of immigrants in the seventies and eighties of the nineteenth century, that Froebel's ideas had their impact. Education of the young child had been seen as a means for reaching and influencing immigrant families isolated by language and cultural barriers, who were clustering in what were rapidly becoming big-city ghettos. Hull House in Chicago and Henry Street Settlement in New York City were typical of those neighborhood houses in urban centers which offered classes for young children as part of their services to families. The teachers were young idealists who taught children in the mornings and in the afternoons visited the children's homes where they provided clothes and shoes, food and advice, and even job counseling and access to medical and psychological assistance. It was their example which was gradually to move the public schools into providing such ancillary services. The public schools had conceived of their role at first as a narrowly academic one and only slowly came to realize that the child who was cold, hungry, ill, or abused was hardly in a position to learn.

But even eighty years later, nursery classes or day care centers of this type were few in number. They could enroll only a small fraction of the thousands of children who lived in the major urban centers and whose families could spare no money for preschool fees. Very often the basic emphasis of these centers was on the child's physical well-being: they fed him, scrubbed him, rested him, checked his immunization and his nutrition, taught him some table manners and hopefully some improved ways of getting on with his peers. The educational component, as in the middle-class nursery school of the same period, was thin at best. Some of the philanthropic operations were excellent, insofar as they went; but some were baby-sitting establishments for which the word "school," even modified as "nursery school," was a misnomer.

During World War II, nursery school classes and child care centers were made available to many children located near war-related industries. Most of these were true learning centers, staffed by experienced teachers and well-supported by federal funds under the Lanham Act. It was clear that "Rosie the Riveter" was not going to get much riveting done unless someone looked after her kids, and since ships and planes were top priorities, funds quickly were made available and nursery schools were set up. Outstanding among the centers run in connection with wartime industry were those in two Kaiser shipyards, Swan Island and Oregonship. They were models of comprehensiveness and imaginative concern, meeting most needs of the shipbuilding families. They ran twenty-four hours a day; whatever shift Mom or Dad worked, the children were looked after. For the tired mother coming off her shift at the end of the day, they provided hot meals which could be picked up with the children and taken home. When new families drove into Portland, tired and bewildered in a strange city, the centers often kept all the children for several days until the parents could find an apartment and become settled. Medical care for the sick child, counseling for the troubled parent, a sense of community for the out-of-state family homesick in an intimidating industrial world, they provided all these and more. James L. Hymes, Jr., director of the Kaiser centers, wrote:

> But perhaps the concept most basic to the Kaiser answer is indicated by the name. These are good nursery schools, but they are more: they are Child *Service* Centers. The premise is that if a shipyard family needs help involving children, the Centers should provide that help. No peacetime precept, no *a priori* rule must stand in the way of service to children, to families.[1]

When the war came to an end, the Lanham Act soon came to an end, too (1946), and the buildings that had been used for nursery schools or day care centers were turned to other uses or stood shuttered and empty. The notion that early education could be available as a right to a broad range of children and their families, rather than as a special program for the few (be these the suburban well-to-do or very small groups of the urban not-at-all-well-to-do) had just begun to take hold when it faded to a memory.

A DECADE OF TRANSITION

The late 1950s ushered in one of the most tumultuous decades in American educational history, a decade that profoundly influenced views toward educating the young child. The testing programs of World War II had revealed academic deficiencies in high school graduates for which the assumed permissive theories of Progressive Education took a large share of the blame. Reform emphasizing the role of academic disciplines, particularly mathematics, the natural sciences, and foreign languages, already was underway when Sputnik (1957) alarmed the American people. Educational change and innovation moved to the forefront of national policy for the ensuing decade.

Curricular Reform and the Bruner Hypothesis

Curricular overhaul, beginning at the secondary-school level in selected subjects, spread horizontally to most fields and downward to the elementary school. The aim almost uniformly was to replace accumulations of content, often lacking order and a sense of priorities, with a few central ideas and processes providing structure to a field of knowledge.[2] To figure out how to teach children and youth well became exciting, intellectually challenging, and important in a way that it had not been since the heyday of Progressive Education. Teachers and academic specialists in all the disciplines who were so often worlds apart began working actively together, observing what worked in selected classrooms, revising material, throwing ideas away, and starting in again. The movement's relevance to young children was established firmly in what might be called "the Bruner hypothesis" (and this must be one of the most quoted educational sentences of the century): "We begin with the hypothesis that any subject can be taught effectively in some intellectually honest form to any child at any stage of development."[3] The importance of this statement lies not in its literal truth but rather in the fact that school was beginning to be thought of again, after a long hiatus, as a significant place of instruction where cognitive powers might be developed; indeed, that learning to think and to know were the most significant occupations of people in school. A belief so powerfully stated, espoused with such a sense of new excitement by teachers and scholars at all levels, was destined to make its mark on views regarding the earliest years of education.

The Bloom Hypothesis

The Bruner hypothesis was a far cry from prevailing ideas of readiness. But it remained more an intriguing concept than a call to action. Five years later, the implications of Bloom's *Stability and Change in Human Characteristics* could not be denied. In what was to become one of the most influential books of the decade, he suggested that up to half of the development present by the late teens is attained by the age of four and up to 30 percent more by the age of seven or eight. Even by age four it may be difficult to change the course of development.

Bloom's study had involved the careful analysis and evaluation by statistical means of all major longitudinal studies done in the United States up to the early sixties. He had looked at many human characteristics, but the mood and concern of the times were such that the central focus was on what he had to say about intellectual development. This made a powerful impact on those already concerned with cognitive development and the education of young children. The crucial material reads as follows:

". . . we would question the notion of an absolutely constant I.Q. Intelligence is a developmental concept, just as is height, weight, or strength. There is increased stability in intelligence measurements with time. However, we should be quick to point out that by about age 4, 50% of the variation in intelligence at age 17 is accounted for. This would suggest the very rapid growth of intelligence in the early years and the possible great influence of the early environment on this development.

We would expect the variations in the environments to have relatively little effect on the I.Q. after age 8, but we would expect such variation to have marked effect on the I.Q. before that age, with the greatest effect likely to take place between the ages of about 1 to 5."[4]

This statement provided at once both an explanation for the observed intellectual limitations of children from deprived home settings and a call to action, since presumably changed settings in the earliest years would result in changed behavior in school and in adult life. Certainly, programs of early intervention, regardless of their theoretical base, more closely approximate the timing of stimulation in the good middle-class home, which we know to be a setting fostering enduring intellectual development.

Urban Decay and Socioeconomic Deprivation

When intellectual forces from within and societal forces from without coalesce, educational change frequently is the result. This was the highly productive combination of the sixties, especially with respect to higher education on the one hand and early childhood education on the other. The impact of ideas such as those expressed by Bruner, Bloom, and others would have been much less and occurred more slowly had there not been rapidly increasing awareness of urban blight and its accompanying conditions.

Though these conditions did not suddenly come upon the scene, full-blown in all their stark reality, we seemed suddenly to be aware of them. The drift to the city had been well under way since Depression days; World War II accelerated it. Affluence for whites in the postwar years provided them the opportunity to move out to the more attractive suburban green. They were replaced in the cities by poor whites and, increasingly, blacks and other relatively impoverished groups unable to pay for the maintenance of facilities, particularly schools. From 1930 to 1960 the national cost of schooling per pupil rose 331 percent, but the per capita value of taxable property in large cities rose only 97 percent.[5] By contrast, the suburbs were able to provide better education at comparatively much less strain to the taxpayer. In his *Slums and Suburbs,* Conant, who was then the country's most respected educational spokesman, described the inner-city condition as "social dynamite."[6]

It is possible to trace all the factors coming together in the mid-sixties to produce an active commitment to compensatory education for disadvantaged children of preschool age. Evidence pointed to the importance of early intervention; the Israeli experience with early education for immigrant children (the "Oriental Jews") provided a glimpse of the possible;[7] the climate of the inner city was explosive; black and other minority-group leaders were becoming militant and raising strident voices. All this produced a political response in the Economic Opportunity Act of 1964 and the Elementary and Secondary Education Act of 1965, two historic pieces of social legislation.

The former created Head Start. The largest project for young children ever backed by the federal government, it combined medical and psychological services with educational services in an effort to help children become ready to succeed in school. By the summer of 1965, over 550,000 children were enrolled in six- or eight-week programs in 2,500 Child Development Centers throughout the country.[8] Since all children eligible for Head Start came from families whose income fell below an established minimum, it was clear that without the program they would not have been in preschool at all. It soon became equally clear, however, that a few weeks or even a full year of compensatory experience before entry into the public schools was not enough to bring about enduring developmental gains. Consequently, a second federally financed program, Follow Through, was added to Head Start to give children who particularly needed it a longer-lasting, more coherent series of educational experiences.

For large numbers of disadvantaged children in many areas of the country, no kindergarten classes were available. Since Head Start was designed to take children directly before their first school entry, it naturally took the place of all or part of the missing kindergarten year. This meant that a majority of Head Start children already were five. But experience and research alike indicated that for children from severely limited backgrounds this was already too late. They could not sustain what they had learned in Head Start when they entered "real" school. If the money, time, and energy poured into the Head Start programs were not to be wasted, the federal programs must be extended downward as well. In 1967, Parent and Child Centers were started in some thirty communities as pilot projects.[9] To these Centers mothers brought their babies and toddlers and stayed with them to observe the care their children received and to be instructed in child-rearing and household skills. Though this program also was largely federally funded, community involvement was stressed, and local attitudes and needs were allowed to shape each Center's procedures in ways appropriate to its locale.

Titles I, III, and IV of the ESEA contributed to early childhood education in a variety of ways, but not all the good intentions were fulfilled. A project growing out of Title IV, of particular promise for the improvement of programs through research, was born deprived into an environment grown less supportive only two short years after passage of the act. This was the National Laboratory in Early Childhood Education, created in 1967. The intent was to fund up to ten or twelve university centers, each with a different focus but each committed to include a full span of activity from research to program development to training and dissemination. A coordinated type of collaboration would assure attention to all major aspects of productive intervention and rapid communication of research and programs. Presumably, such a Laboratory would provide a knowledge base for a national commitment to educating the young.

But funds for fulfillment of these plans were not forthcoming.[10] The debilitating costs of the Vietnam War were taking their toll, drawing resources away from fully implementing the ambitious social legislation of preceding years. The half dozen or so centers and the headquarters office making up the National Laboratory received only a modest trickle of financial support. Meanwhile, a more ambitious proposal for a nationwide effort in early childhood schooling, championed by James C. Russell of the Educational Policies Commission, failed to get off the ground. The intent was to provide nursery schooling for all four-year-olds, beginning with the disadvantaged and ultimately extending to all children, supported by an annual federal commitment of approximately four billion dollars. This proved to be the final educational effort of the EPC which subsequently closed its doors.

One thing that emerges clearly from the period is the shaping impact of federal funding on preschool and particularly prekindergarten education. First-rate scholars were brought into the field and from their work emerged several vigorous theoretical thrusts to guide experimentation and practice. On the immediately practical front, a tremendous amount of growth and change in the availability of preschool education had occurred, particularly over the middle five years of the sixties.

In brief, two remarkable things had happened in the short time span of ten years. First, the young had been discovered, educationally speaking. Early childhood education no longer was an enclave apart; it had moved into the mainstream of inquiry and practice. Second, the focus of attention was upon compensatory education for disadvantaged children. In sharp contrast to the mid-fifties, it was now more likely that a precocious child would be denied rather than granted access to one of a limited number of publicly supported preschool places.

SOME RECENT DEVELOPMENTS

There is no doubt that educational activity in general suffered from decline in availability of federal funds during the late sixties and early seventies. Supplementary educational centers financed under Title III of ESEA through the states virtually disappeared; the regional laboratories and research and development centers financed under Title IV were reduced in both number and funding. Research funds for early education declined markedly. However, although funds available for early education were less than they had been, both the interest and growth in preschool enrollments continued.

In the fifties, the focus in preschool education was on providing kindergarten for thousands of children who normally began their school experience with grade one. Nursery schools enrolled only a privileged few. Today, one of the most rapidly expanding preschool fields is that of the nursery school, enrolling three- and four-year-olds, with the emphasis already shifting to day care for the very young. A dozen years ago, it would have seemed almost bizarre to speak of infants and toddlers in schoollike situations, unless traumatic home circumstances made this obligatory. Now, mothers who have no economic necessity to work, as well as those who must gain a livelihood, are thinking favorably of day care for their very young children.

The U.S. Department of Labor reports that 40 percent of married women in the United States were in the labor force during 1970, and of these some 10,200,000 had children under eighteen. About one-fourth of all mothers with children under three years of age held jobs, and about one-third of those with children between the ages of three and five held jobs. This is an enormous number of children whose mothers are not home, day-in and day-out. Very often the mother works because she must. But, increasingly, middle-class mothers who need not work in order to eat, work to earn income for the extras, or to meet payments on the home, or because they have professional training they want to use, or simply because it is the thing to do and they want to do it. Someone must look after the young children.

Many children are left with relatives or with neighbors on a regular basis for a fee. Some mothers employ baby-sitters; a few, but only a very few, have live-in help. Some children go to private nursery schools (but generally these are only available in urban or suburban areas for well-to-do families). Some hundreds of thousands of children are in Head Start programs, but since these usually are conducted only in the mornings, the mothers must make some other arrangements for after-preschool hours. Consequently, there are thousands of modern Dame Schools; friendly, warm-hearted women who take little groups of children into their homes and look after them. Since they may charge only a small fee, the temptation clearly is to give minimal food and severely to limit materials for the children to use. These "schoolkeepers" typically know nothing about the education of young children. The ideal is to keep them quiet, neat, well-behaved, and clean. These are not characteristics typical of the active, involved, learning child. With rare exceptions, day care in such settings is a custodial operation; a mother is lucky if her child is at least in the hands of a well-intentioned person who is kind and reliable, for many such schoolkeepers are not. Hardly any are equipped to guide those vital early learning years as they ought to be used: for growth and discovery, for joy and security.

The need increases as more and more mothers enter the work force. Some industry-sponsored child care centers give relatively good care with professionally trained staffs and adequate space and equipment. Sometimes, these services are provided free as a fringe benefit negotiated as part of the labor package; sometimes parents pay a small fee. One such operation is run for children of employees and neighboring residents by KLH, a manufacturer of high fidelity equipment in Cambridge, Massachusetts. Started in 1968 with a federal grant of $324,000, the program is now operating entirely on funds from KLH, the Massachusetts Institute of Technology, and the Massachusetts Public Welfare Department, with parents paying a portion of the weekly costs. Welfare services meet the payments of families on welfare.

Skyland Textile Company of Morgantown, North Carolina, 96 percent of whose workers are women, began a day care center in July 1969, and credits the center with "lowering incidence of employee absenteeism, improving productivity, and attracting and holding a more stable group of workers."[11] Other large companies employing many women have begun or are seriously studying such operations. Many universities are beginning to provide them for children of staff, faculty, and graduate students. They are generally funded liberally enough so that pennypinching is not a must, unlike so many of the small proprietary operations, and they can attract competent personnel. Since they often need not break even financially, they can spend the money required for materials, varied equipment, and nourishing food. Their ratio of teachers to children often is set at the federally recommended standard of one adult to four babies or toddlers, one adult to five three-year-olds, and one adult to eight four-year-olds.

With inflated prospects of success, commercial day care chains were making their entry into the preschool scene during the late sixties and early seventies. In 1970, *Business Week* reported that: "At least 25 and perhaps as many as 50 companies are now actively in the field," and went on to say: "Not even the Health, Education, and Welfare Department knows who all the entrants are—or who will offer education rather than simply offering parking lots for children."[12]

Market tests discouraged some companies; some entered and quickly withdrew; others are in deep trouble; and some appear to be making a go of it. There are two alternative plans by means of which commercial concerns have entered the day care market. One is through chains of centers owned and run by a central company, with each center staffed and run by professional and quasi-professional employees. The other is the franchise method, under which individuals purchase each center for a given sum, using the name and format of the parent organization and conforming to its standards, and receive assistance in such areas as advertising, accounting, and (supposedly) staff training. Grave questions may be raised about each method of operation, but franchising seems to be the more fraught with possible ills and abuses.

Verifiable statistics regarding total preschool enrollments are hard to come by; available figures vary widely and change rapidly. Often, they confuse more than they help because of failure to clarify whether some or all types of kindergarten enrollments are included or excluded. It is clear, however, that early schooling now encompasses rather large numbers of children, mostly in urban and suburban communities. Interestingly, and rather surprisingly, we have very little information regarding the day-to-day conduct of schooling in the thousands of installations conducting some kind of educational activity below the level of kindergarten. Descriptions of what transpires in other countries are becoming available[13] and, in 1970, Weber provided an excellent analysis of theories and practices in selected, more experimental centers in the United States, based on first-hand observation.[14] But what goes on in the general run of nursery schools? What kinds of people operate them and what ideas do they employ in conducting preschool programs? To what extent and in what ways have they been influenced by the ferment in early education?

It was in hopes of answering some of these questions that my colleagues and I conducted a survey of preschool installations in nine cities in the United States. The findings are too numerous to be reported here.[15] Suffice it to say that our results indicated that on the whole the day-to-day operations of preschools in the United States bear little resemblance to the practices recommended by experts in the field. Most preschools are still conducted as a warm, safe place for children to play and become socialized to their peers. The decade of ferment and high expectations for using the preschool years for cognitive enrichment have made little impact.

It would be a gross oversight to conclude this discussion of the educational discovery of young children without drawing attention to three conclusions emerging with increasing strength from recent research and practice. First, the school, for any age group, is simply part of the total educational experience, contributing for better or for worse. At best, it can help compensate for home and other environmental deficiencies or enrich an already productive environment outside of school. Second, the very early years are exceedingly formative, setting patterns and directions for much of what will characterize later life. To long-standing interest in early cognitive stimulation has been added concern for a full range of social services contributing to a healthful, sound beginning in life.

These two conclusions lead to an obvious third: that early social and educational services are most effective when joined collaboratively with the home. It is not at all surprising, then, that the political response to early education increasingly is toward support of comprehensive child care programs of various kinds, beginning with prenatal and even prepregnancy parent education and moving on to child care centers providing health and educational services for family units. "Home Start" enjoys the appeal associated with Head Start just a few short years ago. It would appear that the cradle part, at least, of the old saying, "education from cradle to grave," is about to move from slogan to reality.

As a society, we have not yet come to grips with the vital question of what early education and schooling are for. The more various reports and proposals get into specifics, the more we see the seemingly inescapable academically oriented activities of an early school preparing for a later school instead of activities designed with the goal of each child's discovering and expanding himself as a person. Why are we so incapable of envisioning more than a real-life version of Sesame Street?

There is no way of translating into specific recommendations our central concern about the two most fundamental shortcomings of programs in early education. My colleagues and I have had the benefits of extensive observation of nursery school classrooms and discussions with directors, teachers, and early childhood specialists in the United States, England, Israel, and Asia. We have delved into the relevant literature of many lands. What comes through over-whelmingly is a desire to "do good": to keep children safely and happily engaged, to compensate for handicap or disadvantage, to develop the traits of the whole child, and to prepare for school. *What is missing is a sense of what the child is trying to do—perhaps must do—during these formative years, and a sense of the scar tissue he will carry with him throughout life if his early strivings for identity are frustrated by neglect or inept intervention.*

This is not to suggest for a moment that the child, left to his own devices, will mature in wholesome fashion. If this were the case, there would be no need for education and certainly not for school-ing. Even if there were a built-in mechanism for only good unfold-ing—which is not the case—society is not sufficiently benign to assure unswerving adherence to positive development. The environ-ment must be shaped.

The essential elements in this shaping are a set of guiding values infused into every activity and never-failing adult support. For the early phase of schooling, the values to be personified in the adult interest are that the child achieve a sense of personal well-being expressed in his self-confident relationship with objects, peers, and adults; his lack of fear; his confrontations with his occasionally angry, hating, antisocial self; his ability to move in and out of an imaginary world in which knights fight battles with serpents and dragons and win; his transition from narcissistic contemplation of self to interaction with an increasingly expanding environment. These are the marks of the child successfully using his early years, not his level of performance on school-oriented tests. These are the emerging attributes for which he must have unfaltering adult support. These are the goals for the first phase of schooling.

Reading, numbers, and the like are meaningful to the degree they help the child achieve these goals—and very meaningful, indeed, they can be because they are the tools of the human race that extend self-transcendence in limitless ways. But they are not the goals of early schooling. Unfortunately, it is mistaking these mundane means for the ends of education that has corrupted schooling at all levels. Early schools have the best opportunity and the most serious responsibility for maintaining at all times the necessary distinction.

Notes

[1]James L. Hymes, Jr., "The Kaiser Answer: Child Service Centers," *Kaiser Pamphlets for Teachers*, Portland, Oregon, n.d.

[2]John I. Goodlad, with Renata von Stoephasius and M. Frances Klein, *The Changing School Curriculum*, Fund for the Advancement of Education, New York, 1966.

[3]Jerome S. Bruner, *The Process of Education*, Harvard University Press, Cambridge, Mass., 1960, p. 33.

[4]Benjamin S. Bloom, *Stability and Change in Human Characteristics*, John Wiley and Sons, New York, 1964, p. 68.

[5]H. Thomas James, James A. Kelly, and Walter I. Garms, *Determinants of Educational Expenditures in Large Cities of the United States* (Cooperative Research Project No. 2389), Stanford University, School of Education, Stanford, Calif., 1966.

[6]James B. Conant, *Slums and Suburbs*, McGraw-Hill, New York, 1962.

[7]See, for example, Moshe and Sarah Smilansky, "Intellectual Advancement of Culturally Disadvantaged Children: An Israeli Approach for Research and Action," *International Review of Education*, vol. XIII, no. 4, 1967.

[8]Keith Osborn, "Project Head Start—An Assessment," *Educational Leadership*, vol. 23, November 1965, p. 98.

[9]Richard E. Orton, "Head Start Moves Down to Prenatal Period," *Washington Monitor*, September 18, 1967, p. 17.

[10]The Committee, under the chairmanship of John I. Goodlad, had been instructed by officials in the Office of the Commissioner, USOE, to plan for support for the Laboratory in the amount of from $5 million to $10 million per year over a period of from five to ten years. In the short period of

transition from one Commissioner to his successor, the prospect for funds had diminished to zero. The commitment to establish the National Laboratory in Early Childhood Education ultimately was fulfilled, thanks in large measure to the Office of the Commissioner, but at a drastically reduced level of funding.

[11]J. B. Quinn (ed.), *The Business Week Letter,* McGraw-Hill, New York, n.d.

[12]*Business Week,* October 31, 1970, p. 50.

[13]See, for example, Norma Feshbach, John I. Goodlad, and Avima Lombard, *Early Schooling in England and Israel,* McGraw-Hill, New York, 1973; Ruth Bettelheim and Ruby Takanishi, *Early Schooling in Asia,* McGraw-Hill, New York, 1976; and the volumes of the International Monograph Series on Early Child Care, Gordon and Breach, New York, 1972—continuing.

[14]Evelyn Weber, *Early Childhood Education: Perspectives on Change,* Charles A. Jones Publishing Company, Worthington, Ohio, 1970.

[15]A detailed report of the data as well as a summary of current theories of child development and recommendations for the future of early schooling are included in the book from which this chapter is taken. See John I. Goodlad, M. Frances Klein, Jerrold M. Novotney, and Associates, *Early Schooling in the United States,* McGraw-Hill, New York, 1973.

10

Perspective on Accountability

If you think that education's problems will be solved by the accountability movement as it is usually defined where the teacher bears full responsibility for student learning, don't expect much aid and comfort from the following paper. [Editor]

Anyone who has been connected with the schooling enterprise for a quarter century or more has lived through several waves of concern for toughening it up or humanizing it. Each wave has added its own distinctive flotsam to that already cast up by previous waves of reform. And each has sought to build up a swell of sufficient size and force to dwarf the waves of "soft" or "hard" education seen to have preceded.

Books by Bestor, Hutchins, and Lynd[1] in 1953 hastened the demise of the Progressive Education Society, seen to be the villain in soft life-adjustment education of preceding decades. Two years later, Flesch provided a tough but simple solution to what ailed primary schooling: teachers simply had to abandon sloppy word recognition techniques in favor of a structured phonetic approach to the teaching of reading.[2] The launching of Sputnik in 1957

SOURCE: John I. Goodlad, "A Perspective on Accountability," *Phi Delta Kappan*, vol. 57, no. 2, October 1975, pp. 108–112.

convinced us that our schools were not rigorous enough. Academics and the structure of the disciplines would lead us out of this slough of despair.

A decade later, we had been through what probably was the most intensive period of probing and poking at the schools and of seeking to reform them in the history of our common schools. The schools were expected to ameliorate a succession of several social problems,[3] but by the end of the 1960s, the problems appeared to be exacerbated rather than ameliorated. The Coleman Report was the primer in a growing folklore to the effect that schools don't make any difference anyway;[4] and Illich said that society should be deschooled.[5] Doing away with our schools is the ultimate disenchantment—a long way from the view of toughening up here and adding something there which prevailed in the reform rhetoric of the 1950s and 1960s.

A miscellaneous, loosely coordinated, pluralistic array of reforms having failed, apparently, by the 1970s it was time to turn to what many in our society regard as the ultimate authority and remedy: science was to be substituted for ineffectual human processes or, at a minimum, scientific data were to be added to political decision-making processes. The catch-word became *accountability*.

> "Like most metaphors concerning reform, this one covered a variety of disparate elements: performance contracting, community control, management-by-objectives, educational vouchers, management information systems, and educational assessment. . . . American education has been having quite a romance with technocratic approaches to accountability. Seeking better information seems less threatening and more up to date than redistributing political power. . . . In practice, accountability has come to mean reforming government through science."[6]

Taken at face value, the word *accountable* has all the virtuous qualities attributed to words such as God, motherhood, and country. Webster's defines it as "capable of being accounted for" and hardly anyone could object to that. In practice, however, a set of interlocking concepts has been put together to infer a related set of procedures. Michigan's six-step model frequently is cited as illustrative because of that state's experience with accountability and because there already has been some assessment of it.[7] Whatever the controversy about implementation, the plan in concept is not unlike those in various stages of development in other states. Nor is it very different from plans set forth in the extant literature by various advocates.[8] Consequently, it is useful to examine state models such as the Michigan one in the light of their conceptual assumptions and potential implications for practice quite apart from their actual implementation.

The first step is to formulate some common statewide goals. Second, these are to be translated into specific objectives for local schools. Third, there is to be a determination of needed change efforts on the basis of some kind of assessment of student performance in relation to objectives. Fourth, these needs are to be addressed through local innovative efforts directed at the improvement of weaknesses presumed to be revealed through assessment. Fifth, local evaluation capability is to be developed so that some kind of continuing self-appraisal will be built into local improvement efforts. Sixth, feedback from all this to state authorities is then to be used in assisting the state department of education to fulfill its leadership roles, however it may perceive them.

Clearly, all this is very logical and appealing to those who seek full rationality in the conduct of human affairs. But, in estimating the potentiality of such a model for school improvement, several major questions come to mind. For example, does the present state of educational science provide the needed support for drawing the internal connections the model implies? It is a large leap from general statewide goals to behaviorally stated objectives. What evidence is there that those behaviors which are measured bear a reasonably close relation to these goals? The absence of adequate evidence does not destroy the validity of the model for research, but it does raise serious questions about the wisdom of enforcing its use through legislative enactments and monetary sanctions. Other problems arise out of sociopolitical realities in the decision-making process. Plans appearing to substitute scientific rationalism for negotiations among interest groups must anticipate confrontation with or subversion by all those groups whose power or autonomy is perceived to be threatened. Some promoters of accountability plans speak ruefully and even bitterly about the lumps received in the political marketplace. Most surprising is that so many failed to anticipate them, naïvely counting on the logic or even common-sense nature of their arguments to see them through.

In addition to these major substantive and political problems, an accountability model and accompanying processes of the kind described must be prepared to address questions pertaining to feasibility, cost, and potentiality for significant educational improvement.

One fact of educational life must be made clear at the outset in any effort to analyze a movement such as the current one in accountability. Elsewhere, I have made reference to the *soft* and the *hard*—or what Smith has called the *tender* and the *tough*[9]—in characterizing two conflicting normative views regarding the desired nature of education and, therefore, preferred directions for reform. There are those in and out of the education profession who simply reject scientism and what they view as a cult of efficiency in schooling.[10] They reject the bureaucratization of public education and want to reduce the whole as much as possible to a teacher and a group of children. The model of accountability described here is anathema and will remain so in their view no matter what rhetorical and data-based arsenals are mounted in defense.

This group is regarded as *soft* or *tender* by their *hard* or *tough* antagonists. A truce between them can be only that—a respite from a disagreeable period of contention. Although tension between the two has played a significant role in the development of (and in recurring excesses in) American education throughout the twentieth century, tension currently is at a high point, with strong proposals for accountability and equally strong proposals for "more humane alternatives" in education vying for attention.

Consequently, it is appropriate for anyone seeking to analyze accountability as described here to state his or her basic value orientation with respect to these contesting views. In regard to the more extreme protagonists, my position probably can be summed up best by saying, "A plague on both your houses," a view which leaves me, roughly, in the shoes of a stranger who attempts to break up a fight between brothers! The two need each other in the same way a Republican needs a few good Democrats around "to keep his dander up."

There is a place for technology in education and schooling, especially at the instructional level where many neo-humanists abhor it most.[11] But it is unlikely that accountability schemes of the kind presently holding court will operate to improve the decisions made in the essentially nontechnocratic sociopolitical structure of educational affairs or to improve significantly the conduct of schooling.

ACCOUNTABILITY AND EDUCATIONAL SCIENCE

One of the many criticisms directed to current state approaches to accountability is that the common goals are too broad and vague to be of much use. Frequently, there is a simultaneous indication of impatience to get down to the nitty-gritty, namely, the delineation of performance objectives. There is no doubt in my mind that we now have a useful, rather well-developed technology for stating such objectives precisely.[12] But this begs a central issue. What evidence do we have that any eight or ten or fifty behaviorally stated objectives, if attained, add up to some larger human traits of the kind implied in educational aims since the time of Aristotle or in state or locally prescribed goals? The answer is, of course, very little. But, unfortunately, this does not stop the enthusiast, sometimes quite unwittingly, from confusing the technical process of stating precise objectives with the empirical one of establishing real rather than merely assumed relations between a specific performance measured and a human trait desired.

The truth of the matter is that we know precious little about what those performances we stress and reward in school add up to with respect to the characteristics envisioned and expressed in educational goals. Success in the lower grades is a rather good predictor of how a student will perform in higher grades but a dismally poor one of how he will perform on a job or in human relations or of whether he will be truthful, happy, or a law-abiding citizen.[13] The problems raised by such an observation are so formidable that many educators, not surprisingly, say that they are not their business. But, clearly, such problems are at the heart of education itself.

Admittedly, the realms of human experience identified are especially troublesome ones. But even when we move into basic subject-matter fields, no good maps of sequential or logical relations exist. In time, the work of those now toiling in this vineyard and those to follow in their footsteps may help some. At present, however, the rhetoric of pseudoscientism serves to obscure the fact that we do not have the educational science required for translating sociopolitical state goals into properly inferred objectives even though we appear to have the technology for stating the latter precisely. It is doubtful that we ever will be able to do much better in this realm than make some reasonably good logical inferences. Failure to recognize this fact takes a host of well-meaning people, including legislators, down clear, well-marked trails which are unlikely to lead them out of the woods. The disillusionment lying ahead could be monumental.

The accountability model described here ultimately creates rather great expectations of teachers. Whatever the disarming rhetoric to the contrary, it is the teacher who is to be held accountable for remedying deficiencies revealed through assessment. She or he is to be capable of being accounted for—and, indeed, full implementation of the model discussed here logically leads to massive in-service teacher education programs. Leaving aside, for a moment, the questions of who is to pay for this (and this involves fundamental matters of authority and responsibility, not merely finding the cash) and of logistics, given the range of needs likely to be exposed, once again we are confronted with the question of whether educational science is in a position to deliver. In my judgment, a thoughtful answer to this question can only be that it is not and that our expectations for this science must be more modest.

Admittedly, we have some useful knowledge about individual differences, the effects of teacher leadership styles, reinforcement techniques, and the like. But we simply do not now have the educational science almost necessarily inferred from much extant accountability rhetoric. A couple of examples serve to illustrate.

Millions of dollars have been spent in attempting to replace this or that approach to the teaching of reading with another. Although there always is evidence to show that the new method produced marked changes in *some* children, the effect on the mean almost invariably has been disappointing. Admittedly, the Michigan accountability plan, for example, provides teachers with specific information regarding an array of performances for each child in reading. This is considerably more helpful than learning that the class is at the 15th percentile on a norm-referenced test. But the problem now is to have a range of alternatives and know what to expect from them in seeking to produce the desired changes. The onus should be at least as much on the state of the science as on the teacher, but, too frequently, he or she is expected to provide more time and work harder: "Don't stand there, do something." But it might be difficult to get agreement, even among a group of experts, as to just what to do.

Once one moves out of reading and mathematics in the elementary school, the directives from science become even less clear. An emerging goal for schooling in our time has to do with international understanding and attitudes, and state educational goals frequently include attention to this area. A finding drawn from cross-national data gathered under the auspices of the International Association for the Evaluation of Educational Achievement might be of interest to legislators: "Fourteen-year-olds in the United States and Ireland, while reporting moderate frequency of national political discussion with friends and parents, have the lowest expressed interest in such discussion of international matters"[14] (among eight nations tested). How might the accountability model work here?

Any goal statement dealing with international understanding, however phrased, will be vague. But certainly it has implications for schooling which would not be there if no such goal were stated, and so it is not meaningless. But translating it into performance or behavioral terms is, at best, an exercise in logical inference, a process which is not improved upon by the technical one of establishing precision in final statements. Now, let us suppose that the assessment stage suggests deficiencies. What educational practices are to follow? Presumably some kind of international studies are called for. Unfortunately, the seemingly clear path to follow is muddied by some research-based indications that learning more about the ways of people in other lands may not improve attitudes toward these people and, in fact, may have just the opposite effect.[15]

One could cite many more such examples to support the thesis that there is not a science of education sufficient to give credence to the scientism necessarily inferred if any model of accountability of the kind described here is to function effectively. It is an idea whose time is not yet come, whatever rhetorical and political support it is able to muster. But it will be back again, probably in new trappings. The critical question is whether there will be available any more supporting scientific rigor than we have today. The signs are not promising. If one extrapolates from the past experience with this and other recurring themes in American education, many who supported the movement for political reasons will seek a scapegoat in "the uselessness of educational research" and, as in the past, will vote against the very research funds we need if educational knowledge is to be advanced. Ironically, those who expect too much of science usually are strongest in condemnation of it when it fails them. Aristotle had some good advice here which should serve to caution us well: "It is a mark of the educated man and a proof of his culture that in every subject he looks for only so much precision as its nature permits."[16]

ACCOUNTABILITY AND EDUCATIONAL IMPROVEMENT

The accountability model described here presumably is advocated by well-intentioned persons who take a rational, scientific view of the educational process. They approach school reform and improvement in essentially the linear fashion followed by legions of recent and contemporary reformers. They see new curriculum content, materials, organizational structures, or devices as good in their own right. One has only to develop them using the best technology available and put them into the system, school, or classroom. The sociopolitical system of which schools are a part, with all their complex negotiations and regulations, are a mystery and a bother, to be circumvented as much as possible. Ultimately, science will make all such processes unnecessary. During the curriculum reform movement of the 1960s, project directors often sought to do end runs around administrators to get directly to teachers.[17] Then the teachers were sometimes seen as intractable or incapable of changing and so "teacher-proof" materials were the answer.

It becomes increasingly clear that this approach to educational reform has been marked, at best, by limited success. Teachers used the new texts and exercise books but did not use the inductive techniques designed to encourage student inquiry. They accepted the idea of nongrading but translated it into achievement grouping, a familiar and rather soothing approach to the obfuscation of individual differences. They learned how to state objectives behaviorally as they had previously learned many other instructional procedures, but what they did behind the classroom door was their own business.

More and more we are coming to the realization, even if we do not act on it, that principals and teachers have a remarkable facility for taking what is thrust upon them from would-be reformers and wrapping it up in the culture of the school so as to render it benign or impotent. One can only laugh wryly to read in some of the literature on change the straightfaced conclusion that the most successful innovations are those demanding little or no changes on the part of teachers. We know, of course, from biology and sociology that any significant change in a system changes the whole system and, consequently, places new demands on all parts of that system. Sarason said it well when he concluded that any change, to be successful, must deal with the culture of a school and the regularities by means of which that culture conducts its existence.[18] Recently, the National Institute of Education took note of this and similar conclusions in its planning for educational reform.[19] And one reasonably comprehensive review of the research on this subject concluded: "R and D delivery systems aimed at bringing research findings, knowledge and products to the schools have less potential for change than those strategies that emphasize strengthening the capabilities of school districts to actively be responsible for their own improvement."[20]

It appears to me that accountability as a means to educational change and improvement—and surely that has to be its ultimate purpose—at best ignores and at worst flies in the face of these observations and conclusions and, consequently, has only a very limited chance of achieving its purpose, no matter what the sanctions. Even quiet conformity—an improbable eventuality—should be regarded as suggesting subversion or subtle co-opting rather than meaningful implementation. But the almost certain eventuality is organized resistance and the diversion of energy which, all sides would agree, should rightfully go to school improvement. It must be remembered that teachers at least as much as legislators, state department officials, and accountability proponents want to improve schools and have as much or more at stake: they want to live reasonably satisfying lives there each day.

At the front line of obstacles to implementing accountability plans is the fact that large numbers of teachers, when called upon to choose, come down on the side of the soft and tender, not the hard and tough. Accountability advocates may chastise them for being muddled, romantic, or soft-headed, but this will not alter the reality. Consequently, when what could be useful and acceptable information regarding the strengths and weaknesses of their students is couched in the unmistakably clear language of accountability, teachers' backs go up immediately. The target for change has been alerted and defenses are mustered accordingly. The accountability model is in trouble before it is even assembled let alone launched toward its target.

Later, with the new model beginning to function, teachers are called upon to learn new behaviors, often on what is normally time for planning the next day's activities. The education industry, compared to other businesses and industries, is at a primitive stage in the provision of on-the-job training on the time and at the expense of the industry. The cost in dollars, estimated in hours of time to assure implementation of the model described here, should be enough to raise in everyone's mind questions demanding positive assurance that work hours could not otherwise be spent better. (The associate superintendent of a small district in California estimated this cost to be well over $50,000 for the six-month period of time used to define system goals and instructional objectives.) The cost in precious human time surely must give one pause and some reflection on matters pertaining to wisdom and morality.

Still later, with test results coming in, evidence, not surprisingly, reveals near-panic on the part of many teachers. This panic is aggravated when there are monetary incentives or sanctions. As noted earlier, directives for rectifying shortcomings are not at all clear. The science of education provides at best only a few general guidelines to action and, for a host of reasons, there is not out there waiting and ready a well-trained teaching profession. Over the years, the drop-out rate among elementary school teachers has run to 70 percent during the first three years following graduation. In some states, such as California, prospective teachers are restricted to only a very limited exposure to the pedagogic principles and practices which might help at least some perform more effectively—ironically, sometimes because of the legislative enactments of the same legislators now calling for a brand of accountability which demands the highest possible level of professional behavior.

Further, teachers operate within sets of local customs and restraints which may restrict their freedom to do what appears necessary in meeting accountability expectations, such as a pre-scribed approach to teaching reading. Principals may be called upon to see that accountability works, and so are placed in an adversary role with teachers. Increasingly, it becomes apparent that improvement in reading, vocational education, the arts, or anything else depends on the orchestration of many factors such as community enthusiasm, administrative support, peer group collaboration, well-coordinated materials, services, and the like, rather than on some single pedagogical approach for which the teacher alone is responsible. One of the many unresolved issues pertaining to accountability has to do with state versus local domains of authority and responsibility.

It should come as no surprise, then, that teachers fall back to what has been to many an unfamiliar and even unwanted line of defense—namely, the union or teachers' association. They see in the accountability model described here the prospect of their time being controlled for purposes other than teaching. But such specifics may be relatively low in their concern. More important is the prospect of pitting one relatively large, powerful, and impersonal body against another. The arena of conflict shifts, and those who saw themselves reforming education through science suddenly find themselves enmeshed in the very political power struggle they basically view as irrational. One can of worms has been replaced by another.

When events proceed as described here—and I believe that such results are virtually inevitable when the kind of accountability model described is mandated and/or accompanied by monetary sanctions—everyone loses. The potential usefulness of several of the steps as a tool for research, getting information, and making decisions is obscured; there is, unfortunately, excessive retaliation against any such processes for years into the future. Teachers frequently proceed with anachronistic bargaining demands which can lead to such restrictions on their activities that they lose both the freedom they need for creating a satisfying work place and, in the process, any meaningful claim to professional status. Worst of all, those who must work together if our schools are to have any chance of becoming what almost everyone in the struggle would like them to become are hopelessly divided.

In my judgment, the necessary reconstruction of schooling must take place from the bottom up, not the top down. We need state goals for education, of course; goals that reflect the interests of the larger political community and that establish a framework within which the desires of subcommunities are expressed. It is the responsibility of elected government to provide the widest possible forum for articulating these state goals. It is reasonable, too, for the state to sample cohorts of children with respect to what they seem to be learning, much in the fashion of the so-called National Assessment. But, like National Assessment, they should stay clear of gathering and disseminating data on specific communities, schools, and classrooms. There are enough problems, surely, of setting directions and providing support for education at the state level to command the attention of those interest groups that see their course of action demanding the exercise of muscle as well as imagination.

At the local level, we need far more options and alternatives within the framework of state goals than we now have if the varied needs of youngsters in school districts are to be met in any reasonably satisfactory fashion.[21] My colleagues and I worked for some years on developing and simultaneously studying a model of school improvement which both encouraged variability and provided for accountability of the total staff of each school.[22] The model sought to deal with the totality of the school as a culture within which each change of significance affects the system as a whole. Our central hypothesis, which now looms as a basic operating principle in our eyes, was that the school with its principal, teachers, pupils, and parents is the largest *organic* unit of and for educational change. We worked with eighteen schools, each regarded as unique and individual with restraints differentially experienced because each was in a separate district. They were formed into a new social system of communication, peer group assistance, and exchange of ideas called the League of Cooperating Schools and were held together at first by a hub to provide support and encouragement and legitimatization of the right to fail. The hub provided help to principals sensing need for new leadership skills and worked with teachers and principals in developing a process of *dialogue* regarding problems and ideas, making *decisions* following dialogue, *acting* on these decisions, and *evaluating* all these processes and their apparent effects (the process was referred to as DDAE—dialogue, decision making, action, and evaluation). The hub assisted in developing the criteria for evaluating this process of DDAE.

We found that high-level development of the process of DDAE went together with high morale, high sense of power, and high professionalism in creating an atmosphere of openness to change. Teachers sought, were not threatened by, and used a variety of data about themselves and their students derived from their own self-directed evaluation processes and a variety of data-based information derived from the hub. They became admirably accountable to one another, their professional responsibilities, their schools, the community, and the children. We think our work could have proceeded even better and certainly in an environment of less tension had there not been emerging in the state a desire to implement someone else's concept of accountability couched in the language of voluntarism but clearly calling for time and energy which these teachers were now directing enthusiastically to their own schools and classrooms.

It is true, of course, that not all teachers took advantage of this opportunity to become self-renewing. It is true, also, that both teachers and principals sometimes did foolish and, from some viewpoints perhaps, irrational things. This is what some human beings almost invariably do, whatever the source and demands of accountability.

At present, there appear to be few guidelines in educational policy and practice regarding who is responsible for what, to whom, and by what means. What are the proper responsibilities of the state, local school districts, and communities, those employed to run the schools, and parents? Instead of asking of science what it cannot deliver, we should be furthering dialogue about and, indeed, inquiry into such questions. Regrettably, we more often hear the answers given than the questions asked. But at least let us not establish one set of answers over another by legislative enactment or by favoring one special interest group over another, however virtuous the cry of what is best for the children may sound. Neither fiat nor power nor the rhetoric of scientism endows ideas with special truths.

Notes

[1] These were just some of the most influential of a rash of varied books appearing at about this time: Arthur Bestor, *Educational Wastelands*, University of Illinois Press, Urbana, Ill., 1953; Robert M. Hutchins, *The Conflict in Education*, Harper & Brothers, New York, 1953; Albert Lynd, *Quackery in the Public Schools*, Little, Brown and Co., Boston, 1953.

[2] Rudolf Flesch, *Why Johnny Can't Read*, Harper & Brothers, New York, 1955.

[3] The highpoint was expressed in the Elementary and Secondary Education Act of 1965. In introducing it to Congress, President Johnson set the theme in saying that if one looks deeply enough into any problem, education is found to be at the heart of it.

[4] James S. Coleman and others, *Equality of Educational Opportunity*, Department of Health, Education, and Welfare, Washington, D.C., 1966.

[5] Ivan Illich, *Deschooling Society*, Harper & Row, New York, 1970.

[6] Jerome T. Murphy and David K. Cohen, "Accountability in Education—The Michigan Experience," *The Public Interest*, Summer 1974, pp. 53–54.

[7] Ernest R. House, Wendell Rivers, and Daniel L. Stufflebeam, "An

Assessment of the Michigan Accountability System," *Phi Delta Kappan*, vol. 55, June 1974, pp. 663–669.

[8]For an in-depth discussion, see Robert L. Leight (ed.), *Philosophers Speak of Accountability in Education*, Interstate Printers and Publishers, Inc., Danville, Ill., 1973.

[9]Philip G. Smith, "The Philosophical Context," in John I. Goodlad and Harold G. Shane (eds.), *The Elementary School in the United States*, Seventy-second Yearbook, Part II, of the National Society for the Study of Education, University of Chicago Press, Chicago, 1972.

[10]Raymond Callahan, *Education and the Cult of Efficiency*, University of Chicago Press, Chicago, 1962.

[11]A case in point is the computer which, when expertly programmed, has enormous potential for freeing students from many restraints of schooling, such as arbitrary schedules based on the availability of teachers. See John I. Goodlad, "Computers and the Schools in Modern Society," *Proceedings of the National Academy of Sciences*, vol. 63, July 1969, pp. 573–603, reprinted in this volume as Chapter 13.

[12]W. James Popham and Eva Baker, *Systematic Instruction*, Prentice-Hall, Englewood Cliffs, N. J., 1970.

[13]C. Robert Pace, "The Relationship between College Grades and Adult Achievement: A Review of the Literature," in Donald A. Hoyt (ed.), ACT Research Reports, No. 7, American College Testing Program, Iowa City, 1965.

[14]Judith V. Torney, "The Implications of the IEA Cross-National Civic Education Data for Understanding the International Socialization of American Adolescents," paper delivered at the 1974 Annual Meeting of the American Political Science Association, August 30, 1974.

[15]B. Yebio, "World Citizen Responsibility: Some Characteristics of Attitude Development," *Educational and Psychological Interactions*, No. 168, School of Education, Department of Educational and Psychological Research, Malmö, Sweden, 1972.

[16]*The Ethics of Aristotle*, Trans. J. A. K. Thompson, Penguin Books, Baltimore, Md., 1966, pp. 27–28.

[17]John I. Goodlad, with Renata von Stoephasius and M. Frances Klein, *The Changing School Curriculum*, Fund for the Advancement of Education, New York, 1966.

[18]Seymour B. Sarason, *The Culture of the School and the Problem of Change*, Allyn and Bacon, Boston, 1971.

[19]National Institute of Education, *Building Capacity for Renewal and Reform: An Initial Report on Knowledge Production and Utilization in Education* (by Marc Tucker and others), NIE, Washington, D.C., December 1973.

[20]Sanford Temkin (ed.), *What Do Research Findings Say about Getting*

Innovations into Schools: A Symposium, Research for Better Schools, Philadelphia, 1974, p. iv.

[21]For an analysis of some of the problems and issues involved in seeking such alternatives, see John I. Goodlad, et al., *The Conventional and the Alternative in Education,* McCutchan, San Francisco, 1975.

[22]Reported in six volumes (McGraw-Hill) as well as in a series of documentary films (Institute for Development of Educational Activities, Dayton, Ohio). See, for example, Carmen M. Culver and Gary J. Hoban (eds.), *The Power to Change: Issues for the Innovative Educator,* McGraw-Hill, New York, 1973; Mary M. Bentzen and Associates, *Changing Schools: The Magic Feather Principle,* McGraw-Hill, New York, 1974; and John I. Goodlad, *The Dynamics of Educational Change: Toward Responsive Schools,* McGraw-Hill, New York, 1975.

...*And Tomorrow*

Many of Goodlad's major concerns come together in this
section as he considers issues that will continue to be the
subject of debate as we approach the end of this century.
"Reconstruction" is the key word—to face the challenge of the
future, our institutions and our attitudes must change to become
more responsive to pressing needs. Schooling and education
will not only face the task of reconstructing their own processes,
but they will also bear a great responsibility to promote
reconstruction in the rest of society. Thus, chapters in this
section address the need for change in schools in general, in
teacher education, in technological processes of schooling,
in educational research, and in attitudes promoted by schooling.
The section concludes by laying out the alternative futures that
are desirable and possible—and necessary.

Several themes run through most of the chapters. Goodlad
asks what education is. Is it the classic paradigm of someone
doing something to someone else, or the emerging value of
the individual accomplishing whatever he wants and needs,
or is there a place for both "learning" and "being educated"?
What are the school's responsibilities to its community, and
when do the concerns of the larger society and, indeed, the

global community supersede those of a local constituency? Who should participate in making the decisions about what a child should be exposed to, and who will protect the interests of the child and preserve his right of access to the accumulated wisdom of humankind?

11

An Ecological Approach to Changing Schools

A major part of Goodlad's attention over the past ten years has focused on the problem of bringing about change in schools. It was obvious that traditional methods—passing laws, writing books, bringing in consultants, and publishing new curricula—had failed to bring about significant change in the ways schools structure themselves or the programs to which students are exposed. Instead of trying once more to make these methods work, Goodlad proposed a new direction involving a cooperative endeavor among a group of schools and a research institute. The theory was tested in the five-year Study of Educational Change and School Improvement conducted by |I|D|E|A| under Goodlad's direction. This chapter presents the rationale behind the study and some of its findings. The theory and the study are discussed in detail in Goodlad's *The Dynamics of Educational Change: Toward Responsive Schools.* [Editor]

William Ralph Inge once said that "There are two kinds of fools: those who say, 'This is new and therefore better' and others who say,

SOURCE: John I. Goodlad, the Abraham M. Wechstein Memorial Lecture, New York University, March 8, 1975; and John I. Goodlad, "The Uses of Alternative Theories of Educational Change," Phi Delta Kappa Meritorious Award Monograph Number 1, Phi Delta Kappa, Incorporated, Bloomington, Ind., 1976.

'This is old and therefore good.' " Succinctly, he highlighted a vexing problem for schools: to conserve and preserve on one hand and to be responsive to new expectations and knowledge on the other. The problem is vastly complicated by widely diverging perceptions regarding what should be preserved and what should be changed. And it is even more complicated by disagreement over how best to conserve, change, or effect some productive tension between the two.

Answering the "what" question is virtually a national pastime; everyone is an expert. But relatively few people concern themselves with the "how." Presumably, we assume that exhortation or legislative enactments will suffice or that reforms will be absorbed through a process of osmosis. We seem to forget that institutions are collections of people and, therefore, that they contain all the people problems of changing. And institutions contain even more: the residue of their adaptations to earlier expectations as well as the realities of current adaptations by those who keep them functioning.

Changing schools means, then, not merely changing the teachers, principals, and superintendents who run them, difficult as this is. It means, also, changing the institutional arrangements which, in large measure, determine the "school" behavior of all these persons, individually and collectively.

THEORIES OF CHANGE

In both traditional and contemporary thought, there have been two major views regarding how people change. Ekstein has this to say:

> "Ideas about change have always seemed to divide men into two polarizing groups. Some believe that in order to change man must change his outer reality—society. Others say that regardless of how much one changes the culture, the external world of men, unless one can make that change reach the inner man, one will not succeed."[1]

There are those who interpret the process of education as implying that someone in the role of teacher or tutor does something to make someone else learn. One teaching theory derived from this view involves a teacher clarifying what is to be achieved by the tutee, determining what this means for pedagogical operations, and then proceeding to employ the necessary reinforcement and extinction mechanisms. Somebody with the authority of knowledge or power does something to somebody else.

The second view implies a much more self-determining role on the part of the individual. Applied to education, in its most extreme form it assumes that "nobody can teach anybody anything."[2] It does not rule out a second party in the process but only sees him as a helping hand, a temporary crutch to lean on. The tenets of psycho-analysis come close to this view. The analyst serves for a time as a nonjudgmental accomplice in the search for self-understanding as the individual gropes for increased control over daily existence. Only recently have psychoanalytic concepts begun to creep into teaching and teacher education.

A good many models of change have been derived from these two sets of views, most associated with some derivative of the first rather than the second. Until recently, these models have been applied almost exclusively to individuals and small social groups—tutoring, teaching, supervising, group therapy, and the like—but not to educational settings such as schools or colleges. Apparently, we did not adequately appreciate the significant role of institutions in modifying individual behavior. The emergence of sociology as a formal discipline directed attention to institutions, early work focusing to considerable degree on organizational malfunctioning in the same way that psychology initially paid so much attention to human abnormality.

It was social psychology that put the individual-institutional interaction under scrutiny. Theoretical work moved relatively quickly into management theory and practice, intruding into the field of educational administration by the 1950s.[3]

But there were very few practitioners and, indeed, only a small colony of professors of education who thought in these dual terms when the post-Sputnik educational reform movement was getting into high gear. Improving the schools was conceived as developing certain competencies in administrators and skills or knowledge in teachers. The institution, to the extent that it was thought about as an entity, would benefit incidentally.

Interestingly, however, it was schooling, not usually the teachers, that came under attack in the 1950s. The school, it was charged, needed to be returned to a position of authority and significance in the lives of young people. Analysis of attacks on soft progressive education, however, reveals that "the school" was seen less as that functioning local entity than as a symbol for some less visible "they"—teachers' colleges, the NEA, the interlocking education establishment. The school was merely a convenient euphemism for something more abstractly deficient; it was not being referred to as a concrete setting.

The dominant change strategy to emerge was espoused by the National Science Foundation and was applied primarily to the development of new curriculum materials to be placed in the hands of teachers. Administrators and the peculiarities of schools were at best a nuisance and at worst an obstacle to be bypassed in some ingenious fashion. In time, teachers fell into the same category for some reformers and "teacher-proof" materials were to save the day. The U.S. Office of Education subsequently adapted the model for a wider range of proposed educational reforms.

This model, dominating educational reform of the 1960s, came to be known as RDD: research, development, and diffusion. The Elementary and Secondary Education Act of 1965 added the necessity of evaluation for the RDD activities flowing from it. Although many of its proponents argued that the model was not intended to be employed in precise linear fashion, this was the way in which it was largely interpreted and used.[4]

By the end of the 1960s, there was growing suspicion that the reality of reform at the target end, behind school and classroom doors, fell far short of matching the rhetoric.[5] A few years later, retrospective evaluations suggested that the intended users simply had not been taken sufficiently into account in the process.[6] They had been treated as largely passive recipients, expected, at worst, to be only midly resistant.

One reason for our unproductive efforts to improve the schools is that we are almost blindly caught up in this single model of change which stems directly from our Western rational bias. This bias, highly productive in its application to business, industry, and the military when resources appear to be unlimited and when the race favors the strongest and biggest, until recently has been so to our advantage as to be scarcely questioned. Indeed, to do so has been and, in many quarters, still is regarded as unpatriotic, if not seditious. But the Vietnam War, investigations into the role of the

CIA, Watergate, unemployment, and declining raw materials now give us pause. The day is drawing close when not to recognize the need for new national orientations will be commonly regarded as not in the best interests of the country and certainly not in the interests of humankind.

The rational bias of our Western industrialized, highly technological culture places purpose before activity in linear fashion. Such a view dominates the military, industrial, and business domains, as previously noted, but also spills over as the prevailing perspective in religion, education, rites of passage, and a host of personal relations, especially those deemed essential to economic success. Even courtship and marriage are still, for many people, instrumental to other "more basic" considerations.

For much of what actually takes place under these rubrics, however, there are no specific predetermined purposes to be met. Clarifying goals may be as far away from what touches on daily existence as the setting of precise behavioral objectives for savoring a good meal (although the advent of expense accounts and the business purposes for which they were created certainly have done much to diminish the purely aesthetic and gustatory delights of relaxed dining). For some people, especially in non-Western cultures, a sense of intense *being* rather than a clear purpose is quite enough.[7] Education, too, is as much a way of life as it is a set of goals to be achieved. It is conceivable that a bias admitting to the importance of activity qua activity, whether or not purpose arises or comes later, has much to say to reforming the schools. Because the Western rationalist bias is so pervasive and so exclusive of other rationalities, however, gaining credence for any alternative will be a monumental task.

In the United States, as in most Western nations, the purpose-before-activities orientation is generally accepted as *the* rational approach to schooling. To the virtual exclusion of any other, it guides the formulation of federal and state policy, the development of curricula, most processes of research and evaluation, proposals for school reform and educational accountability. In relatively rigorous form, it has stimulated programmed instruction, various other approaches to individually prescribed instruction, performance contracting, program planning and budgeting systems (PPBS), and competency-based teacher education. Clearly, it is an exceedingly useful orientation for many things, providing needed system and rigor in the preparation and dissemination of a wide array of tools, techniques, materials, and organizational arrangements.

This is an engineering production model with an impressive philosophical and methodological lineage. Although implicit in some pedagogical practice for a long period of time, it received widespread favor following World War II, especially in large-scale federal involvement in educational reform in the 1960s and, subsequently, in evaluative efforts to appraise the effects of supplementary expenditures for a host of special programs. Now, when one speaks of RDDE, it is not some general image of research, development, diffusion, and evaluation that comes to mind but a specific paradigm associated with curriculum development projects supported by the National Science Foundation and a wider array of reforms and innovations supported by the U.S. Office of Education in the late 1960s and early 1970s and by the National Institute of Education today.

As a general theory of intelligence and means of both individual and social improvement, what I have been describing has many uses. It has attracted many first-rate minds and harnessed human and material resources for the betterment of humankind. But, as in many things, its obvious strengths have given rise to abuses and misuses. The abuses have pertained primarily to narrowness and singleness of purpose while attacking complex problems. Consequently, there has been overextension of expectations and applications. For example, an exponent of a useful limited theory of learning becomes so enamored of this tool that he extends it to a wide array of human processes, allowing a few instances of success to block out the failures. Now, the rhetoric of claims to virtue and justice becomes grossly overblown. Of course, these vices are not the exclusive prerogative of this particular model. But it is the inherent claim to rationality, to exclusive rationality, that lends such irony to the excess.

The foregoing suggests a second major misuse of the engineering/ industrial model which sets purpose before activity and assumes efficiency as defined by the input-output ratio as the prime criterion of value and effect. It lies simply in lack of awareness of alternative views of man, nature, change, and improvement. In effect, the very pervasiveness of the Western industrial view of man and his world imposes cultural blinders which simultaneously exclude for many people the possibility of alternative views and condone allegiance to what becomes not just one tentative model but truth, virtue, and justice. The response to crises is virtually galvanic; more and better become as one; the social response and, therefore, the rewarded individual activity is "try harder; don't just stand there, do something." But be rational; that is, conform to the model.

Ironically, although this model is essentially expansionist and is well described by the slogan, "Think big," its very dependence on singleness and clarity of purpose tends to blind it to danger signals such as delayed side effects and diminishing resources. There is room for industrialist and nature-lover alike when huge forest resources are only being trimmed around the edges. But sharply different interests come out of the woods when resources dwindle and more devastating techniques for extracting them emerge. The so-called energy crisis poses the issues sharply. The environmentalist loses ground rapidly when oil for the lamps of home and factory is in short supply. Most people now find themselves less tolerant of an alternative ethic and respond to the consumer-oriented drumbeat in the face of such crises, whatever the long-term costs.

Thoughtful men and women who have dared to look down the road apiece, learned men and women who are aware of alternative value systems, and futurists who have extrapolated the future in a straight line from the present, see much danger and, indeed, disaster in continued adherence to the model of intelligence which has served us well in the past, judged by its own inherent criteria.[8] They see a need to suspend or relax some of the conventional rules of Western rationality and progress in order to explore the possibilities of alternative rules.[9] This is not a new vision; it is as old as civilization itself.[10] However, the present urgency brings not only fresh formulations of the human condition but also alternative views of change and improvement enriched by knowledge of our own cultural traditions as well as growing awareness of those of the rest of humankind.[11]

I believe education and schooling to be suffering from both abuse and misuse of the conventional model of change stemming from the Western rationalist bias, and I believe that it is essential to examine and use alternative views. However, the record will show that I have advanced the conventional model's cause over the years, albeit blindly at times, and that, space and time permitting, I could mount a strong case in defense of its merits. It does not lack in strong defenders and proponents and needs little in support from me. But to shift a critical mass of attention to alternative explanations, theories, and models and to open up fresh options for research, development, and evaluation in education will require Herculean effort.

It must be recognized that in previous efforts to reform the schools the expectations for change and, indeed, for the role of the schools in reforming society were quite unrealistic. They could result only in disappointment and failure. However, it is also fair to say that the prevailing conceptions of how to effect change were inadequate. In effect, they said that one intuits and researches a need, researches and develops a solution such as new materials or structures, and then "puts them into the system." What was largely ignored is that the system is not a target, a box, or merely brick and mortar. Nor is it only a collection of people who happen to be associated and who can be changed significantly and individually by a product, special training, or both.

No, the system is an institution or collection of institutions characterized by rules, regulations, roles, functions, and activities. Each school, then, has what Sarason has aptly termed a "culture."[12] This culture is survival-oriented, not goal-oriented. Rewards and even personal satisfaction often are perceived to come from maintaining equilibrium in the system, not changing it. In general, RDD personnel and personnel in schools and school systems live in profoundly different settings. To think that the former can change the school by injecting into it some new ingredient, however rationally attractive, is seriously to misjudge the problem of change.

When outer-directed strategies for change appear to have had a hard time of it, the inner-directed alternative is dusted off and polished up. The shortcomings of the former are used to strengthen the latter. Those of us who have survived a few cycles and counter-cycles of impassioned rhetoric of reform brace ourselves for a new excess replacing the one recently discredited. Caution is in order.

Griffiths has argued effectively against the proposition that the educational system can and will reform itself.[13] Tye and others note the effectiveness of middle management in keeping things as they are.[14] It would appear that, for change to occur, there must be some combination of internal responsiveness and external stimulation. For change to prevail as an ongoing characteristic condition, there must be some continuing productive state of tension between these two essential sets of forces. The achievement and maintenance of such a state of tension should characterize the change process.

DEVELOPING A NEW CHANGE STRATEGY

A hypothesis regarding schools and change began to take shape in my mind in the 1950s,[15] subsequently matured into the status of a principle during the 1960s, and then was implemented and tested in a loose field experiment with 18 schools over a period of five years. A series of personal experiences and inquiries between the initial formulation and testing transformed the hypothesis to the status of a principle, the condition which Conant states is prerequisite to pursuing the often-tedious work involved in testing.[16] Perhaps it is more accurate to say that a set of related concepts emerged, each of which could be stated as a hypothesis, and that these lent themselves to developing and testing a strategy for change in existing field settings. At a minimum, they included the following.

First, the optimal unit for educational change is the single school with its pupils, teachers, principal—those who live there every day— as primary participants. The interactions of these people, the language they use, the traditions they uphold, the beliefs to which they subscribe, and so forth, make up the culture of the school. This culture is part of a larger ecosystem that includes the community. It is not necessarily a healthy ecosystem, but it exists, often with surprising tenacity.

Second, under certain conditions, a school changes. Presumably, then, *under certain conditions,* it could change itself so as to be more satisfactory and satisfying to those who are part of its culture. This implies some change-oriented activity on the part of these primary participants.

Third, it follows that, *under certain conditions,* the school might be able to change so as to be more satisfactory and satisfying to all the people in the school-community ecosystem. This suggests the need for some reasonably sensitive information and communication structures.

Fourth, although a school has some elasticity and considerable tenacity, it is in conventional economic terms a consuming economy. The "systems" of which it is a part exercise enormous constraints—constraints which are essentially conservative and which seek to discourage change and innovation. The systems are not only the formal political ones of state and local educational organizations, they are also informal, exerting subtle pressure by way of implicit and explicit expectations for schooling and for the behavior of teachers and administrators.

Fifth, if change within the school is going to proceed more rapidly than changes within the larger system or is in any significant way to deviate from the expectations and procedures of that system, the school will require the goodwill of that system or some compelling different drummer or both. Presumably, these requisites constitute some of the conditions implied above.

Sixth, since the school is in some ways an isolated, fragile culture, often with tenuous relations to the larger ecosystem, efforts to change probably will require a supportive reference group, preferably made up of peers. Put bluntly, effecting change is essentially a very lonely business. Linkage with others reduces individual loneliness through sharing it.

Seventh, changes of any significance will require new knowledge, new skills, new ways of doing things. Threat and insecurity are bound to be accompanying conditions. The overall process or strategy of change must anticipate both the need for training and the necessity of coping with tension, probably without knowing in advance what the specifics will be.

Eighth, if the threat and insecurity are great—and they are bound to be substantial if the subsequent changes are seen as significant— then the alternative drummer must be perceived as exceedingly salient as well as likely to have longevity. A temporarily waxing and waning drumbeat will not suffice. School people have been disillusioned on this score before.

It is readily seen that these concepts differ markedly from those guiding the RDD model described earlier. They differ not merely in degree, in that they pose an alternative approach to changing somebody or something. They differ in kind in that they pose fundamentally different assumptions and, indeed spring from a different theory. The language is different, specifically eschewing the implication that somebody who knows the good acts on someone else for the latter's good. Rather, some people going about their daily business in the usual fashion, perhaps with little thought given to alternatives, become aware of other possibilities or perhaps only the promise of such. Their interest is aroused.

Both positions have their respective biases. RDD is merely one application of the rationalist bias that assumes purpose preceding action. The second position does not begin with the assumption that purpose exists before activity begins. Goals, to the extent that they do become important later, might very well be discovered or perhaps even invented after the fact to justify actions in the eyes of a probing rationalist. Goals and reasons, perceived in retrospect, might even take on a certain elegance, perhaps for their aesthetic as much as for their explanatory characteristics. The purist's extreme bias is that change begins and ends within, through a process virtually of immaculate conception.

My own bias is clearly evident. It favors beginning as close as possible to and with the culture that is to undertake change. But it does not exclude external forces or even rational plans. There must be a drummer, relations with peers from whom one might learn, and a support and communications structure. To repeat an earlier condition, there must be a productive tension between inner and outer forces.

The several concepts, put together in some reasonably inter-locking fashion, produce what might be called a *responsive ecological model of change*. The culture of the school, preoccupied with its own maintenance, learns, perhaps fortuitously through its connections with the larger ecosystem, of some alternative activity or way of doing things or new relations. This could occur through its own searches but not necessarily. Some other organism, with purposes of its own, might have sought out the school. In fact, it is even conceivable that there was a proposal from the constraining system, a proposal which, at long last, elicited curiosity in some part of the school's culture. At the beginning, the source of new ideas probably does not matter very much.

However, returning to the symbol of the drummer, what happens subsequently depends on many factors about which we know very little. The drummer must have credibility and be perceived as having "staying power." Ultimately, there must be an alignment of self-interest on the part of the collective known as school with whatever expectations or activities are perceived. Since both the drummer and the school have self-interests, since both presumably perceive potential activities, and since both sets of self-interest and perceptions probably are different, the problem of changing schools begins to take on considerable complexity. This complexity, especially as it relates to the self-interests of those in schools, has been largely ignored or at best inadequately understood, I believe, by those who have tried to change schools.

IMPLEMENTING THE STRATEGY

It was with this full range of complexity that my colleagues and I attempted to deal in a structure created for that purpose named the League of Cooperating Schools. The League represented a rather unique symbiosis in American education, that is, the living together in more or less intimate association of two dissimilar organisms. Although one of the two—the eighteen League schools—should not be described as a single organism, nonetheless it constituted a class of organisms or cultures, and even though we sought out very different schools in regard to the conventions of size, age of faculty, socioeconomic status and ethnicity of pupils, types of buildings, and so on, the differences are in degree not kind. The other organism was a newly created institution, the Research Division of the Institute for Development of Educational Activities, Inc. (|I|D|E|A|), an affiliate of the Charles F. Kettering Foundation. Although unknown and untested, |I|D|E|A| gained credibility from being perceived as associated with or at least endorsed by UCLA.

Although negotiations regarding the proposed relation between these two dissimilar organisms went on for months and resulted in a written agreement between |I|D|E|A| and each of the eighteen districts in which the schools were located (one to a district), the League was in many ways an instant innovation. It suddenly came into being and was launched with a name, an identifiable formal structure, and a ceremony involving superintendents, principals, and Foundation trustees and officers. But if anyone had asked all those involved what was being launched, there would have been many different answers; some would have had little or no idea.

Presumably, the schools had some interest in improving themselves, though it probably would be a mistake to say that this was a strongly held interest. Undoubtedly, there were stronger motives for belonging to the League, especially on the part of principals: prestige, pleasing others, appearing to "be with it" during a time when innovation was the name of the game, expectation of Foundation funds (although there was much initial contrary rhetoric and no funds were given). |I|D|E|A| was verbalizing an interest in promoting "constructive change in education"; its Research Division was committed to studying change, not to developing and disseminating specific innovations.

The written agreements were vague, addressed more to responsibilities and commitments of the cooperating parties than to goals. (Are goals essential to or even appropriate for symbiosis?) The quid pro quo was stated: |I|D|E|A| would help the schools help themselves; in return, the schools would cooperate as we studied the whole process. But just how all this would be done was not stated. I had formulated some of the underlying concepts in an unpublished report to the Kettering Foundation and in a few in-house memos; these were reiterated in initial meetings with superintendents and principals; and, later, they were prepared for publication.[17] The only clearly formulated aspect was the structure,[18] but even here many details were to be worked out in the collaborative enterprise.

In summary, there were three institutional elements comprising the League: the individual school, the eighteen schools as a collective, and the |I|D|E|A| offices. The idea of the single school as the largest and the key unit for educational change was paramount. From the outset, the principal was viewed as strategic, perhaps as much for blocking as for leadership potential. Collectively, the eighteen were viewed as a peer group entity, with enormous potential for developing into a legitimatizing, reinforcing new social system with sufficient salience to endorse countervailing change activity in individual schools. Obviously, we had considerable interest in the development and accompanying study of such an innovation. Our office, the hub, was viewed as a source of some tangible support in the form of people, materials, a meeting place, and so on. Our resources were committed primarily and increasingly to inquiry.

But to call these ingredients "The League of Cooperating Schools"—as many people are now inclined to do—would be a grave misinterpretation. The League was also relations and sets of relations. If one perceives the League physically as a large wheel with a diameter of several hundred miles, the spokes convey relations between the hub and each of the eighteen schools. One can then draw a rim connecting the eighteen. The idea was to strengthen the school-to-school relations represented by the rim (the new social system) and de-emphasize the spokes (the conventional relation). But there were many more potential relations all of which ultimately materialized: among clusters of schools within the eighteen, between the principals as a total group and as clusters within it, between teachers, and among various clusters of our staff and various clusters of teachers and principals. And then, of course, there were relations between various groupings of these and various components of the larger ecosystem.

The League was, then, only in its most primitive origins a symbiosis. It was conceived to be a synergism with multiple potential interrelations and ripple effects. Further, these interrelations and effects were not and could not be preperceived or predirected, let alone planned. Some were sought; some of the most significant were serendipitous. Just as RDD has been posited and employed as a change model, so might serious attention be given to SSS—symbiosis, synergism, and serendipity. What happened and what we found out, both viewed from a reasonably broad range of perceptions, cannot be reported, obviously, in one brief paper. A documentary film, in four segments, and several volumes seeking to provide such information are available.[19] Some highlights must suffice here.

Clearly, there was some considerable early appeal. Perhaps it was simply a matter of novelty. After all, the League was a kind of instant innovation—there it was. It both provoked and tolerated almost any kind of reaction, from the customary "these things too shall pass" to enthusiasm on the part of those seeking something new, to mild amusement on the part of the skeptical. In retrospect, the hypothesis that appeals to me is provided by March:

> ". . . what we need . . . is playfulness. Playfulness is the deliberate, temporary relaxation of rules in order to explore the possibility of alternative rules. . . . In effect, we announce—in advance—our rejection of the usual objections to behavior that does not fit the standard model of intelligence."[20]

At the outset, the rhetoric to the effect that we would only help the schools help themselves, that we would not be technical consultants on pedagogical problems, that we offered no specific innovations, and that there was no formal agenda of topics and procedures was scarcely heard. As one principal said later, "We knew that, at some time, John Goodlad and his staff would tell us what to do." When, after a year, we still had not, there was growing, uneasy disbelief and, ultimately, anger. The dawning of the realization by the principals that a good deal of what was to happen in the schools was up to them was exceedingly painful—"We have met the enemy and he is us."

The principals met together, with some of us involved, one Monday each month. These became very special sessions for them and for us. We do not fully realize the loneliness of the principalship, caught as it is between conflicting sets of pressures. Nor do we realize the inadequacy of principals to perform leadership roles.[21] These sessions took care of some of the loneliness and, in time, provided many of the needed skills and understandings. And, in time, many principals developed a gratifying sense of self-worth, of being able to make a difference.

The schools were slow to take off. By the end of the first year, many had scarcely moved or been touched. But then something began to stir. In faculty meetings or in small informal clusters, teachers began to talk about the possibility of some kind of change— a period of "unfreezing."[22] Then, some activity ensued and was accompanied by varying degrees of excitement. This was followed by questioning: of what they were doing, of themselves, of one another. Some kind of program took shape. It was accompanied by dissatisfaction and the asking of more basic questions. There was considerable desire at this stage, particularly, for ideas, and heavy demand for materials and references was placed on us. Later, there was strong interest in finding out what others, especially in other League schools, were doing about similar problems.[23]

This cycle, clearly followed in most of the schools, is quite unlike the rational process of stating objectives, developing a means for carrying them out, and evaluating their attainment. It illustrates that actions do, indeed, precede as well as follow goals.

The process was unsettling for some principals—in fact, for most of them. It was unpredictable and, initially beyond their span of control. Attempts to administer it sometimes brought forth resentment from teachers. But inability or unwillingness to intervene also elicited resentment, as one of our filmed sequences clearly shows. Rising feeling of potency on the part of teachers clearly was threatening to principals' feelings of self-worth. They needed their peer principals badly; their meetings together took on added importance and became more interesting.

All this began to put a severe strain on our staff. Principals and teachers posed "client needs" to warm a consultant's heart. We were wooed; some of us were seduced. Several would have turned the hub completely into a field-oriented center devoted exclusively to servicing the schools. A few decried our somewhat detached inquiry as immoral: "Those people out there need us badly." The do-unto-others mode of helping is deeply ingrained in our educational culture.

Our staff was very much divided as to how to proceed. It was decided, by no means unanimously, to draw back as much as possible from a consultative role and to massage the existing structure for peer socialization and help. This structure already was working for the principals but was functioning only spasmodically, at best, for the teachers. Increasingly, our office served as a switching station to put those teachers who wanted help or wanted to give help in touch with their appropriate counterparts. A good deal of interschool visitation preceded and accompanied this in-service education of and by peers. At first, the hub managed the process of communication and interaction, but, increasingly, schools and teachers initiated and followed through on their own. The network began to function in synergistic fashion.

Increasingly, through the hub, we fed back research data to the schools. This had been part of our agreement from the beginning, but it took time for this type of resource to be seen as useful.

One of our major collaborative undertakings was the clarification and refinement of a process referred to as DDAE—dialogue, decision making, action, and evaluation. In research terms, it ultimately became our measured variable. All groups came to see this as the way to conduct our respective and cooperative enterprises. Principals, teachers, and members of our staff worked on criteria for productive DDAE and developed an instrument for examining its functioning. The data gathered using this instrument were fed back to the schools.

In high DDAE schools, we found some interesting, apparently associated, characteristics of teachers: high morale, high professionalism, high sense of personal power and potency.[24] Where these sets of characteristics clustered, we found a certain resilience in the face of severe disruptions such as a change in principal. We found, also, a relatively high level of what might be called innovative behavior. Interestingly, however, innovations as such were not regarded with awe or as "a big thing." New organizational patterns (team teaching, nongrading, the integrated day, etc.) and new products were used like conventional resources—to get a job done. In what we perceived to be the most smoothly operating primary units, for example, planning among teachers occurred as the need to plan was sensed—at recess, after school, on the run.

We eschewed the standard measurement of pupil effects, at first as a rationalization because of limited resources but later as a matter of principle. American education and especially change and innovation suffer badly from CMD—chronic measurement disease. We pull up plants to look at them just as the roots are taking hold and we measure nutritional effects on plants that either were never planted or were never watered and fertilized. We shake our heads and commit to oblivion innovations that never existed.

In the League project, we measured a few pupil traits or behaviors that seemed important to us, mostly having to do with attitudes toward school. In general, pupil attitudes were more positive in schools where there was a clustering of high DDAE, teacher morale, teacher professionalism, and teacher sense of power.

If one must think in conventional experimental terms, the schools, not the pupils, were the dependent variable. Our interest was in helping the schools develop dynamic cultures. The assumption is that a healthy ecosystem will be healthful, in turn, for all associated with it.[25]

TOWARD AN ECOLOGICAL MODEL OF SCHOOLING

It is important to reflect on self-renewal in schools as an attainable, sustainable condition. My present persuasion is in the negative. This position arises primarily from my inability and unwillingness to view a school as a self-contained entity, with all the necessary ingredients for a fully self-renewing culture.

"The school as a culture" is merely a convenient metaphor but an enormously useful one for coming to understand schools better and especially in seeking to improve them. It helps to remind us that becoming involved in changing a school probably will contribute more to our own understanding of schools than to any school's improvement—at least if we can forget the missionary role long enough to become learners.

The school is too interdependent with its larger ecosystem to be a clearly identifiable self. The people in a school make up only a temporary culture; for part of the time they occupy other roles (some of them perceived to be more important) in the same ecosystem. If the culture of the school is to become dynamic, to the point of enjoying the hyperbolic description "self-renewing," those in it must perceive their roles, activities, and rewards there as significant. This is what happened, I think, to a gratifying degree in the League. But we must take care not to deceive ourselves into thinking that the concept of a self-renewing school or of the culture of a school, is anything other than a metaphor.

The culture of the school is an exceedingly useful metaphor for conceptualizing and testing appropriate decision-making roles in the ecosystem of which the school is a part. The new dogma in schooling, as in many other things, is "citizen participation." There is a myth abroad in the land that if we simply get lay citizens into the act, all good things will follow. But grim experience suggests otherwise, even though the idea has a great deal of merit and obvious potential benefits. We need a variety of social experiments designed to work out the respective decision-making roles and the logistics before we go plunging into still one more deep, dark pool of disillusionment. We already should have enough experience and evidence to know at the outset that some kinds of intervention by those who are not primary participants imperil certain fragile and exceedingly important elements of a school's ecosystem.

We must understand, too, that the concept of a school-community ecosystem also is only a metaphor, useful for some understandings but not as a comprehensive model of assumed reality. Currently, "community" is a much-abused concept. It is being redefined so as to have only the most parochial of connotations—my neighborhood, my class, my race, my school.[26] There is a much larger community and it, too, has a stake in those "community schools." Likewise, a child has a right to be educated in and for a community going beyond what he can see and touch and smell. It is the school's responsibility to conceive of itself as part of the nation's and, indeed, humankind's ecosystem and to educate in those inalienable rights for which unseen and unknown citizens have fought and died. Some of them had better ideas than each child's parents have about how and in what to educate.[27]

Each of us owns an interest in every school. And so there must always be both an inner and an outer force in changing schools. The problem is to create and maintain a productive state of tension between the two. The League of Cooperating Schools represents a modest contribution to the understanding of what is required. It promises no easy instant rose gardens, only the planting and caring thereof.

Notes

[1]Rudolf Ekstein, "Toward Walden III," *Reiss-Davis Clinic Bulletin*, vol. 1, no. 1, Spring 1974, p. 13.

[2]W. R. Wees, *Nobody Can Teach Anyone Anything*, Doubleday, New York, 1971.

[3]J. W. Getzels, "A Psycho-Sociological Framework for the Study of Educational Administration," *Harvard Educational Review*, vol. 22, no. 4, 1952, pp. 235–246.

[4]Ernest R. House, *The Politics of Educational Innovation*, McCutchan Publishing Corporation, Berkeley, Calif., 1974.

[5]See, for example, John I. Goodlad, M. Frances Klein, and Associates, *Looking Behind the Classroom Door*, revised edition, Charles A. Jones, Worthington, Ohio, 1974.

[6]National Institute of Education, *Building Capacity for Renewal and Reform: An Initial Report on Knowledge Production and Utilization in Education* (by Marc Tucker and others), NIE, Washington, D.C., December 1973.

[7]In Western culture, the writings of Martin Buber neatly differentiate between a full sensitivity to the present experience and libertinism.

[8]Hannah Arendt, *The Human Condition*, Doubleday, Garden City, New York, 1959.

[9]James G. March, "Model Bias in Social Action," *Review of Educational Research*, vol. 42, no. 4, Fall 1972, pp. 413–429.

[10]Val D. Rust, "Humanistic Roots of Alternative Education," in John I. Goodlad et al., *The Conventional and the Alternative in Education*, McCutchan, Berkeley, Calif., 1975.

[11]W. Warren Wagar (ed.), *History and the Idea of Mankind*, University of New Mexico, Albuquerque, 1971.

[12]Seymour B. Sarason, *The Culture of the School and the Problem of Change*, Allyn and Bacon, Boston, 1971.

[13]Daniel E. Griffiths, "Administrative Theory and Change in Organizations," in Mathew B. Miles (ed.), *Innovation in Education*, Teachers College, Columbia University, New York, 1964, pp. 425–436.

[14]Kenneth Tye, Charles Wall, and Judith Golub, "The Principal as a Change Agent: A Concept Revisited," unpublished paper.

[15]John I. Goodlad, "The Individual School and Its Principal," *Educational Leadership*, vol. 13, October 1955, pp. 2–6.

[16]James B. Conant, *Two Modes of Thought*, Trident Press, New York, 1964.

[17]John I. Goodlad, "Educational Change: A Strategy for Study and Action," *National Elementary Principal*, vol. 48, no. 3, January 1969, pp. 6–13.

[18]John I. Goodlad, "The League of Cooperating Schools," *California Journal for Instructional Improvement*, vol. 9, December 1966, pp. 213–218; Virgil M. Howes, "A Strategy for Research and Change: The League of Cooperating Schools," *Childhood Education*, vol. 44, September 1967, pp. 68–69.

[19]The film, entitled "The League," is available from |I|D|E|A|, P. O. Box 628, Far Hills Branch, Dayton, Ohio 45419. The books, |I|D|E|A| Reports on Schooling, Series on Educational Change, six in number published in 1973, 1974, and 1975, are available from McGraw-Hill, New York.

[20]March, op. cit., p. 425.

[21]Kenneth A. Tye and Jerrold M. Novotney, *Schools in Transition: The Practitioner as Change Agent*, McGraw-Hill, New York, 1975.

[22]Kurt Lewin, "Group Decision and Social Change," in Guy E. Swanson et al. (eds.), *Readings in Social Psychology*, Henry Holt and Company, New York, 1952.

[23]For a discussion of the change cycle in schools documented in our studies, see Ann Lieberman and David A. Shiman, "The Stages of Change in Elementary School Settings," in Carmen M. Culver and Gary J. Hoban (eds.), *The Power to Change*, McGraw-Hill, New York, 1973.

[24]For a detailed discussion of DDAE processes and accompanying research, see Mary M. Bentzen and Associates, *Changing Schools: The Magic Feather Principle*, McGraw-Hill, New York, 1974.

[25]For a report on the entire project, within the context of an analysis of the recent history of change in our public schools, together with the outline of a more comprehensive strategy than we developed and studied, see John I. Goodlad, *The Dynamics of Educational Change: Toward Responsive Schools*, McGraw-Hill, New York, 1975.

[26]Robert M. Hutchins, "The Great Anti-School Campaign," in *The Great Ideas Today, 1972*, Encyclopaedia Britannica, Chicago, 1972, pp. 114–227.

[27]John I. Goodlad, "Transition: Toward Alternatives," in Goodlad et al., op cit. Reprinted here as Chapter 16.

12

The Reconstruction of Teacher Education

Again, we are given arguments for team teaching, differentiated staffing, and other "innovations," this time in the context of their utility for improving pre-service and in-service teacher education. Experience with the League of Cooperating Schools provided the basis for many of the ideas presented here. [Editor]

The most striking feature of any effort to improve education is its piecemeal character. The curriculum reform movement of the 1950s began auspiciously with both the production of new materials for elementary and secondary schools and the reeducation of teachers to deal with new content and methods. Within a very few years, unfortunately, the teacher education component was falling by the wayside. As a consequence, much of the intended thrust of what might have been a comprehensive effort at curriculum reform was lost in the classroom. Similarly, there have been significant efforts to restructure the school both vertically and horizontally, so that pupil progress will be more continuous and so that teams of teachers will work with students as individuals and in groups of various sizes.

SOURCE: John I. Goodlad, "The Reconstruction of Teacher Education," *Teachers College Record*, vol. 72, no. 1, September 1970, pp. 61–71; and John I. Goodlad, "Staff Development: The League Model," *Theory Into Practice*, vol. XI, October 1972, pp. 207–214.

Regrettably, however, these efforts at school reorganization have not been accompanied by the kinds of curricular and pedagogical changes needed to effect them fully. In general, teachers have not been prepared for nor educated in these redesigned schools and classrooms but, rather, are trained in and for yesterday's classrooms. Forward-looking administrators have difficulty finding the innovative teachers needed to redesign schools. Forward-looking teacher educators, on the other hand, experience comparable difficulty in seeking to identify innovative schools in which to prepare new personnel. More often than not, efforts to improve the schools and efforts to improve teacher education proceed with very little mutual awareness. The interlocking character of the system serves to keep it clanking along but provides neither for effective communication nor for reconstruction.

Ironically, within this system of extreme complexity, specific proposals for improving teacher education are conveyed in the rhetoric of complete and relatively simple solutions. The classic panacea is the teaching of more "liberal arts" courses to end the assumed proliferation of "methods" courses—and sometimes this panacea is offered when there are no methods courses at all. A sad consequence of this folly is that teachers are turned out for the elementary school who have little idea, for example, of how to teach reading. Many of the same people who blindly recommended more liberal arts courses now condemn the teachers for their inability to teach children to read. A favorite set of recommendations pertains to student teaching. There should be more of it, or it should be placed earlier or later, or it should occur at several times in the teacher education sequence. There has been a lot of debate, too, as to whether the introductory course for teachers should be historical, philosophical, or sociological in orientation or whether it should combine all these into something called cultural foundations. The debate includes whether the course should be at the beginning or at the end of the sequence or whether it should be before or after student teaching. Imbedded in all these proposals are significant issues which must be resolved and resolved more effectively than in the past. It is the preoccupation with them, however, at the expense of all else, that gives one pause. Teacher educators must get above this myopic dialogue to face the fact that the solution to any one of these issues, no matter how sound or profound, is minuscule in the face of the gargantuan problems of educational improvement now facing us.

Nothing short of total reconstruction will suffice: of the courses in education, the relation between courses and practice, the "mix" of faculty conducting the program, the school setting for practice, in-service education of teachers, the school year, and all the rest. We must develop comprehensive change strategies which take account of the fact that pre-service teacher education, in-service teacher education, and the schools themselves are dependent, interrelated, and interacting components of one social system, albeit a malfunctioning one.

STATE OF THE FIELD: SOME OBSERVATIONS

After long participation in and scrutiny of the so-called professional education sequence for teachers,[1] I conclude that most of the courses in it have developed out of accretions of knowledge presumed to be relevant to education rather than out of fresh observations and interpretations of teaching and schooling as naturalistic processes. Courses in education, with a few notable exceptions, are very much like the courses in most other departments of the university in that they are *about* something—in this case, about education. As such, they probably are no better or no worse than these other courses. There is a place for them in teacher education, just as there is a place for courses about things in medicine, business management, and law. But the subject matter must be as relevant as possible to teaching and the promotion of learning. There must be courses devoted directly to this practice, courses which involve the student in it and which are "about something" only to the degree that they seek to improve and develop understanding of what he is doing right now as a beginning teacher. In effect, then, the teacher education program must be both academic and clinical in character. The future teacher must teach individuals in groups; he must manage a class; he must become a participating member of a faculty group seeking to change a segment of school practice; and he must, simultaneously, inquire into all these as he experiences them. The courses about education, in turn, must place all this in perspective without losing either figure or ground.

But this is not how teacher education courses have been constructed and taught. One result is the substantial disillusionment of the students who come into them. They expect to get their hands dirty and their feet wet in real classrooms with real children or youth. At least this is what literally thousands of young men and women told us when we interviewed them during James B. Conant's study of the education of American teachers. Instead, they find themselves to be largely passive recipients of learning fare not too unlike that in psychology, philosophy, history, or whatever. Consequently, they condemn their education courses, not so much for their intellectual impoverishment as for their failure to bring them into the nitty-gritty of teaching itself.

A glaring aspect of this irrelevance has come sharply into view in recent years. Until very recently, most teacher education programs were conducted as though urban blight and human inequities did not exist. Except in a few urban universities, future teachers were protected from harsh environments and the problems pertaining to them by being placed in safe, homogenized city or suburban schools for their student teaching assignments. All this is now changing, but the reconstruction required to make the courses relevant to social realities is formidable, indeed.

Another area of neglect is in "pedagogy." Students study principles of learning in their educational psychology courses. Rarely, however, are they provided an opportunity to carry these learnings directly into teaching situations where they may test them and receive constructive feedback regarding their efforts. The problem is partly—but only partly—one of numbers. Classes in educational psychology and methods of teaching usually are large. At the very time the future teacher needs a truly clinical orientation he often finds himself in a lecture class with very little opportunity to see and analyze let alone participate in teaching processes employing the principles being studied. It must be admitted, also, that educational psychologists frequently are far removed from the classroom in their own work and interests and not well equipped to spell out the practical implications of what they teach.

Another set of problems in the teacher education sequence arises out of the several differing sets of values with which the future teacher must cope as he or she moves through introductory courses into student teaching in neighboring schools. No consistent, agreed-upon set of values or approaches to valuing pervade the preparation program. In chameleonlike fashion, the student adjusts to one set of values pertaining to the use of theory, research, and inquiry within the university context and then to another pertaining to survival and the perpetuation of existing practices during his or her apprenticeship. Since the student hopes and expects to be employed by the school system in which this apprenticeship is obtained, the values of the school and classroom where he or she is placed are powerful and pervasive. In general, then, the student is directed not toward what schools could be but toward what they are.

Professional attitudes in teaching—like many of the professional skills—are left in large measure to chance. In the majority of teacher-preparing institutions, the future teacher takes a few scattered courses in education as an undergraduate while pursuing his degree. The education courses are regarded by many simply as necessary requirements to be met. For vast numbers of students, teaching is not yet a firm goal but is rather a kind of insurance—though the option of falling back on teaching if nothing else works out is rapidly disappearing in a time of shrinking enrollments and oversupply of teachers. Securing the degree is the major goal, and teaching—at least until the student enters into the student-teaching part of his program—is secondary, at best.

We know that it is exceedingly difficult to change the behavior of young children. It is many times more difficult to change the behavior of young adults. Nonetheless, we proceed on the implicit assumption that significant change will and does occur through a process of osmosis involving lectures, textbooks, and independent study. These techniques are reasonably effective in promoting low-level cognitive changes. It is exceedingly doubtful that they make any profound differences in attitude formation. A student motivated toward the attainment of the degree, dividing her time between this pursuit and scattered courses in education, will develop only by happy chance the commitment necessary for effective teaching in modern society.

Certain conditions built into the conduct of teacher education programs and into the professorship also work against the development of professional attitudes and skills. In major universities there is a high premium on inquiry designed to advance knowledge. This probably is as it should be, since there are few other institutions in our society assuming such a role. Conscientious professors are troubled by a schizophrenic situation in which they see little possibility for research productivity if they give to future teachers the attention professional development deserves. To move beyond anything other than lecturing in seeking to individualize instruction is to take on an exceedingly difficult role and not certain recognition. Assistant professors learn from older colleagues the fate of

idealistic young teachers who chose to go the individualized instruction route in teacher education programs. Others are insightful
enough to realize that their academic preparation to be students of
the educational process is not adequate preparation for the clinical
role of guiding neophytes in pedagogy. This latter situation, which
many professors caught in the dilemma will quickly recognize, is not
likely to be dissipated simply by placing more stress on and giving
greater recognition to teaching in universities. Improvement will
come only when we recognize that teacher preparation is not
something to be done on a mass basis but is akin to other professions
in its demands for individual instruction. To educate teachers
properly will require financial outlays for academic and clinical
personnel of a kind not yet generally contemplated in educational
planning.

IN-SERVICE TEACHER EDUCATION

Turning to in-service education of teachers, we find little to
reassure us that constructive educational change is likely to result
from it. Large numbers of teachers on the job prepare themselves
not to become better teachers but to leave the classroom. Large
numbers of teachers enroll in graduate programs to prepare to be
administrators. It is questionable that preparing to become an
administrator, when no prospect of employment is in the offing,
constitutes a sound basis for teacher morale or professional improvement. It is worth noting, also, that securing a degree in educational
administration usually serves just as well as a degree emphasizing
teaching in gaining salary advancements.

Our study of sixty-seven elementary schools in the United States[2]
revealed a formidable gap between the in-service educational
pursuits of teachers and the critical problems of the schools as
identified in interviews with principals and teachers. A substantial
number were engaged in some kind of extra-school activity, such as
an evening class in a neighboring university, a research project with
a professor, or some kind of district committee seeking to make
recommendations for curricular improvement. But we found few
instances of planned faculty attack on the vast array of problems
identified by the staff as critical. In only four of sixty-seven schools
was there anything resembling a critical mass of personnel engaged
in systematic planned attack on these problems. It would appear

then that relatively few school faculties are actively engaged in reconstruction. Given this fact, we cannot expect our schools to do a more effective job in their communities simply by doubling and redoubling the kind of in-service education currently under way. A more carefully designed strategy focused directly on the problems of the schools themselves is called for.

CONDUCT OF SCHOOLING

In the same way that certain conditions surrounding the professorship and the education of teachers in universities are not conducive to change, certain conditions surrounding the conduct of schooling contribute more to maintaining the status quo than to facilitating effective change. Education probably is the largest enterprise in the United States that does not provide for the systematic updating of its personnel. After basic requirements for certification are met, further study often is optional and at one's own expense. Forward-looking industries, by contrast, make certain that their employees are updated in the latest ideas and techniques, on company time and at company cost. Employees who do not take advantage of these opportunities find themselves unemployed or stalled on the advancement ladder.

Schooling is geared to self-maintenance and not to change. Tackling the problems facing schools today demands teamwork. But the principal and his staff are engaged in essentially individualistic activities which keep them occupied and separate from morning until late afternoon. It is unrealistic to expect a staff, with tag ends of energy left over, to enter enthusiastically and vigorously into the business of changing schools after school is out. Keeping school is, in itself, exceedingly demanding. It is not at all surprising, then, that the efforts of school staffs, under present conditions of limited time and energy, result in peripheral but not basic changes.

Studies suggest that principals are chosen, not because of their recognized leadership abilities, but with the expectation that they will maintain the system. A nationwide prejudice against women as administrators—changing very slowly—results in the selection of men over women regardless of qualifications. Many elementary school principals have had little or no experience in the classroom and simply are lacking in ability to help teachers with their pedagogical problems. In general, the training of school principals has not been directed toward the development of leadership skills needed for unleashing the creative talents of teachers. Consequently, the principal often tends to routine matters of keeping school while teachers work largely independently of each other in classroom cells. The time, setting, leadership, and resources for reconstructing the school too seldom come together in such a way as to produce the fundamental changes our times and problems demand.

Because only a few school faculties are systematically engaged in improving the school environment for learning, we have in this country surprisingly few models of what redesigned schools could and should be like. The thrust of significant changes recommended for American schooling during the past decade or two has been blunted on school and classroom doors.

When one brings into perspective all these conditions—pertaining to pre-service teacher education, in-service education, and school improvement—one sees that the total system is designed for self-maintenance, not self-renewal. Teachers for schools of today and tomorrow are trained in settings encrusted in the mold of yesterday. Shaking free of this mold necessitates the injection of change into each component part of the system. Because envisioning and dealing with this system as a whole is so essential, each of us must make the effort to rise above myopic concentration on minuscule portions of immediate but relatively minor importance. My colleagues and I have conducted and studied one attempt to do so.

THE LEAGUE STRATEGY AND TEACHER EDUCATION

The League of Cooperating Schools project, briefly described in Chapter 11, sought to focus on the culture of the school as of central importance to understanding and effecting educational change. The individual school was assumed to be the organic unit for change, and a network of cooperating schools was created to provide a new social system committed to change. This social system legitimized and created a "press" for change, with all that this implies for new expectations, roles, activities, relationships, and rewards. The inherent significance for teacher education, especially at the in-service level, becomes apparent. Rather than each teacher receiving in-service training as an individual, the focus was on development of the staff as a whole.

What perhaps is not quite so apparent, however, is that new demands and new resources for staff development were created. What was sought in the League was for each school to become self-propelling with respect to improvement: diagnosing its problems, formulating solutions, taking actions on recommended solutions, and then trying to get some evidence as to the effects of action. For research purposes, a process termed DDAE (dialogue, decision making, action, and evaluation) was identified. Clearly, then, the initial goal of staff development was refinement of DDAE in each school.

This is a distinct shift in expectations for and activities of most in-service teacher education. Traditionally, staff development has meant in-service education for the individual teacher. The teacher has been regarded as important to the virtual exclusion of other factors. Consequently, teachers have been expected to engage in so many "units" of in-service education per year and have been rewarded in salary for so doing, often *whether or not the activity pertained to their teaching*. Most in-service education activities approved by school districts take the teachers away from the problems of their schools. Griffin's study, for example, suggests that curriculum planning is more neglected at the institutional level (the level of the local school) than at societal and instructional levels of decision making.[3] The strategy described here turns teacher attention to the school and its problems.

One of the prime tasks undertaken by principals and teachers in the League was preparation of a set of guiding criteria for promoting, monitoring, and evaluating DDAE in the schools. These criteria were directed to such elements of school planning as processes of group interaction, going to the literature for ideas and research evidence, pre- and postplanning of faculty meetings, and conducting faculty and small-group meetings. The principals imposed upon themselves leadership training sessions to prepare for the new leadership roles required. And total school faculties and subgroups more and more imposed upon themselves in their school improvement efforts the processes implied by their own criteria. School improvement and staff development became virtually synonymous. Interestingly, research showed that as teachers became more involved in these processes of DDAE, they also placed staff development high among areas of needed self-improvement.

The League as a new resource for staff development became

increasingly powerful with each passing year. A newsletter published by the |I|D|E|A| offices contributed significantly to the mutual support and assistance roles which were envisioned relatively early in the project. Each school appointed a reporter who submitted brief "League reports," recounting successes and difficulties. A classified ad section ultimately emerged, through which schools advertised assistance available to other schools or help wanted with a problem. Sometimes, communication occurred directly from school to school; sometimes it was facilitated by our staff in what we called the hub. The result usually was a short training session between interested parties. These became commonplace during the fourth and fifth years of the project.

Three patterns of help to schools or groups of teachers emerged. Quite early in the League's history, teachers from schools which had forged ahead quickly were in demand as group leaders for workshops and staff institutes in neighboring school districts (rarely in their own, at first). Likewise, a few of the principals were called upon relatively early for leadership roles in summer conferences and institutes. Somewhat later, usually, both principals and teachers served in such capacities in their own school districts, learning that it is easier to become an expert in a neighboring school system than at home. Paralleling these developments, teachers in the League both visited each other and engaged in mutual assistance.

Some enlarging and restructuring of the League, with termination of the initial project in 1971, brought new elements into staff development. One of the recurring themes in teacher education invokes the old chicken-and-egg analogy. Schools seeking to change turn to the colleges and universities for that mythical teacher-innovator. Teacher-preparing institutions look to the schools to provide observation stations for largely nonexistent innovative practices. Teachers continue to be prepared for the status quo.

UCLA, one of the initial partners in the League, had been effecting certain structural changes in its teacher education programs while the project was taking shape. These were joined with substantive changes in 1971–72, when the clinical component and some of the campus classes were moved out into League schools. Student teachers suddenly had access to changing school environments. Teachers in the schools suddenly had access to courses taught by university personnel for their students but open also to experienced teachers. Student teachers were assigned to schools for an array of teaching experiences and not just to the classroom of one supervising teacher. They, like the experienced teachers, had access to ongoing programs of staff development in their schools. Much of the distinction between pre-service and in-service teacher education was wiped out. There simply were more and less experienced teachers in the schools.

The collaborative effort in staff development described here, with its more recent blending or merging of pre- and in-service education is still in embryonic form. The League itself was created as much to study what happens when school personnel attempt to change themselves and their schools as to effect educational improvement. Already, some next steps and attendant problems are emerging.

First, the concept of teachers helping each other in individual and total staff development has been scarcely exploited. Teachers learn a great deal from the demands of teaching each other and take readily to instruction by peers, with whose experience they readily identify. It seems reasonable to assume that cooperating school districts through a mechanism such as the League might provide a series of "pedagogical service stations," temporary in-service institutes staffed by teachers released from teaching duty and attended by teachers currently involved in their own schools with problems related to offerings of the service stations. Both groups would receive in-service education credit; most teachers would serve at some time in their career as staff members. The costs need not exceed current expenditures for in-service education.

Second, much remains to be done in working out the appropriate contributing roles of universities and school systems in the approach to teacher education suggested here. Experienced teachers in the schools might take over some of the "pre-service" functions now assumed by the university. In return, however, university personnel could contribute much more than they currently do to in-service staff development and school improvement. In the process, the universities would be presented, as never before, with an array of phenomena and problems calling for research. The kind of sharing suggested appears to be very appropriate, given the declining need for new teachers and the growing need for continuous self-improvement of schools and their personnel. One begins to see the possibilities for a relation not unlike that of schools of medicine and teaching hospitals. When one envisions the prospects for some of these teaching centers being in the inner-city, simultaneous school improvement and teacher education look particularly promising and timely. Merely assigning student teachers to inner-city schools accomplishes little and sometimes leads to increased disillusionment on the part of both schools and teacher-training institutions, to say nothing of the tender student teacher.

Some grievous hurdles remain to be overcome. The kind of collaboration suggested here calls for a balance of power between schools and colleges or universities. Is an intermediate, third party called for? If so, what is to be its relation to both and to the state's teacher certification structure?

How is all this to relate to the growing interest in performance criteria for evaluating and perhaps even certifying teachers? And is teacher performance to be judged on the basis of pupil achievement, demonstrated ability to use a variety of pedagogical procedures, contributions to the improved health of the school's culture, or some combination of all these?

Looking to the immediate future and only to the problems arising out of our experience with the League, it becomes apparent that staff development and school improvement of the kind described here must be legitimized by the school district as approved and rewarded in-service activity. Otherwise, the questionable cycle of adding "Brownie points" for more and more courses and more and more lectures on teacher institute days, whether or not related to teachers' problems and growth, will not be broken.

There are implications here, too, for the all-year school. Keeping school and changing the schools simultaneously are tasks of gargantuan proportions. The schools appear to grow less and less responsive to rapid social changes and new demands. Increasingly, it becomes apparent that "responsible parties" in schools need more than a few hours each month for the processes of DDAE required for continuing improvement. At least a core of career staff members should have weeks of time in any given year for the necessary processes of curriculum development, school reorganization, and institutional retreading.

Focusing on the individual school as the organic unit for educational improvement departs more abruptly from conventional approaches than at first is apparent. The most difficult aspect of this departure is that it calls for us to lift our eyes and efforts temporarily from customary teacher education practices which focus only on individual teachers. What we learned in the League of Cooperating Schools and are just beginning to develop in the teacher education program at UCLA is only a start toward the needed reconstruction of teacher education and, with it, the schooling enterprise.

A STRATEGY FOR IMPROVEMENT

Although it is obvious that no single change or innovation is adequate to cope with this complex array of problems, we must proceed on the assumption that an interrelated series of proposals, if effected, might bring about significant improvement. Most of the proposals enumerated below have been set forth, at one time or another, for the improvement of teacher education. It is not the virtue of any of them that is significant here. Rather, significance rises out of the potentiality for manipulating simultaneously all or most of the major components of an interacting system.

The first recommendation calls for admission of future teachers into a program requiring full-time commitment. The student accepts the fact that he is entering, full time, upon a professional program designed to prepare him to teach in schools. In the process of engaging in such preparation, he may complete a bachelor's degree in the arts or sciences. But this is now a secondary rather than a primary goal. Whether taking a course in education or in a subject field such as mathematics, the goal is to learn to teach and to become a functioning member of a faculty responsible for the education of young people. This is different from the kind of commitment that usually characterizes participation in a teacher education program today.

Having been admitted, the future teacher immediately joins a teaching team in a teacher education center—a collaborating school—affiliated with the college or university in which she is enrolled. At the outset, participation is limited but specific with respect to authority and responsibility. The student receives a small but ascending stipend as a teacher aide. With increase in responsibility, he or she then moves to the role of intern and, ultimately, resident teacher, with the stipend steadily increasing at each level of preparation and responsibility. Even as a resident teacher, however, her salary is substantially lower than that of a beginning teacher today. The concept being implemented here is that passage from the status of college student to schoolteacher is accompanied throughout by responsible involvement and financial recognition, with both advancing commensurately.

Just as beginning teachers in training are apprentice teachers, collaborating personnel in the schools are apprentice *teachers of teachers.* In the preceding analysis of the current teacher education scene, the point is made that professors of education often are ill-prepared to provide the clinical component which is so critical in the education of future teachers. The best potential source of such personnel is the schools. Consequently, schools of education must recruit from the schools those persons who appear to offer promise for becoming clinical members of the faculty. Clinical faculty members so recruited would retain their basic appointments in the schools while affiliated with colleges or universities. It is character-istic of many good teachers that they simply lack the capability of transmitting their skills or the reasons underlying them to those in training. It would seem appropriate, therefore, that schools of education seek to bring out these talents by assisting outstanding teachers to interpret their procedures to beginning teachers on the job. Those experienced teachers in the schools who prove to be most competent in this process should be selected as short-term or part-time clinical faculty to work with the academic faculty of teacher-preparing institutions. We see then the emergence of a teacher education effort shared appropriately by persons trained in research and inquiry and persons possessing unusual skills in teaching and, ultimately, ability to transmit these skills to beginners.

It is proposed next that the academic and clinical faculty join in the development and conduct of seminars organized around prob-lems encountered by beginning teachers in the schools. The substance of teacher education courses must emerge not from the analysis of subject matter assumed to be relevant and selected from appropriate disciplines but from continuing analyses of the real world of teaching. Then we turn to appropriate source disciplines. Although problems of the beginning teacher constitute the initial focal point for bringing to bear relevant knowledge, such problems constitute only the beginning and not the end. It will be the responsibility of the joint faculty to bring into juxtaposition both the theoretical knowledge and the clinical skills needed to cope with the specific problem at hand and related problems likely to emerge in the future. Thus on the surface the curriculum is organized around pressing problems of teaching. Looking deeper, however, one discovers that these problems are merely departure points. Begin-ning with them, the student is brought into knowledge from many disciplines increasingly seen as relevant to teaching.

To develop a required sequence of courses out of such a process, however, is to return us, ultimately, to the sterility and irrelevance now prevailing. Beginning teachers do not encounter problems in orderly sequences. It is unrealistic to believe that any sequence of courses, however carefully prepared, will suffice for all students. Therefore, it is recommended that the faculty prepare a number of interchangeable modules on teaching designed to provide specific knowledge and skills pertaining to the needs of beginning teachers, needs identified through a feedback system. These modules might include instruction in teaching to specific goals or elements, evaluation, application of learning theory, use of audiovisual aids, teaching of specific aspects of various subjects, and so on. Stored on video tape, filmstrip, microfiche, and programmed lesson, such modules would serve to satisfy specific needs of individual students arising out of their guided teaching experience.

Next it is recommended that students participate regularly in critiques of teaching taking place daily in their schools. Each day, one or more lessons taught by academic or clinical faculty, teachers, aides, or interns would be subjected to critical analysis by some member of the total team. This activity is missing from the conduct of schooling today. Because it is likely to be threatening to experienced teachers, it is suggested that initial critiques be conducted on the lessons of volunteers. Subsequently, more and more teachers would be willing, experience suggests, to permit their teaching to be used for critical analysis. In time, the teacher education center becomes a place of inquiry into teaching.

A major responsibility of the academic faculty, in the reconstruction proposed here, would be to join the staffs of teacher education centers in the business of school improvement. Specialists in the teaching of reading, the preparation of curricula, the organization of schools, and the role of values in making decisions would regard the teacher education centers as laboratories for extending their academic interests to the schools. The prime in-service activity of each staff member in the teacher education centers would be the identification and resolution of the central problems residing in their schools. The goal would be to engender a process of self-renewing change in which college professors, experienced school-teachers, and beginners at several different stages of preparation would play their respective roles.

For such a proposal to become functional, it is necessary that considerable responsibility for decision making now centralized in school districts be decentralized to individual schools. I have long believed that a single school with its principal, teachers, students, and parents is the largest organic unit for change in our educational system. If individual schools are caught up in dynamic self-renewal, then the school system as a whole is potent. If the school is to be the key unit for change, then the principal must become the key agent for change, since he or she occupies a position through which change can be effectively blocked or facilitated.

If the principal is to provide constructive leadership for change, she or he must be trained in what is required. It is unrealistic, however, to' expect the principal to possess all those pedagogical skills required for assisting the staff to teach. In the structure proposed here, this is quite unnecessary. But it is essential that the principal understand the interacting social system of which she is a part and the dynamics of effecting planned change. Instruction in these matters should be at the heart of leadership training.

As stated earlier, the structure of schooling effectively restricts the kind of staff planning required for educational improvement. There simply is not time both to maintain the ship and to redesign it. Consequently, it is proposed that teachers be employed on a twelve-month basis, with at least two months of the year devoted to both personal improvement and total school planning. There are many ways of implementing such a proposal. Under the scheme, teachers teach for six weeks, have a planning week with children out of school, teach for an additional six-week period, engage in a period of planning, and so on throughout the twelve-month year. With teachers employed for twelve months (with a month's vacation) and with children attending school only nine months, approximately two months of nonteaching time are available for the planning activities essential to the self-renewing school.

If teachers are to make effective use of this period of nonteaching, however, they must be part of a team-teaching structure. By teaching in teams, it is possible for members of each group to devote a considerable proportion of their time to planning, preparing instructional materials, evaluating, and replanning. Whatever other arguments there may be for team teaching, a critical one is that it provides the kind of flexibility necessary for effective planning to proceed. Also, it is difficult to see how beginning teachers can be introduced into responsibility for teaching on a limited basis unless they are members of teaching teams.

Clearly, the commitment and involvement of teachers-in-training called for here requires a substantial period of full-time preparation. It is recommended that the total time span from entry to graduation as a full-fledged teacher be from two to three years and culminate in a terminal professional degree. One possible alternative is to begin the teacher education program with the senior year in college. Students would receive the baccalaureate after one year in the program but would continue into an additional year of postbaccalaureate work. Another alternative is to begin such a program at the postbaccalaureate level with the candidate pursuing two years of work leading to the master of arts in teaching degree. To repeat, it is essential that students enter into a full-time commitment at the outset and that all other goals become secondary. It is essential, also, that the degree awarded be regarded as terminal. From this point on, the educational system should provide for professional updating at the cost to the enterprise. Persons desiring to move into some other aspect of education would leave teaching in order to pursue advanced specialized professional education.

It is recommended, also, that there be moderate salaries throughout the training period. Initial stipends would be increased gradually to a level of perhaps several thousand dollars below present first-year salaries. With completion of the program, however, and admission to the teaching profession, truly professional salaries would prevail. The net effect would be to attract committed persons into a profession of lifelong reward and appeal.

The reader is reminded that the reconstruction proposed here results in reducing the ratio of full-fledged professional teachers to children. The proportion of adults in the pupil-teacher mix is more than made up, however, through the inclusion in each team of aides, interns, and residents, all assuming some responsibility for instruction. Cost estimates reveal that such staffing patterns cost little or no more than conventional arrangements.

A program of the kind outlined here necessitates nonspecification of courses for certification. Approval of individuals for teaching by a state agency would be replaced by approval of teacher-preparing consortia involving colleges and public schools. The decision to award teaching certificates to individuals would belong to the collaborating faculty, after careful observation and evaluation of candidates. Reliability of such appraisals could be improved through periodic use of outside evaluation teams.

Finally, at the heart of the whole, there should be a research center committed to the study of the entire enterprise, much like the hub of the League. Such a center would engage in studies of pedagogy, the effects of experimental programs, the efficacy of various self-renewing strategies in the schools, and so on. Instead of there being a monolithic program, there would be several experimental ones, each with differing entrance requirements, course arrangements, and balance of academic and clinical work. Every component part of the teacher education enterprise would be conducted as a hypothesis to be tested rather than as established assurance of what is effective education of the future teacher.

CONCLUSION

No part of what is proposed here is startling or unusual. Every element has been proposed; many have been tried. What is unique and unusual, however, is the proposition that all these ingredients be put together simultaneously in a single collaborative enterprise designed for the in-service and pre-service education of teachers and the improvement of schooling.

Clearly, the tasks proposed, taken together, are enormous—perhaps overwhelming. There are two ways to cut down the size of any problem. One is to eliminate some of the component parts and focus on a few. The other is to focus on the whole by reducing the order of magnitude with regard to each component part. The second alternative is proposed here. The first has been tried and found wanting.

This means then that the arena in which the component parts are to develop, interact, and be studied must be kept as small as possible. Instead of many teacher education centers at the outset, there should be only a few. Instead of spreading the resources of the academic faculty across dozens of schools in an ad hoc process of school improvement, energy and talent should be focused on the few schools selected to serve as teacher education centers. Instead of endeavoring to move the entire teacher education program on an even front, existing programs should be allowed to phase out while new programs of a controlled and experimental sort are phased in. Instead of endeavoring to serve many individuals at varying stages in their preparation to teach, teacher-preparing institutions should focus on precise delineation of the group to be served, which is admitted at a specific time in the college or university hierarchy with provision for individualization taking place within a defined structure. The principle of unity of structure and diversity of programs thus emerges.

There is no way of knowing at the outset whether a commitment to the kind of attack suggested here will correct the current deficiencies in schooling and teacher education. Nor is there experimental evidence to commend the directions proposed. But until one has created alternatives, there is no way of comparing alternatives. The problems which the strategy proposed here is designed to correct are formidable and of long standing. Redoubling our efforts to deal with them along present lines of endeavor will not suffice. The time is come to break out of old molds, to get beyond immediate preoccupations, in a comprehensive effort to deal with the whole.

Notes

[1] The observations in this section are based primarily on direction of or participation in the following studies: the organization of schooling (1963) for the Center for the Study of Instruction of the NEA; James B. Conant's study of the education of American teachers (1963); two studies of the curriculum reform movement (1964 and 1966); a study of school and classroom practices in sixty-seven elementary schools (1970, revised 1974); and a study of the process of change in eighteen elementary schools (1975).

[2] John I. Goodlad, M. Frances Klein, and Associates, *Looking Behind the Classroom Door*, revised edition, Charles A. Jones, Worthington, Ohio, 1974.

[3] Gary A. Griffin, "Curricular Decision-Making in Selected School Systems," unpublished doctoral dissertation, Graduate School of Education, University of California, Los Angeles, 1970.

13

Computers and the *Schools* in *Modern Society*

Computers are not only an exciting instructional tool. They also offer the potential for redesign of the entire educational enterprise. [Editor]

Some components of "modern" educational technology have been with us for some time: films, filmstrips, records, radio, and television. One might expect that these components would be in widespread use in the schools today. Surprisingly, they are not.

In visits to approximately 250 elementary school classrooms in sixty-seven schools,[1] my colleagues and I found little evidence of a technological explosion in the classroom. In fact, there was little evidence that the "golden age of instructional materials" is here. For instruction, teachers depend heavily on telling and questioning, with the primary exchange being between teacher and child, child and teacher—not among groups of children with the teacher as observer and participant. While there are striking classroom examples to the contrary, the predominant impression is one of traditional teaching techniques with traditional textbooks as the prime medium of instruction.

SOURCE: John I. Goodlad, "Computers and the Schools in Modern Society," in "Symposium on Computer-Assisted Learning," *Proceedings of the National Academy of Sciences*, vol. 63, no. 3, July 1969, pp. 573–603.

One is forced to ask why. Undoubtedly, the quality of the newer media often has been poor. Many educational films are pedantic, precious, and "holier than thou." Too often, they tend to talk down to children; certainly, they do not grip the viewer. A first-rate film library for schools is developing, but slowly.

But quality does not fully explain the fact that teachers have eschewed audiovisual aids. There is no doubt that teacher training and tradition are enormously restraining influences, but it is clear that audiovisual aids have almost always been advocated as *extensions* of the teacher. The cant in audiovisual education is that the audiovisual presentation is to be an extension of conventional teaching procedures. Too seldom is it assumed that students should be free to use such materials on their own initiative: to cut tapes and records, to produce films, or to use any of these which are available. Almost invariably, the teacher intervenes in some way between student and learning device. Herein, I think, lies the heart of the problem. So long as the interface is not a direct one between student and material and so long as the teacher himself must make the material available, the audiovisual device enters as a fifth wheel. We must move, rather, to the notion that almost all the educational processes can and should be a direct interface between student and stimulus, with the teacher only a guide. Use of the material or device must lie completely within the ken and freedom of the individual learner.

We are now entering into a new phase of instructional technology made possible by the advent of the computer. The unique contribution of the computer is that it clearly needs little, if any, intervention on the part of the teacher. The computer marches on in its relentless way, students are plugged in, and the teacher is free to stand back from and appraise the learning that is under way. In fact, if the teacher seeks to monitor the computer as a teaching aid, in the conventional sense, the teacher's actions are dehumanized. The teacher becomes a human robot, always outstripped by the mechanical one which is indefatigable and, for most purposes, more efficient. The central problem, then, in the use of the computer in instruction is to develop a team-teaching situation, with human and electronic teachers each performing the most appropriate role.

The computer lends itself to at least three sets of functions: (a) management of masses of educational data, (b) management of the educational enterprise, and (c) instruction.

Large school systems, in particular, are faced with formidable problems of storing and retrieving data pertaining to pupil records, teacher records, payroll, test results, and so on. These data can be managed much more efficiently by computers than by humans. A single computer, programmed for storing and retrieving such data, has an enormous appetite—too large an appetite, usually, for small and intermediate school systems. Therefore, this aspect of computer use in schooling lends itself well to cooperative endeavor among several neighboring school systems sharing a common computer. School systems are surprisingly stubborn and individualistic, however, in regard to the way in which such data are classified and otherwise identified. There are no strong arguments for one system of classification over another. Nonetheless, neighboring school systems stick stubbornly to their own methods when a little "giving" could result in both savings and improved efficiency in regard to data control.

In a large school system, the option is to use the computer not only for these more mundane tasks, but also for somewhat more experimental endeavors. The office of research, for example, might be able to conduct broad-scale research and evaluative activities which otherwise would not be possible. The city of Chicago represents an early example of this dual use. During the day the computer is available to persons who have various individualistic concerns, and at night it is devoted to handling routine matters. The possibilities of putting the computer to work at night is too little recognized by school personnel. Many major universities run their computer facilities twenty-four hours a day, with students and faculty members gaining access to the facilities around the clock.

The second function might be described as *management of the educational enterprise.* There are several types of activities under this rubric, but two of them, in particular, should be mentioned. First, the computer is increasingly entering into the management of student programs. A well-known system is that generated by Stanford University which, using a module of time, individually schedules students located many miles away. Printouts from the computer tell each student where he is supposed to be and what he is supposed to be doing at any time during an instructional week.

But a much more sophisticated management activity lies just around the corner, one already extensively used in other fields and, particularly, for research purposes. This is the process of feeding data to decision-making processes. Administrators and teachers make hosts of decisions during a given day, most of them not based on data but on hunches and intuition. Human intuition needs to be enriched by data. For example, when teachers move into new patterns of school organization, such as nongrading or team teaching, decisions which were formerly not theirs to make now lie before them.[2] Since modern management techniques have not caught up with these new decision-making processes, teachers become frustrated because of the unavailability of the data they need. What is called for here is a conceptualization of the educational decisions involved in any aspect of the enterprise; the identification of the kinds of data needed for these decisions; the classification and storage of these data for easy recall; and the recall of the data at the point of decision making. Thus, an instructional team considering the class or group placement of a given youngster for the following term should have at its disposal salient data pertaining to that child: adjustment to the present group, learning accomplishments in various fields, difficulties with peers and adults, and so on. These data are then taken into account in making the appropriate educational placement. Even more sophisticated management techniques using the computer are on the horizon for schools and teachers.

The educational function appropriate for computers which has attracted most attention is *instruction*. The computer is a tireless, relentlessly evaluating teacher which has several modes of instruction at its disposal: sound, sight, and touch. A properly programmed computer is able to present words to be spelled, sounds to be made, and instructions to be followed. It is able to present images and symbols to be responded to by touch. It is able to evaluate pupil performance and to direct the student backwards, forwards, or sideways, for appropriate learning activity. Almost all the computer-assisted instruction currently under way is experimental in character. Significant are the experiments in the teaching of spelling, reading, arithmetic, and so on, at the University of Pittsburgh, the University of Texas, the University of Illinois, and elsewhere. The program in computer-assisted instruction at Stanford University depends upon carefully worked out "software" in basic instructional areas. These programs use both "on site" computers and remote terminals.

There are many technical problems still to be resolved in computer-assisted instruction: the development of computers which can handle a large number of terminals; the refinement of communication to remote terminals; and on and on. Two other problems are more significant at this point in time. The first is cost, but rapid gains are being made here. The second is the human variable. There needs to be developed an enormous readiness on the part of the educational profession to build the computer into the instructional process.

COMPUTER-ASSISTED LEARNING

The two key characteristics of computers which promise to change education in schools and society are *efficiency* and *availability*. The most dramatic changes in the conduct of education are likely to be more the product of the availability characteristic. The computer is ready, willing, and able—twenty-four hours a day, seven days a week, $365\frac{1}{4}$ days a year.

Before turning to these characteristics of efficiency and availability, let me say a little about the prognosis for early widespread use of computers in the lower schools. First, there is not likely to be widespread use of computers for teaching and learning during the next decade. This view is in contrast to many of the wide-eyed claims for computer use in instruction. The reasons for my conservatism include those usually cited. The costs of computers and computer terminals already have been identified. Wherever terminals are remote, a major cost item is the telephone communication system. It is in this realm that breakthroughs are anticipated, so that costs may be reduced markedly in the relatively near future. Nonetheless, costs in general and the costs of transmission from computers to terminals in particular will continue to be restraining factors, if only because the *image* of cost will continue to exist. And, of course, actual cost factors also will continue to be formidable for some time. This problem is compounded by the fact that estimates of real costs are difficult to come by and vary enormously with respect to any given cost factor.

It must be remembered, too, that school (and university) budgets are relatively inflexible. In California, 80 percent of the budget in a local school system is locked in to mandated specifications, with over 60 percent of the total outlay in elementary education going to teacher salaries. It must be remembered that many of the potential savings in the use of computers occur only after computers have been installed. Consequently, there is a period of time during which a school system must suffer under dual budget outlays. It is difficult to amortize this kind of financial outlay. No matter what the computer may replace in the future, it is laid on over whatever exists at the outset.

But the most subtle difficulty with early introduction of computers lies in simultaneously changing and maintaining the educational system. Innovation is difficult, not just because this is its character but because the existing system must be maintained while the new one is being introduced. The educational ship is not brought into dry dock but must remain on the high seas while repairs are effected. It is not surprising, then, that educators tend to tinker with the rigging—raising and lowering the sails, polishing the brightwork, or swabbing the decks. Meanwhile, it is the hull that really needs changing, but it dare not be tampered with for fear the ship will sink. Consequently, most educational change is at the periphery and, as a result, is inconsequential. To introduce a real change into the system is to change the whole system. Consequently, to introduce computers for instruction is threatening. Teachers must then work harder to facilitate a process which they fear will replace them. This difficulty will remain for some time as the least penetrable.

This problem suggests that the computer will enter into the schools at those points and in those ways that require a minimum of mediation by the teacher. This brings me back to where I started with respect to audiovisual aides in general. Most audiovisual aids used to date have involved considerable mediation by the teacher. Skillful administrators who wish to see the computer used increasingly in the schools should devote some of their attention to how the computer can be introduced so as to require only a minimum of new behavior on the part of the teacher. We may expect to see the computer used as a teaching device in segments of the curriculum where there are rather well-agreed-upon skills or bodies of content that can be programmed for direct computer-student interface with little or no teacher participation. Already we see this to be the case in the teaching of reading, mathematics, and spelling. Where teachers are involved in close communication with the computer, one is depressed to note that the teacher tends to be robotized. He often engages in a perfunctory handling of printouts that might just as well be handled directly by the student. It is when the student encounters problems which are not programmed that a more sensitive kind of relationship is called for and when the human teacher should be sought.

In brief summary, then, I am saying that the use of the computer in schools will be delayed primarily by the subtle difficulties of simultaneously changing and maintaining the educational system. To the extent that teachers do not have to carry the double burden, the computer is as likely to be welcomed as rejected.

Now let me return to the efficiency characteristic of computers. These have been summarized in many places. First, the computer is capable of presenting a response sequence of learning opportunities, uncontaminated by nuances of speech or by mannerisms characteristic of the varying human teacher. Second, it tends to extinguish errors and to reinforce correct responses. Third, it provides for individual rates of speed, with students usually able to control the rate of presentation and of response. Fourth, the computer provides individualized schedules, permitting students to exercise idiosyncratic behavior without further confounding the energy restraints of the human teacher. Fifth, the computer eliminates or holds the potential for eliminating a host of routine pupil-teacher contacts which add little or nothing to the learning process. It is doubtful that meaningless routinized human interactions are better than no human interactions at all. And it must be remembered that it is difficult for most human beings to be truly human in the best sense, hour after hour, all day long, with a passing parade of students.

But the efficiency characteristic of computers poses some problems which are rarely identified in the literature. The first is for theory and research. There are conceptual problems, to be checked out empirically, pertaining to the parts of the curriculum which should be allocated to computers and the parts which should be allocated to human beings. It is quite likely that there are certain kinds of human processes which should remain in the exclusive domain of human beings, but it is not at all clear what these might be. It is a kind of inquiry which may not be very popular in education but which must be carried on.

The efficiency characteristic also poses problems for teacher self-respect. The computer is more efficient in most of what teachers now do. Research has shown that, even in classrooms rated as superior with respect to instruction, an enormous amount of teacher time is devoted to the purely routine. But this is not at all surprising.

Human beings seem to need a considerable amount of routine to fill in the time between less frequent creative efforts. What will the teacher do if not directing routine? Articles and books on computer-assisted instruction end with the captivating notion that the computer will enable human teachers to do those truly human things. What are they? And will teachers be able to do them all day long? Our divorce rate suggests that it is exceedingly difficult even for two people to establish a productive human relationship. How, then, is the human teacher to establish such a relationship with thirty other human beings and maintain it throughout five or six hours of an instructional day? Most teachers would be in a state of collapse at the end of such days. Clearly, if teachers, given computers, are to move to more intensely human instructional activities, the nature of the instructional day must be completely rethought. The kind of teaching day in elementary and secondary schools probably ought to resemble the kind of teaching day in institutions of higher learning. Perhaps a forty-hour work week for teachers should include only twelve to fifteen hours of direct instructional time. This will not be easily understood by the lay community.

Quite apart from the theoretical research and affective problems involved under the rubric "efficiency," there are problems of logistics and politics. Teachers and computers must learn to work productively side by side in the school environment. But we have not yet been outstandingly successful in developing teams of human teachers. Ahead of us lies the logistical problem of developing teaching teams which will include the computer as one component of the team, with the electronic teacher performing the tasks appropriate to it and the human teachers engaged in other kinds of activities and only rarely monitoring the computer terminals. There are implications here for school building design, teacher allocation and utilization, and so on. Is the cost of adding a computer to be absorbed by reducing the size of the human teaching staff? The computer is not likely to add to the economic efficiency of education if what it does efficiently is merely added to what human beings do inefficiently. And inherent in all of this are implications for the role of teacher unions. Will we arrive at the day when teachers teaching only twelve or fifteen hours a week are paid by union contract a full week's wages for whatever they may do in their remaining hours? Might this mean that the potential additional time for planning, for preparing more effective lessons, for counseling with students, and so on, will go by the board? There are many intangibles here which cannot be predicted and which might very well change the nature of the teaching profession as we know it.

While the efficiency characteristic of computers offers promise of better performance in conventional educational tasks, the availability characteristic offers a promise of fundamentally changing or eliminating conventional educational tasks. The possibility emerges when we realize how much of the conduct of schooling is geared to, or dependent upon, the limited availability of human energy.

It is possible to think of many specifics of school practice which depend, perhaps implicitly, on our awareness of the limits of human energy in a schooling situation; for example, entrance age really has little to do with a child's readiness to learn. It is now becoming clear that children are ready to and, indeed, do learn for many years before coming to school.

Entrance age, then, whatever it may be, has no real educational justification. It simply is difficult for teachers to look after twenty-five or thirty youngsters who are not toilet-trained, who are very little socialized, who need to eat relatively often, and who tend to carry on many of their pursuits in rather short bursts. No, leave them home, we say, during this potentially troublesome period. Similarly, there is no educational justification for a 9 A.M. to 3 P.M. school day. Such a period roughly coincides with the time when most human beings go to work and return. Why should school be any different? It is not easy for it to be any different so long as instruction is tied to human beings and their conventional utilization of energy. Likewise, children are placed in a grade because this, supposedly, limits the need for high ceilings and low floors of expectancy and provision for learning within any class group. Of course, the grade is not really like this, but we can pretend. The egg-crate school building, with its 30:1 ratio of children to teachers in each classroom and the continuous interaction process suggested thereby is related to notions of how many children can be handled at once and how many children can be within the hearing and seeing range of the teacher. High school faculties are put together in order to provide for a balanced curriculum at any one time. It is possible that balance in the curriculum has more to do with the availability of human energy than educational rationality. Likewise, there is an orderly progression from elementary to secondary school, with the former tending not to tread on the domain of the latter. None of these accepted conditions of schooling is necessary when one introduces the concept of energy available at any time of the day or night to any age group throughout the year. The learning stimulus is always there; one needs only to tap it. This is not the case with human teachers.

Perhaps the most significant aspect of the computer with respect to education, then, is that an altogether new kind of energy is injected into the educational process. It is energy which has nothing to do with the night before, with viruses, with unmanageable children, or any of the rest. Subjects missed this year can be picked up next year. Single subjects can be pursued intensively for periods of time related only to the whim of the learner. The fifty-year-old need not humble himself by going back to school with twelve-year-olds in order to get what he needs and wants. He may go directly to the energy system, which is insensitive to age, color, or origin of birth.

The moment that we make teaching energy available throughout the twenty-four hour span of the day to all individuals in any place, most of the conventions of schooling explode; school need no longer be what we have known it to be. And so it is the characteristic of *availability* of the computer which holds the potentiality for fundamentally restructuring, if not eliminating, school as we know and have known it.

It is quite reasonable, of course, to conceive of a school which is unnecessary for the purposes it has served traditionally as being necessary for latent functions which we have not, up to now, chosen to recognize. Consequently, school may be thought of as a place where children are known to be, where parents and guardians can locate them at will. They are accounted for, so to speak. It could be a place where students fulfill certain social functions, testing their peer relationships with members of both sexes. It could become a place where human beings are brought together not for the formalities of learning but for a higher literacy going far beyond reading, writing, and arithmetic. But clearly with the advent of computers for learning, unless schooling is rethought it is unlikely that students, particularly at high school levels, will see school life as the kind of life that is most meaningful for them. And this brings us to another potentiality of the computer.

If terminal and transmission costs are brought down to a reasonable point so that the purchase of computer time and terminals is not unrealistic for schools, and if the production of software is vastly enhanced, then one major obstacle to computer-assisted instruction in schools is removed. But these economic advances apply equally to homes. Consequently, the reduction of computer terminal costs for school use open up home use. In fact, there are many more potential purchasers of home-based terminals. All that remains for computer terminals to be installed in homes is the availability of adequate supplies of software. The home becomes a most interesting potential market for computer companies and the large commercial education complexes.

We have not begun to tap the potentiality of the home as the locus of a much wider array of human activity. Thousands of commuters suffer through traffic jams in order to get to offices in which they operate in cells, with only occasional interaction with other human beings. A substantial part of the work force spends much of its time and does much of its business on the telephone. Much of this might as readily be done by remaining at home and forgetting the traffic problems. The same could be said of schooling.

The only thing now standing in the way of an enormous amount of productive learning occurring via television is the quality of programs. Envision a computer terminal, with a wider variety of instructional resources, available in the home in the same way a television set is available now. Given the rapid advancement and rapid outmoding of knowledge, age is a poor criterion for knowing or for needing to know. Consequently, one can envision families comprised of many age levels learning together from computer terminals in the home. This does not mean that members of the family will refrain from going outside for other kinds of learning activities, but it does suggest that both basic learning and updating, as appropriate, might very well be effected through home communication with a central learning unit generating to many computer terminals. Home budgets are more flexible than school budgets and, therefore, can be adjusted to take care of additional expense. And the social system is a relatively simple one. There are few problems of getting through it or into it.

Now, let us put together computer capability for storage and retrieval, management, and instruction. It is possible to conceive of a computer programmed to provide instantly, at a home terminal, continuously updated information about the total educational resources of a community. In some sections of the country these resources already are abundant, but the communication system regarding them is inadequate. A member of a family might very well secure a printout of what is coming up in the way of art shows, museum displays, athletic events, plays, lectures, and so on, and where and how these educational and cultural resources might be reached. Some programs would come directly into the home via computer terminal. Included in this repertoire of cultural resources would be a library of educational programs spanning the whole gamut of human interest. Envision a cultural community center in which the totality of learning resources available is "programmed." And envision an individual record-keeping system by means of which the segments of this, uniquely assembled for any given individual, are managed. Then envision human teachers with special skills located in various centers available to those who need or call for them. Finally, envision guidance centers staffed with individuals uniquely equipped to counsel on individual learning interests and problems. Within this complex, "teachers" would play a diversified set of roles. Some would spend hours and hours in preparing a single lesson, to be viewed within the lifetime of that lesson by thousands or even millions of individuals over a wide age span. Others would be engaging in those group interaction processes which we might label intellectual dialogue. Others would staff the counseling centers referred to previously. Still others would engage in presentations viewed and responded to on home and "community" computer terminal screens. Others would evaluate in order to determine the effectiveness of instructional programs.

This is not "education 1980." But it very well could be "education 2000."

We cannot envision or bring about very much of this if we fail to realize that the changes potentially inherent in modern technology will change systems as we know them. Change is not just a matter of tacking on something new. If a change is significant—and computers hold the potentiality for significant change—then it will affect the entire organism. The system will enter into disequilibrium and all its parts then become subject to change. Consequently, all its parts can be redesigned. It is the availability of new energy—energy which can be held stable over long periods of time; energy which is unfaltering; energy which stores and retrieves; energy which responds to and sustains the input of human energy—that promises to change the school as we have known it. It is this energy which promises to eliminate the unfortunate alienation of much of schooling from education and to make the boundaries between the two indistinguishable.

Notes

[1]John I. Goodlad, M. Frances Klein, and Associates, *Behind the Classroom Door*, Charles A. Jones, Worthington, Ohio, 1970; revised and retitled *Looking Behind the Classroom Door*, 1974.

[2]Hugh D. Lawrence, "Placing Children in Learning Environments in a Nongraded School," unpublished doctoral dissertation, University of California, Los Angeles, 1975.

14

Thought, Invention, and Research in the *Advancement of* Education

The paper on which this chapter is based was originally prepared as Goodlad's presidential address to the American Educational Research Association in 1968. It can be construed as a warning to his fellow researchers to remember that they need to be as concerned with the utility of their work in the real world of schools as they are with the elegance of research designs or the effort to fit all studies and outcomes into preexisting models. [Editor]

My central thesis here is that innovation in educational practice offers unique but unexploited opportunities for the advancement of educational science. For reasons which completely escape me, we too often assume virtually by definition that direct study of educational practice is applied research. It is not the problem that makes education an applied or a basic field. It is what we seek to gain from the problem and the frame within which we approach it. Substance, process, and product are the closest we have in education to natural phenomena. It is in the study of these as natural phenomena that educational science will be forged, if it is to be forged at all.

SOURCE: John I. Goodlad, "Thought, Invention, and Research in the Advancement of Education," *The Educational Forum*, vol. XXXIII, November 1968, pp. 7–18.

What follows can be summarized in a series of topic sentences. First, our daily thoughts and actions, progress in social affairs, and advance in any field of inquiry involve a mixing and blending of deductive and inductive reasoning. Second, there is, certainly, no one-to-one relation between human decisions, including educational ones, and specific research findings. Third, always to insist on research findings as prerequisite to action is to inhibit invention and to endanger both human progress and dispassionate scientific inquiry. Fourth, the possibility of being able to differentiate the effects of compared alternatives presumes the existence of or preexistence of genuine alternatives. Fifth, the failure of an alternative to deliver gains on certain criteria (including some traditionally assumed to be of great importance) may be irrelevant with respect to decisions as to whether to continue, discontinue, or propagate the alternative. Sixth, the rational advance of educational thought and practice is seriously impeded by inappropriate expectations for and methodological deficiencies in the study of educational phenomena.

I turn, then, to the first of these topic sentences, that pertaining to two modes of thought, the deductive and the inductive.

THOUGHT

I take the phrase "two modes of thought" from the title of a little book by James B. Conant, published in 1964.[1] In it he develops several observations having enormous implications for the study of education, which currently is in danger of becoming lopsided; for the practice of education, which recently has been somewhat inventive; and for the relation between the two.

The natural sciences, Conant observes,

". . . are the result of the empirical-inductive method of inquiry together with the imaginative use of the theoretical-deductive. In the last one hundred years in all branches of the natural sciences, the advances have been a consequence of the collaboration of scientists with two different outlooks."[2]

He points out not only that some men and women work in one or the other tradition of thought but that the greatest scientists often use both. He refutes the popular use of Darwin's work as an example of how the accumulation of "empirical facts" led to generalizations.

Darwin had been unable to explain how each species fits its environment until he chanced to read Malthus' *Essay on Population* and "the idea of natural selection suddenly rose to my mind." Conant comments,

"Such are the flashes of genius that result in a great scientist's conviction that a working hypothesis is far more than an hypothesis—that it is a principle, that is correct. Unless he is armed with such a conviction, he will not proceed with the laborious testing of the deductions from the generalization. . . . The empirical-inductive is by itself insufficient to generate advances in scientific theory. On the other hand, the theoretical-deductive mode by itself is too often barren; for advances in the practical arts, it has been in the past quite unnecessary."[3]

He then goes on to use the work of the nineteenth-century inventors to show how discoveries have been made with a minimum of theory even in the age of science. Conant sums up his views with the following:

"There should be places within the whole range of the offerings of a university for those who from early youth desire to study human problems by empirical methods and also plans for those who are interested only in broad speculative theories. . . . In the past the tendency of the empiricists to dismiss the writings of all theoreticians as meaningless nonsense and the tendency of theoreticians to talk as though all empirical research were beneath contempt has polarized the total academic world as regards both research and education. . . . Just as man needs two legs to walk on, the social sciences need two types of thinkers if the advance is, as it should be, to meet the needs of a free and highly industrialized society."[4]

In *The Sources of a Science of Education,* John Dewey expresses some similar views.[5] Interestingly, he too refers to Darwin, pointing out that philosophical inquiry regarding evolution preceded Darwin. Darwin may not have encountered these earlier writings but he did encounter Malthus. Some quotes and paraphrases from Dewey round out those from Conant and add to the conceptual structure I shall use.

"Galileo's experiments and measurements form the basis of modern science. . . . Galileo had, however, first performed an experiment in *thought* [italics mine]. . . . It was this general idea, arrived at by thinking, that gave point to his experiment in Pisa. . . . It was his preliminary hypothesis framed by thought which gave revolutionary impact to his measurement of rolling balls. . . ."[6]

Like Conant, Dewey employs the term "working hypothesis."

"They are *working* ideas; special investigations become barren and one-sided in the degree in which they are conducted without reference to a wider, more general view. . . . No matter how these are obtained, they are intrinsically philosophical in nature. But if a philosophy starts to reason out its conclusions without definite and constant regard to the concrete experiences that define the problem for thought, it becomes speculative in a way that justifies contempt."[7]

Educational science cannot be constructed simply by borrowing the techniques of experiment and measurement found in physical science. . . . *This principle is particularly important at the present time* [italics mine]. . . . The lack of an intellectually coherent and inclusive system is a positive warning against attributing scientific values to results merely because they are reached by means of recognized techniques borrowed from sciences already established and are capable of being stated in quantitative formula."[8]

". . . educational practices provide the data, the subject-matter, which form the *problems* of inquiry. They are the sole source of the ultimate problems to be investigated. These educational practices are also the final *test of value* of all researches. To suppose that scientific findings decide the value of educational undertakings is to reverse the real case. Actual activities in *educating* test the worth of scientific results. They may be scientific in some other field, but not in education until they serve educational purposes, and whether they really serve or not can be found out only in practice. The latter comes first and last; it is the beginning and the close; the beginning, because it sets the problems which alone give to investigations educational point and quality; the close, because practice alone can test, verify, modify and develop the conclusions of these investigations. The position of scientific conclusions is intermediate and auxiliary."[9]

While Dewey stresses the importance of thought, of the generation of working hypotheses, he decries the emptiness of thinking which takes place remote from the source of intellectual supplies. Similarly, he decries practice-related research that lacks working hypotheses, the big ideas. A researcher so engaged is likely ". . . to occupy himself with isolated and relatively trivial problems, a kind of scientific busy-work, and yet may expect his results to be taken seriously by workers in the field."[10]

Finally, in the context of my first topic sentence pertaining to thought, I draw upon Joseph Schwab's notions of short-term and long-term syntax.[11] These are, respectively, the syntax of stable and fluid inquiry. About the former he says:

"If the current principles of physiology are organ and function, the stable researcher in physiology busies himself discovering the function of first one organ and then another. The principle guides the inquiries but is never, itself, the subject of any inquiry."[12]

Fluid inquiry or long-term syntax, on the other hand, is attuned to the inconsistencies in short-term inquiries that suggest imperfections in the principles guiding them and seeks to provide either alternative or more comprehensive structures. The salience of these new structures, in turn, sets off new short-term inquiries. In the process, a field can be torn apart and rebuilt.

Most of the scholarly inquiry in a field at any given time is of the short-term variety. Consequently, the intrusion of new conceptual structures into the field is upsetting—particularly to those short-term inquirers who have mortgaged a chunk of their lives in a grant tied to the structures now being challenged. We should not be too surprised when the "dispassionate, rational" world of science suddenly erupts and is marked by acrimonious outbursts. The advancement of vigorous fields often is characterized by a veritable cacophony of sound.

We should not be surprised, either, that fluid inquiry—its vital significance notwithstanding—often has a hard time of it. Schwab's comments are insightful:

". . . there are some scientists who would deny the very existence of fluid inquiry because they deny the existence of conceptual frames as underpinnings of their work. Many men feel much more emotional stability and readiness for work if they permit themselves to believe that the notions that guide their work represent 'the facts' and are stable and eternal. It was once possible to maintain the fantasy of such stability for a lifetime. . . . This is no longer the case."[13]

One of the crosses to be borne by the fluid inquirer, especially in a field that only grudgingly recognizes the necessity of long-term inquiry, is what Schwab calls the "political-rhetorical-scientific hard work of obtaining acceptance of a new conceptual scheme by one's fellow scientists. This task . . . is as much a part of the scientific enterprise as obtaining data. . . ."[14]

Unfortunately in a field such as education, characterized by short-term inquiry and embracing very few distinguished theoretical educationists who serve to legitimatize long-term inquiry, the political-rhetorical demands of gaining acceptance for new constructs use up available energies. The substantive enterprise of gathering and interpreting the essential hard data suffers accordingly. And promising alternative structures in education frequently go begging and remain empty because they fail to become salient for short-term inquiries. It is lamentable that the field of education which so desperately needs bold working hypotheses is as yet ill-adapted to risk taking.

INVENTION

I turn, next, to invention in educational practice which, properly studied, offers unusual opportunities for advancing education as a field of study. I find the rationale for such a statement in thinking about the preceding roughed-in ideas of Conant, Dewey, and Schwab. Making some of these explicit here outweighs, I think, the risks of repetition. First, advancement of a field calls for productive interplay between two modes of thought: the theoretical-deductive and the empirical-inductive, often within the mind of one scientist. Second, educational practices provide both problems for educational inquiry and "the field" for testing and verifying conclusions. Third, fluid inquiry reshapes a field, serving to monitor the course of stable inquiry, pose alternatives, and maintain the necessary tension of productive uncertainty.

To these three notions, I add a fourth. Inventing or innovating in the *practice* of education involves a blending of theoretical-deductive and empirical-inductive inquiry, however primitive in their development the two modes of thought may be.° Invention in practice provides articulation of persistent educational problems. And it poses alternative concepts, modes, and principles for conducting practice. In effect, invention provides for educational practice a kind of fluid inquiry in that old concepts and old ways of doing things are challenged. Is it not conceivable, then, that the study of invention would provide for educational science, also, a much needed stimulus to fluid inquiry? The perplexing fresh research demands posed by educational invention would serve thereby to accelerate education as a field of study. Certainly, the proper study of invention would be good for educational practice. But, if Dewey was even close to the target, such study also would be proper for the advancement of educational science.

We are not likely to have invention in educational practice, however, let alone advances in educational science, if we demand research on the effects of an invention as a prerequisite to its creation. We are asking an ambiguous question, if not the wrong one. We are asking for information that cannot yet be given on criteria that rest only in our minds and which may be quite inappropriate. Perhaps worse, we invoke the sacred mysteries and prestige of "research," equipping practitioners for whom the invention is intended (and probably threatening) with formidable defenses against changing anything, more formidable defenses than they would think up if left to their own devices. Thus, the invention never rises to the level of being a serious viable alternative. Its effects are never studied, simply because there are no effects. Fluid inquiry is thwarted, stable inquiry along traditional lines continues, and education is the poorer.

But to seek for justification of the invention—the structures on which it rests, the observations which gave rise to these structures,

---

°I use the terms "invention" and "innovation" synonymously for my purposes here. Webster's definition of innovation neatly summarizes what I have in mind: something that deviates from established doctrine, practice, or forms. I speak, then, to the invention of new forms, not to the adoption of forms ready-made in which only replication is involved, and to innovation in which something new must be invented.

the problems with which the invention seeks to cope, in effect, the entire thought process which produced it—is quite another matter. This can be an enormously difficult undertaking, especially since the inventor invariably took intuitive leaps and usually is unable to retrace his steps. The identification and analysis of these leaps as well as of the hard data employed, constitute part of the process of determining whether further development should be undertaken. They are part of educational science, a part with which logicians and philosophers of science are comfortable. They are quite foreign to the training, interest, and temperament of many empiricists and yet absolutely essential to long-term empirical inquiry.

To carry on our empirical inquiry in ignorance of the need for such philosophical inquiry is to assure the irrelevance of much of it. Simultaneously to conduct theoretical-deductive inquiry which is equally devoid of the empirical is to assure sterility in educational science.

Let me illustrate what I am driving at here with a much-talked-about recent educational innovation, team teaching. Viewed within the long-term frame guiding much current stable inquiry, team teaching is, indeed, trivial, as Lee Cronbach several years ago pronounced it to be.[15] Viewed within another frame, however, team teaching is seminal in its implications for both practice and research.

In 1955, several of us met in an office of the Ford Foundation to discuss teacher education. But we were not interested in exploring teacher education within familiar long-standing frames. We were concerned about how to differentiate rewards for teaching so that outstanding teachers would not find it financially necessary to moonlight or to enter administration during mid-career; about how to assure self-renewal for the overburdened teacher in the elementary school's self-contained classroom; about how to bring highly specialized resources into that classroom; and about how to induct neophytes meaningfully into teaching when their supervising teachers already are burdened with "keeping school." We focused on a paper prepared by Francis Keppel, dealing not with the usual conventions of preparing teachers but with the horizontal restructuring of the elementary school. That paper provided a rough approximation of what many educators today term "team teaching."[16]

Team teaching is intended to secure maximum flexibility in the horizontal organization of the school and must be viewed within this context. It seeks to redesign a significant part of the instructional environment. If it is viewed within the frame of quickly improving the subject matter accomplishments of, say, third-graders—as it usually is—then it is an enormously complicated way of achieving such a goal. And to expect, in choosing team teaching in practice or for study, significant and rapid advances in achievement as a result, without also specifying concomitant *instructional practices,* is both to apply the wrong criterion and to assure inconclusive outcomes.

No, team teaching posed for us an alternative structure to the long-standing organizational structures of departmentalization and the self-contained classroom, both of which appeared to us to hamper needed developments in teacher education and one or the other of which always seemed to be cyclically in or out of fashion. Team teaching was seen immediately as threatening to the stated goals of established groups. The idea of hierarchy of personnel runs counter to the monolithic character of the teaching profession and was attacked by both the NEA and the AFT. The idea of children being exposed to a team of teachers shocks some exponents of the self-contained classroom who support the strange notion that children need two adults at home but can stand only one at a time in a school.

Team teaching is for educational practice what a broadly comprehensive new construct pertaining, say, to the acquisition of knowledge might be for educational science. But, according to Dewey, we will not find such constructs in speculation alone, nor in other disciplines. We will find them in the context of educational practice. Team teaching, like a few other unshackling innovations, confounds current stable researchers, introduces possibilities for developing new long-term syntactical structures, and promises to redirect stable inquiry. For example, the concept of team teaching includes so many variables in the teaching-learning environment that most of the studies comparing departmentalized and self-contained classes, so religiously reported in our encyclopedic reviews of the literature, are revealed to rest in the context of a differing conception of "school." Its potential flexibility provides new possibilities for both innovative and classical approaches to studies of, for example, sex, age differences, group structure, and socialization factors in learning, to say nothing of more direct studies of educational efficiency.

Looking into the future of educational practice, team teaching opens up the school to further innovation: in school building design, personnel utilization, teacher education, programmed instruction, educational guidance, and computer use. These, in turn, challenge the established long-term syntax of educational research. Studies into man-machine relations in education, for example, with all the theoretical-deductive and empirical-inductive relations involved, are facilitated in environments where humans learning to differentiate their teaching functions are ready to further differentiate with machines in the instructional partnership.

Scholarly research and discourse into the effectiveness of established team teaching models derive their relevance from the relevance of the criterion measures used. But even when initial research on relevant criteria shows no gain or perhaps even a loss, the decision as to whether to continue, discontinue, or even to propagate team teaching is not yet dictated. A science of education promises no such easy answers to the questions of thought and action inherent in human invention and the specifics of educational practice. It promises, rather, to raise the level of practical wisdom—the level of intelligence, if you will—with respect to the conduct of education.

RESEARCH

Any innovation that upsets stable educational practice presents new research problems and, therefore, fresh opportunities for advancing education as a science. Dewey has pointed out that educational science cannot be constructed simply by borrowing the techniques of experiment and measurement from sciences already established. When the practice of education is not being reconstructed, however, it is somehow easier to rest within the blissful security of borrowed techniques, especially if the lending discipline is a prestigious one.

But unless, as researchers, we are aware of the clash of fluid practice with conventional ways, we tend not to reexamine our stable researches, proceeding quite unaware of the anachronisms which could be involved. The advancement of education suffers accordingly. The sadly ironic part of it all is that we remain unaware of the possibility of playing in the wrong ball park. And if journals continue to publish our output and colleagues to reward our efforts, we may remain quite ignorant of the irrelevance of what we continue to do.

An innovation promising to upset traditional ways often is complex, if only because it proceeds from different, unfamiliar assumptions. Further, it rarely appears full-blown. An innovation in thought does not retain any credence for long unless implemented in some form somewhere, even if in name only. The inventor, almost in spite of himself, becomes involved too early in the political-rhetorical demands of his calling before his conceptual model is fleshed out. And conceptual work often is misdirected early by the harsh tests of practicability, the demands of relevance. Perhaps this is as it should be, but the researcher had better be aware and beware. He simply must not trust what is claimed in practice. There may be no relation between the innovative practice and the innovative concept this practice is supposed to reflect. In fact, on looking closely, the researcher may find no innovation at all but simply old ways under new labels. There is little point in studying the nature or effects of what is not there—in studying nonevents.

As an example, I turn to nongrading, an innovation with which I have had a romantic attachment for some time. More than twenty years ago, after several years of teaching incarcerated delinquent boys, I began to question whether the high nonpromotion rates among them achieved what presumably had been intended. Doctoral studies brought me to research which strengthened these suspicions and to a study of my own. My findings were statistically significant, coming out clearly in favor of promoting rather than retaining slow-learning first-grade children. But these findings, even when added to parallel findings in other aspects of pupil progress, brought me no comfort. Detailed analysis of the data on individuals revealed that the experiences of some children in the favored promoted group left much to be desired, highly significant group superiority notwithstanding. And so, with empirical-inductive work behind me, new theoretical-deductive inquiries began.

These inquiries led me to a substantial body of knowledge about individual differences which, in turn, led me to question grade standards and expectancies as adequate for describing, encompassing, or evaluating the pupil activities of a class. My habitat—the University of Chicago—brought me together with Robert H. Anderson and to a plan called "the ungraded primary," established in some Milwaukee schools in 1939. A few years later, I wrote an article entitled, "To Promote or Not to Promote?" questioning not so much the efficacy of nonpromotion as a long-established practice of adjusting the child to the graded mechanism but, rather, the viability of the graded school itself, which poses only unsatisfactory alternatives of pupil progress.[17] Ten years later, a nongraded alternative was in full bloom under my direction at the University Elementary School, UCLA.

But what happened during the intervening decade and subsequently is highly relevant to discussions of research on innovations. In 1957, I made a grave mistake in judgment and, in 1959, Anderson and I compounded it. In first an article,[18] and then a book,[19] the terms "nongrading" and "reading levels" were inadvertently associated with each other. We used "nongrading" to imply little more than the absence of grade levels, coining it deliberately so as to avoid the use of "ungraded" which was being applied to practices which did not fit our budding conceptual model. The use of reading levels rather than grade levels as a basis for determining pupil assignments and progress in reading had a certain appeal because the practice suggested criterion-referenced standards rather than norm-referenced standards,[20] a condition that is now essential to my model of nongrading.

I completely overlooked the tendency of teachers in the primary grades to use reading measures as a basis for clustering pupils and the cyclical return of "homogeneous" class-to-class grouping as the assumed panacea in seeking to organize schools horizontally. I should have known better, since I have lived most of my career close to these problems in practice and in the literature. I failed to predict that teachers and administrators would reach eagerly for the catchy innovative label and that nongrading soon would be used to describe pitifully tired old practices of interclass achievement grouping.

And it should have dawned on me that many researchers, subsequently comparing graded and "nongraded" schools, would fail to realize that nongrading is a vertical, not a horizontal, pattern of school organization and, therefore, has nothing to do with conventional practices of homogeneous interclass grouping. But this theoretical-deductive error is more to be expected among stable inquirers than the empirical one of failing to identify genuine alternatives before seeking to differentiate the effects of compared alternatives. As a consequence of both kinds of errors in inquiry which, in turn, reflect similar misconceptions in practice, we are beginning to get a literature of research on "nongrading" that unfortunately advances neither educational practice nor educational science.

The first pitfall to avoid then, in studying innovations, is the assumption that what is claimed in practice is, indeed, a reasonably accurate working model of the innovation being proclaimed. Carbone, for example, compared pupils in several graded and "ungraded" schools.[21] Then, almost as afterthought, he visited the schools which had been selected initially on the basis of label. The only broad differentiation in practice which he was able to identify was a greater use of ability and achievement grouping in the so-called ungraded classes. Clearly, Carbone compared two groups of graded schools, one group of which practiced more homogeneous grouping in the name of ungrading. But there were no differences in vertical organization; there were no nongraded schools in the sample. Carbone had the good sense to point out that the schools were different but not in what they claimed to be. His study was really another in the long series on homogeneous grouping. His contribution was in the form of a by-product, a warning to the unwary.

The second pitfall to avoid in studying innovations is the assumption that a new label automatically implies new practices. Hopkins, Aldridge, and Williamson studied twenty ungraded and twenty-five graded classes, finding no differences between pupil groups.[22] Without a conceptual or descriptive definition of nongrading and a check for congruence in practice, however, there is no way of knowing how or whether the two groups of classes differed in concept and practice. There is a hint in the statement, ". . . the ungraded program tended to cluster the leaders more," that these "ungraded" classes, like Carbone's, were grouped homogeneously. Apart from this, we know only that some classes carried the ungraded label. If label were the only thing changed, however, we could not expect to find differences between pupil groups.[23]

The ironic sequel to this study is that, following it, school personnel decided to return to the conventional graded organization! They returned to what they may never have left, not knowing that what they had sought they never achieved. Shall we go around again?

Researchers simply must take cognizance of the fact that innovators are not always diligent in building conceptual models of their thought patterns. In fact, as stated earlier, the conceptual models of educational innovators have little chance to mature prior to the introduction of operational models in practice. Researchers must remember, too, that educational practices are primitive and pragmatic, rarely reflecting conceptual models even when available and when faithful reflection in practice of such models is claimed. Researchers must take any such claims with a grain of salt, coming to realize that labels can cover anything or nothing. There is enormous slippage from conception to implementation of most educational ideas. When one inquires, then, into the effects of an innovation, he frequently knows not what he studies, especially if he does not bother to examine it.

The implications of these observations for appraising educational innovation and for advancing educational science should be reasonably clear. But let me make one of them explicit. A seminal innovation is countervailing in concept. Implemented, it is countervailing also in practice. The researcher simply cannot go in with his stable research—his conventional criteria, his time-worn measures—and expect to contribute to the advancement of educational practice and science. By doing so, he endangers both.

No, he must come to grips with the conceptual underpinnings of the innovation, the fluid inquiry underlying practice. For it is in the countervailing implications of new practice that many fresh research insights will be gained, new methodologies will be forged, and fluid inquiry will be nurtured. The leaders in this long-term educational syntax will be model builders who create and manipulate abstract constructs and who adduce to them the characteristics causing one model to differ significantly from another.

It is in this adductive thinking that the theoretical-deductive and the empirical-inductive modes of thought are merged so as to constitute a unique and, in its ultimate form, a unified mode of thought. The fluid inquirer thus builds his mental model, a model which reflects both theory and practice but is neither. The mental model stimulates and is stimulated by the simulated model, an interplay now facilitated by availability of the computer. This kind of model development places us in a position to test the true nature of supposed or inferred relations—the congruence of conceptual and operational models—and to engage meaningfully in empirical research. Without such models and the careful checking of congruences, research on innovation is virtually meaningless.

FINIS

Educational science has not yet come of age. If it can be said that 95 percent of all the scientists ever born are still living, similarly it can be said, with equal confidence, that 99 percent of the educational researchers who have ever lived are still living. But I do not believe that increased age alone will mature the field or its members. There must be several corollary conditions—and I go out almost where I came in.

First, we must deliberately redesign our institutional, associational, and research structures so as literally to force an interplay of the theoretical-deductive and empirical-inductive modes of thought. Second, much of this interplay is assured when our inquiries begin and end in the stuff of educational practice. Third, we must fashion our research designs both in the quiet recesses of our minds and in the turbulence of changing practice, especially innovative practice. Fourth, we must come to understand that advancing long-term educational syntax calls for a kind of fluid intellectual movement from mental to simulated to operational models and back again. Fifth, short-term inquirers, although they need not be model builders, must be aware of the need to check the fit and the parallel with respect to conceptual and operational models lest their research be barren. Clearly, the new research in which the stable researcher will engage calls for close collaboration with the conceptually oriented activist and the forward-looking practitioner.

Sixth, we can and should expect of educational science an increasingly positive influence on the level of intelligence used in conducting the educational enterprise. An aspect of this intelligence is found in not expecting of research findings easy "yes" or "no" answers to the viability of complex educational innovations which, by their very nature, need time for refinement and seasoning. In this regard, we have much to gain from the history of relations between data, decisions, and human progress. It is sometimes useful to remember that the train lost its first race with the horse.

Notes

[1]James B. Conant, *Two Modes of Thought*, Trident Press, New York, 1964.
 [2]Ibid., p. 2.
 [3]Ibid., pp. 30–31.
 [4]Ibid., pp. 92–95.
 [5]John Dewey, *The Sources of a Science of Education*, Horace Liveright, New York, 1929.

[6]Ibid., pp. 23–24.

[7]Ibid., pp. 54–55, 56.

[8]Ibid., pp. 26–27.

[9]Ibid., pp. 33–34.

[10]Ibid., pp. 43–44.

[11]Joseph J. Schwab, "The Structure of the Natural Sciences," in G. W. Ford and Lawrence Pugno (eds.), *The Structure of Knowledge and the Curriculum*, Rand McNally, Chicago, 1964, pp. 31–49.

[12]Ibid., p. 39.

[13]Ibid., pp. 41–42.

[14]Ibid., p. 43.

[15]Had Cronbach chosen to formulate his position carefully and to publish it in, say, *Phi Delta Kappan*, his words would have had some effect, since he is a legitimatizing figure in American education. However, his view was only an aside in a letter of counsel to Ole Sand, then directing the NEA's Project on Instruction (ca. 1962). As author of one of the Project's volumes, I used his helpful comments but chose to ignore the remark on team teaching.

[16]A team teaching plan closely approximating in rationale and design the one we discussed that day had been formulated several years before by Francis S. Chase who was a key participant in the New York meeting. See Francis S. Chase, "More and Better Teachers," *Saturday Review*, September 12, 1953, pp. 16–17.

[17]John I. Goodlad, "To Promote or Not to Promote?" *Childhood Education*, vol. 30, January 1954, pp. 212–215.

[18]John I. Goodlad and others, "Reading Levels Replace Grades in the Nongraded Plan," *Elementary School Journal*, vol. 57, February 1957, pp. 253–256.

[19]John I. Goodlad and Robert H. Anderson, *The Nongraded Elementary School*, revised edition, Harcourt, Brace and World, New York, 1963.

[20]For an excellent discussion of the significant differences between the two, see Robert Glaser, "The Design of Instruction," *The Changing American School*, Sixty-fifth Yearbook of the National Society for the Study of Education, University of Chicago Press, Chicago, 1966, pp. 239–240.

[21]Robert F. Carbone, "Achievement, Mental Health, and Instruction in Graded and Ungraded Elementary Schools," unpublished doctoral dissertation, University of Chicago, 1961.

[22]Kenneth D. Hopkins, O. A. Aldridge, and Malcolm L. Williamson, "An Empirical Comparison of Pupil Achievement and Other Variables in Graded and Ungraded Classes," *American Educational Research Journal*, vol. 2, November 1965, pp. 207–215.

[23]For an excellent treatment of this and other problems in nongrading and in research on nongrading, see William P. McLoughlin, *The Nongraded School, A Critical Assessment*, University of the State of New York, State Education Department, Office of Research and Evaluation, Albany, 1967.

15

Educational cAlternatives

The following chapter is adapted from Chapters 1 and 11 of
The Conventional and the Alternative in Education. Goodlad
first lays out a typology of alternatives that can be developed
in education. Then he draws out the implications of these
alternatives and presents several scenarios for a future in
which education and schooling have become one. [Editor]

Education is a process through which behavior—ways of thinking, feeling, and acting—changes or is modified over time. (Some would say that feeling is a special kind of thinking, but we shall not join this issue here.) Definitions almost invariably stress growth or expansion, processes requiring time. Consequently, any discussion of education must encompass the formulation of characteristic or dispositional behavior and the circumstances most likely to produce it. A formal curriculum or course of study may or may not be a part of the learning environment.

Usually, the educative process simply modifies emerging characteristics, but sometimes it completely replaces established ways of

SOURCE: John I. Goodlad, Chapter 1, "A Typology of Educational Alternatives," and Chapter 11, "Transition: Toward Alternatives," in John I. Goodlad et al., *The Conventional and the Alternative in Education*, McCutchan, Berkeley, California, 1975, pp. 3–27 and pp. 241–268.

behaving or adds new behaviors to the existing array. There are, potentially, so many ways of behaving and of changing behavior that alternative ends and means for education are virtually limitless. For the welfare of individuals and humankind, it would appear desirable to keep the options open. When access to options people see as desirable, for whatever reasons, begins to close down too tightly, the drive to keep options open tends to intensify. Sometimes, new alternatives open up in the process. However, most efforts to create alternatives are post hoc responses to the perception that freedom of choice has become restricted.

Of course, the matter of access is not the only issue in considering educational alternatives. There is also the issue of whether existing alternatives are relevant to the needs and interests of the people. And then there is the question of efficiency, especially relative costs. Many recent innovations in schools of the United States, for example, have little relevance for developing countries either because they are too expensive to maintain or because they are not addressed to educating more people at less cost.[1]

FREEDOM IS THE ISSUE

This paper focuses primarily on the issue of retention, restoration, or expansion of individual freedom to learn. Much of the recent rhetoric on openness, free schools, no schools, and the like takes this issue as its theme, which is understandable in the light of the extent to which most schools seriously limit the options and perpetuate certain inequities of a class-oriented society. Paul Goodman, John Holt, Edgar Friedenberg, Jonathan Kozol, Ivan Illich, and others have spoken eloquently to these realities. (Their names and their works are now too well known to require references.) In effect, they have given us new glasses with which we are able to see at least a little way through the cultural smog surrounding us.

In another context, Norman Cousins has stated, "Human societies have gone into decline not because people were indifferent to dangers but because they were oblivious to signs."[2] The erosion or limitation of personal freedom in education appears to bear a rather direct relation to the requirement that large numbers of people learn what others have decided will be good for them and that the majority accepts this situation as desirable or, at least, is resigned to it. The so-called romantic and radical reformers see educational institutions as embodying this combination of conditions and as villainous accomplices in a continuing restriction of educational freedom—and, in fact, of freedom defined more broadly. Most are impatient with educational alternatives conceived only as better ways for schools at all levels to perform a narrow range of traditional functions and, when pushed philosophically, accept as legitimate only those processes and resources that help people learn what they want to find out.[3] Since the discussion of alternatives today includes reconstruction of the schools as well as their elimination, this paper deals with both classes of alternatives in education.

Any consideration of individual freedom is dangerously incomplete, however, unless one is very careful to include the matter of collective freedom—the rights and welfare of peers, the aged, the unborn, neighbors, neighborhoods, fellow citizens, communities, the globe, humankind. Futurists have serious doubts about the welfare of all these and, therefore, of the individual if the future is not planned or, if you will, shaped. And, if the future is to be shaped, does this not mean that the individual must help shape it and in the process be shaped by it? Does this, in turn, imply that the welfare of the individual must be subjected to the welfare of all and, therefore, probably to a considerable degree to the direction of "leaders?" And that preparation for the future necessitates an early stage of life being instrumental to a later, the child a disciplined platonic father to the man? Or is some kind of balance possible, a house with many mansions here on earth, with open access to the house and all its mansions and human processes within mansions fully conducive to individual freedom and dignity?

Our Utopia seems to become, then, a learning society supporting learning individuals. Hutchins defines it as one that had transformed

> . . . its values in such a way that learning, fulfillment, becoming human, had become its aims *and all its institutions were directed to this end.* This is what the Athenians did. . . . They made their society one designed to bring all its members to the fullest development of their highest powers. . . . Education was not a segregated activity, conducted for certain hours, in certain places, at a certain time of life. It was the aim of the society. . . . The Athenian was educated by the culture.[4]

One has little difficulty in placing much contemporary concern for alternatives in education within Hutchins' concept of the learning society. It embraces at once concern both for what goes on as institutions seek to fulfill the educational functions assumed by them and what should go on in a society concerned with education as a way of life. The concept opens up the search for alternatives in education as being more important than the search for alternative modes of travel, heating, and entertainment. It even opens up the search, through educational processes, for alternative images of humankind, such as man as part of an ecological system rather than as exploiter of an ecological system from which he is somehow detached.[5]

Another possibility is an evolutionary transformational process which is not a linear extrapolation from existing societal trends—about which Toffler warns us in *Future Shock*[6]—but which could represent a marked departure from them (as Toffler suggests for survival and growth). Hutchins' concept suggests that doing better what we are now doing in schools falls far short of the mark. It also brings to mind the old cliché that education is too important to leave to the educators—at least those now caught up in Ichabod Crane roles as keepers of America's schools. Such a concept also reminds us, soberly, of how threatening education properly conceived is to those in our midst who would keep educators stereotyped as Ichabod Crane. More than the educators, they know the power of education and are aware, intuitively perhaps, that it is, properly conducted, the most powerful tool for democratization ever conceived.

The central educational issues in providing alternatives can be subsumed under two classical questions: (1) For what shall we educate? and (2) How shall we educate? The significance of both has been at least implicit in the foregoing. Before proceeding to a kind of typology of alternatives in education, however, a further word on the how is in order.

The issue is a moral one. I have assumed that attainment of a learning society requires the commitment of a substantial number of citizens to it who understand and value it and are fully aware of its importance to their own individuality and the welfare of humankind. Presumably, there has been in their own development a process of transcending self to embrace others and of transcending society to become autonomous. Presumably, such dual-transcendence is both learnable and educable. Is a philosophy of learning adequate that embraces as legitimate only those processes and resources that help people learn what they want to find out? Are there phases of life during which such transcendence is more easily achieved? Is it fair to the individual not to intervene at such times, even when he or she senses no need for such learning and no awareness of its significance?

Regarding the morality of anyone trying to do anything to anyone else in the name of education (that is, to educate), my position is that both learning and being educated are necessary at this point in time—and into an indefinite but not necessarily infinite future. I am not ruling out the possibility of a learning society bringing ". . . all of its members to the fullest development of their highest powers." But that society is not yet here. To deprive one of "being taught," therefore, may be as immoral as to impose one's will on another. In effect, I accept education as a moral alternative and, as a consequence, method has a great deal to do with it and alternative ends and means become exceedingly important.

With Frankena, I rule out one common set of alternatives: indoctrination or

> the use of example, habituation, suggestion, exhortation, propaganda, and sanctions like blame and punishment in such a way as to inculcate certain rules or virtues and with the purpose of insuring behavior in conformity with them, not of preparing the way for reflection and spiritual freedom.[7]

With Frankena, I endorse "a more properly educational way" of

> promoting the achievement of reflective, personal autonomy, self-government, or spiritual freedom, even if this leads the individual to criticize prevailing ideals, principles, or rules (in a way, this aim has two parts: autonomy and reflectiveness).[8]

I accept education as a moral alternative and regard alternatives in education, both ends and means, as a priceless freedom.

OPTIONS

In education, there appear to be four classifications of practice and potential practice:

1. common ends and common means
2. common ends and alternative means
3. alternative ends and alternative means
4. self-selected open ends and means, including the freedom of not deliberately choosing

The total array of educational resources and decisions, in turn, may be classified as *instructional* (tutors, teachers, books, responsive machines, etc.), *institutional* (institutions with education designated as primary function), and *societal* (aspects of living having potential for serving an educational function).[9] This kind of classification gets us around the problem of drawing a line between schooling and education, since education is a process and a function which can go on at many times, in many ways, and in many places, including schools. It also helps us around some invidious problems of stereotyping and judging by association. Thus, teachers in public schools are, by some strange processes of stereotyping, less humane than teachers in private homes or teachers in ski schools. Similarly, schools are malignant but homes and job-related educational activities are benign—the high incidence of parents beating and mutilating their children and the need for child labor laws notwithstanding. These are matters frequently passed over far too lightly by some of our romantic reformers.

If one opts truly for openness in regard to alternatives,[10] the two-dimensional grid implied above takes us somewhat away from popular either/or distinctions, as well as away from the error, noted above, of mistaking, for example, "free" schools as necessarily and logically more humane than the little red schoolhouse of yesterday or P.S. 2002.

Figure 4 presents the grid, with the cells a *tabula rasa*. Filling them in is a task of monumental proportions going far beyond the dimensions of this paper. Literally dozens of items could go in most of the cells except those under "common ends, common means." The possibilities for varying the what, who, where, how, and when of education are virtually limitless. Even when the educational system promulgates a single set of ends and means, societal decisions as to *who* is to be educated *when* sharply restrict or considerably expand the options. In developed countries, the vastly greater expenditures per student for tertiary over primary education represent an interesting value choice. Pervading alternatives of substance, place, and time are the philosophical aspects of *how*.

Alternative Groupings of Alternatives in Education	Instructional	Institutional	Societal
1. Common Ends Common Means			
2. Common Ends Alternative Means			
3. Alternative Ends Alternative Means			
4. Self-Selected, Open Ends and Means			

Figure 4. Two-Dimensional Grid for Classifying Educational Alternatives.

There are proper and improper educational means in the human sense. Schools that foster or permit the tyranny of older children over the younger have lost their way, whether or not "free," just as surely have schools whose mechanistic straight-line reinforcement techniques contribute equally to cheating and attainment of reading skills, whatever their results in achievement scores. Similarly, the teaching of literature is no more humane than the teaching of physics simply because one is classified under the humanities and the other under the natural sciences.

Common Ends, Common Means

One cannot speak of common means except in an approximate or relative sense; there is no such thing. In a society committed to the inculcation of cultural imperatives in the young, even prodigious efforts to specify substance and praxis (there are countries with syllabi spelling out in detail precisely how daily instruction is to be conducted) are modified, distorted, and changed by vagaries of pupil mix and teacher personality. This is so even with the tribal functionary and the group of boys he inducts into the privileges and responsibilities of manhood.

The alternatives built into a common ends/common means concept of education tend to be of an either/or sort. In the classroom, there are pass/fail marks (or more differentiated systems such as A, B, C, D, E or F) and promote/nonpromote decisions with respect to moving through the system. For the institution as a whole, it is "out" or "in," with this decision often made early, followed by a waiting game until 14, 15, or 16 (depending on school-leaving laws). For society as a whole, the alternatives are the determination of when to begin (usually with more alternatives for the affluent), when to leave, and a sorting process regarding eligibility for subsequent noncompulsory segments of secondary and tertiary education. Motivation for going on is maintained by requiring educational credentials for entry into the economic system.

The maintenance of a system of schooling with such limited alternatives, many of them punitive, seems to require a good deal of accompanying baggage directed to rationalization, justification, and legitimatization. Testing systems develop and external examinations hang on long after considerable opposition to them has developed. These frequently are used as weapons against innovation. When an innovation is suggested, there is a sudden interest in what research (based on test results) has to say about it, even before it has been tried. But there is a corresponding lack of interest in research questioning the system: for example, research on the effects of failing marks or nonpromotion. The dissemination of such research is offset by increasing the rhetoric regarding the dangers of "soft" education and the need to protect a common cultural heritage (even when it is by no means common!). In effect, when the system is threatened, the ceremonial rain dances pick up speed.

Common Ends, Alternative Means

Most efforts at educational reform in this century, especially during the past two decades, have been directed toward finding alternative (hopefully, better) ways of achieving a set of educational aims deemed essential for all. Proposals have far exceeded trials or implementation in practice. The literature on these alternatives is so extensive and so well known to most readers of educational journals that there is no point in citing sample references. Likewise, most of the ideas and forms are sufficiently well known to negate the need for definition and description.

Instructional alternatives include programmed instruction through books, nonresponsive machines, and responsive machines such as computerized television consoles; pedagogical approaches such as problem-solving techniques, small-group instruction, individual pupil diagnosis and prescription, and multimedia presentations; and an array of individualized alternatives for pupils requiring very little or no teacher intervention. Institutional alternatives include simultaneous operation of several distinctly different models of curriculum organization (single-subject structures, integrated subjects, activity oriented to student interests); introduction of multigrade, multiage, and nongraded patterns of school organization; varying ways of grouping pupils and/or teachers, including team teaching; use of modular scheduling or less complicated variations in length of class periods, timing of recess and lunch periods. Societal and systemwide alternatives have included experimentation with greater decentralization of authority and resources; creation of out-of-school activities; performance contracts with educational consulting firms; and even so-called alternative schools freed of systemwide requirements regarding means.

All these fit into one or more of just a few basic kinds of manipulations: varying time available for learning (by mastery learning and nongrading, for example), varying place (leaving the school for some educational purposes), varying pupil mix (pupil grouping), varying teachers (team teaching), varying external restraints (decentralization), varying approach or style of learning (changing teaching methods). Many of these have now become rather standard ways of proceeding. Several have become *the* standard way in some schools, thrusting aside what was there before and thus replacing monolithic practice with monolithic practice. Those innovations which have been most successful in gaining acceptance are the ones representing only minor deviations from long-established practices or those most readily modified and homo-genized so as to be palatable. The most acceptable innovations are those requiring little or no modification in teacher and adminis-trator behavior. In effect, they are not changes at all. Nothing changes but the appearance of change.[11] Very often, the innovation as conceived is powerful enough, but its significant elements are lost in a process of smoothing out the potentially indigestible lumps—a process of immaculate adoption. As one superintendent remarked to principals and teachers, "Innovate all you want, but don't change anything."

The desirability, validity, and morality of unresearched alterna-tives are as relevant to this discussion as to the previous one regarding common ends and means. Is not the absence of research support here as much of an indictment as its absence in the previous discussion? The answer is no. In order to secure relevant data on the relative effects of alternatives, we need alternatives. These need care and feeding until they are strong enough to warrant compari-son—and then on criteria relevant to both the new and the old. (Usually, the new must stand the test of criteria relevant only to the old.) What I object to is legislative or administrative fiat designed to legitimatize one practice over another as though there were, indeed, unequivocal evidence to support it.

The promulgation of unproven alternatives can be defended if their use is not required by law or by various mechanisms designed to punish for nonconformity or to reward for conformity. We are back to our concerns for freedom again. It is one thing to insist on single practices for teachers when there is powerful evidence for them; quite another to prescribe by law or protect by fiat when no such evidence exists. In a field of human endeavor lacking such evidence in almost all areas, it is the better part of wisdom to create alternatives, publish their strengths and weaknesses for various purposes, and encourage teachers to use whatever seems to work best under the circumstances. Teachers, like other human beings, tend to respond positively to such a challenge, especially when there are nonthreatening opportunities to learn, to exchange ideas with colleagues, and to advance professionally as a result.[12] Encouraging the use of alternatives should be accompanied, of course, by sustained research on their effects in both experimentally controlled and field situations far in excess of anything we have known to date.

In spite of the rather exciting spate of proposed reforms in curriculum, organization, and instruction, the common ends/ common means orientation to formal education hangs on tenaciously. Maintaining this system of education protects many elements of stratification and segregation in our society. Planned change is, at best, difficult. But when problems of logistics are complicated by the implication of consequences for those who threaten what exists, which is always the case, effecting change becomes no way of life for the inept or faint-of-heart.

Alternative Ends, Alternative Means

Although the implementation of alternative means regarding the what, how, where, who, and when of education has been disappointing, the importance of and need for innovation are broadly accepted. The moment one introduces the concept of alternative ends, however, debate quickens. Fears range from concern that "the tools of the human race" will not be taught to apprehension about the promulgation of ideologies threatening to "the national interest." Much of the controversy centers on how much choice should be available to individuals at various stages in the educational or life cycle.

In current practice, the picture of educational freedom resembles an inverted triangle, narrow or limited at the bottom and broadening as one progresses upward in time. Generally, the goals are common for all at the primary level; one may explore a few options at the secondary level; and selection of scientific, aesthetic, or literary goals is more or less open at the tertiary level. This is not a steady, even progression, however. In general, kindergartens offer more alternatives than the second grade;[13] for most students, the senior year in high school is more open than the freshman year of college; and, although choice of a profession is open to many college graduates, professional education itself is usually sharply prescribed. Nonetheless, the system operates on the general assumption that increasing freedom of choice is a right earned through earlier mastery of a narrow range of core goals.

Regarding these core goals, Hutchins says the following:

> The barbarism, "communication skills," is the contemporary jargon for reading, writing, figuring, speaking, and listening—arts that appear to have permanent relevance. . . . They are the indispensable means to learning anything. They have to be learned if the individual hopes to expand his individuality, or if he proposes to become a self-governing member of a self-governing community. Learning these arts cannot be left to the choices of children or their parents.[14]

This view is a far cry from that of viewing as legitimate only those processes and resources that help people learn what they want to find out. Hutchins articulates the most common position regarding the role of schools found in this country and throughout the world.

In general, the drive for alternatives with respect to goals has had two foci: balance or emphasis and timing or placement. Today, virtually any listing of goals for American education would be encompassed by the following categories: intellectual development, enculturation, interpersonal relations, personal autonomy, citizenship, creativity, aesthetic perception, self-concept, emotional well-being, physical health, and moral and ethical character. Free schools, alternative schools, and the like are created, frequently, because people perceive regular public schools as neglecting or underemphasizing several of these.

A great deal of controversy surrounds the question as to whether some of these categories are more important for one stage of personal growth than others; whether there is greater psychological readiness at one stage rather than another and, consequently, a potentially compatible fit between teaching and learning; and whether it would be more appropriate and/or efficient to emphasize a few goals at a time rather than this whole range of commitment but still touch on all of them within a year or two. Such innovations as modular scheduling, single courses taught in great depth and breadth over a semester, and "schools within schools" in which students enroll for exclusive work in a field or cluster of fields for several months or even longer are directed at this last concern. Regarding the second, Hunt and others have argued for early intervention in the cognitive development of children, especially when a disadvantaged milieu is likely to cause retardation.[15] Thinking of this kind has resulted in a recent "educational discovery" of the young child.[16]

In regard to balance and emphasis, I have been developing a "phases" concept of schooling in which nongraded phases of from two to four years in length overlap each other in a series of progressions from early childhood through all the years of formal schooling.[17] Each phase has dominant or priority functions to be emphasized, each function derived from assumptions about the nature of the developmental/environmental interface and its implications for educational ends and means. For a decade, the University Elementary School faculty at UCLA has sought to define and conduct such a phase-oriented program.

Self-Selected, Open Ends and Means

Even though educational programs based on the common ends, common means approach differ markedly from models providing differential selection of ends and means, all seem to be on a continuum from rigidity to increasing flexibility. Regardless of where a program fits on this continuum, however, it appears to retain certain conventions. We hang on to the conception of school as a place, for example, and of education being something that takes place in school buildings during certain hours. In the United States, at least, even career education generally is pursued inside school when it probably could take place better in other work places. The self-selection of ends and means appears to break with this continuum, however, and to be in the realm of more radical alternatives.

Some educational innovators would argue that self-selection is an option in some of the alternatives already mentioned. The response to this observation depends on what one means by self-selection. Admittedly, many open and alternative schools allow and even encourage pupil choice among alternatives. But, except in very rare instances, there remains a set of implied norms with respect to choice. For example, when a teacher says, "What shall we do today?" the intended options are drawing, dancing, reading, story-telling or perhaps hunting for insect creatures in fields or ponds. If there were, indeed, no restrictions regarding choice, then self-selection (within the general option of school) would be operating. But most advocates of self-selection do have a set of norms in mind, norms internalized by children at an early age. Even in the schools so much lauded by reformers—namely, the British Infant Schools— the available range of alternatives quickly becomes apparent and one is seldom surprised by radical departures. Eisner reports an absence of group discussion and planning in the schools he visited.[18]

True self-selection of goals as well as means demands societal and institutional alternatives going far beyond the largely instructional freedom so commonly recommended by reformers in recent years. The voucher system, for example, appearing to provide maximum freedom of choice to parents and their children, offers choice only among places still bound by the conventions of schooling referred to above—and this choice, in turn, is sharply defined geographically for most people. A major argument for the voucher system is that it will encourage innovation through free enterprise. There is little or no evidence to support this assumption for education, and one must even question its validity for aspects of business and industry. Witness, for example, the rigidity of the automobile industry in this country. Our private schools are not markedly deviant. Private nursery schools are about as free of outside controls as one could conceive schools to be and yet they resemble each other and public nursery schools very closely.[19]

We will approach a situation of true self-selection when one may choose among options (which might or might not include schools) whether or not they offer a core of "cultural essentials." This means that school in any form no longer would be compulsory. Likewise, none of the options would be supported by special sets of coercive contingencies. Such a situation must not be confused with freedom, however, because the available range of options still might not parallel the range of human needs and interests though, presumably, society would move toward such a fit.

It is now useful to return to the grid (Figure 4) in order to provide a summary of the preceding discussion regarding ends and means. Figure 5 provides such a summation, with several examples in each cell. This typology is very arbitrary, admittedly. The distinction between institutional and societal is not always precise, for instance, but this is largely because there is not in our society any clear-cut delineation as to what should be left to local institutional autonomy and what decisions should be retained by centralized controlling agencies.[20] Likewise, an innovation such as nongrading could be placed in three of the four institutional cells. Consequently, any given cell should not be regarded as necessarily fully discrete from all the others.

Further, it could be argued that the alternatives suggested for the common ends, common means category belong under common ends, alternative means since no alternatives whatsoever are possible under the former. But this strict interpretation destroys the approximate intent of the analysis. Its purpose is to suggest a flow from utmost rigidity to utmost freedom in a learning society as one moves downward on the chart.

The bottom right-hand cell depicts both the widest array of alternatives and the Utopian ideal of the individual's drive for knowledge and skills being satisfied within the framework of a learning society. Within this cell or extrapolated from it to the right and off the chart lie an indeterminate number of educational possibilities. A rich array for all other cells already exists or at least has been envisioned by someone. Although examples in the bottom row are hard to come by in practice, they can be described. Summerhill fits the description of the middle cell, for example.

It appears, then, that we are not hard up for alternatives to the conventional in education. Although the search for the new and, one would hope, better will continue to be challenging, it recently has diminished sharply and will maintain a lower profile for some years to come. The challenge is to make what already is envisioned more widespread, to accelerate the pace of change.

ALTERNATIVE SCENARIOS FOR ALTERNATIVE EDUCATION

Space limitations prevent my entering upon the intriguing path of endeavoring to conceptualize a variety of ways in which the structures, contents, and processes of reconstructed schools might differ from the conventional ones we know. The purpose here, rather, is simply to sketch two somewhat different scenarios for a combination of schools and other educational options we could have in a relatively near future, let us say, circa 2000. All the components have been described elsewhere; they need to be put together in systemic form.

One scenario suggests a comprehensive role for a much-changed and extended school. Essentially, school becomes a concept rather

Alternative Groupings of Alternatives in Education	Instructional	Institutional	Societal
1. Common Ends Common Means	intra-class ability and achievement grouping; promotion or nonpromotion; marking systems	inter-class ability and achievement grouping; suspension and expulsion criteria and procedures	ages for entering and leaving; matriculation requirements
2. Common Ends Alternative Means	individualized and small group instruction; variety of learning modes; programmed instruction; mastery learning	team teaching; nongrading; multiage grouping; modular scheduling; variable patterns of curriculum organization	decentralization of decision making; out-of-school options; performance contracts; alternative schools; curriculum guides suggesting varied

3. Alternative Ends Alternative Means	interest; selection from an array of individualized stimuli (e.g., programmed instruction in literature rather than math)	geared first to one set of goals and then another; schools within a school; partial voucher plans	schools; easing up of requirements for entering tertiary education or economic participation in society; public educational television
4. Self-Selected, Open Ends and Means	no required instructional program; choice of teachers and areas of emphasis (the instructional program now becomes entirely personal)	no institutional requirements; learner does or does not take advantage of it with no fear of punishment or retribution other than personal consequences	vast variety of formal and informal institutions committed fully or partially to education; school as a place might or might not be one of these; a learning society

Figure 5. A Typology of Educational Alternatives.

than a place, more or less guiding utilization of a host of settings for learning on a twenty-four-hour-per-day basis. As merely an extrapolation from the six-hour-per-day school we now have, it would be a bureaucratic monstrosity. However, stress on considerable local initiative and absence of state laws designed to legitimatize certain competing ideas rather than others would encourage open competition among views and the periodic correction of excesses. The other scenario suggests a sharply limited role for the school as just one of many institutions providing options for choice. There is no reason why, in the future, both scenarios and a variety of alternatives between them and options within them should not flourish side by side in our society. Some are more appropriate to certain communities than to others. For example, educational alternatives invoking use of a wide variety of institutions outside of schools is more easily realized in urban settings. Rural communities seem more likely to move toward the school as the center of educational, recreational, and cultural life. But in urban communities, a great deal of enlightened human engineering must occur before they will be able to provide many safe educational adjuncts to or extensions of schools.

What follows is based on the assumption that these scenarios will not result only from efforts to improve education. Rather, educational changes will follow or accompany changes in the larger society. Planners and policy makers must be convinced, however—and educational processes should play a role here—of the importance of building educational provisions into the process of environmental change. This may prove to be the most difficult and unlikely proviso in seeking to create educational alternatives.

Scenario One: The Schooled Society

One scenario, then, is for all the educational components to be encompassed by something called school. Presumably, there would be a Commissioner of Education and Culture with broad powers to guide the development and utilization of the educational possibilities inherent in all the city's resources. Many of our museums, galleries, and, indeed, in some places even libraries (although the last decade or so of enlightenment in this sector is encouraging) are custodial and archival. But in the scheme envisioned here, a significant part of their public support would depend on availability and service for educational purposes. Similar expectations would prevail for YM- and YWCA buildings, recreational halls, and the like, most of which now go unused for large portions of the day. Similarly, school buildings would be brought into twenty-four-hour use, seven days each week.

A school building would be the base of operation and the planning center in making educational provision for the surrounding community. But it would be only one of many settings used throughout the day and might very well not be the site for some students for long periods of time. The local school would have access to all the educational resources of the immediate and larger community in planning the total offerings available to the successive groups of students entering and moving through the institution. Within this framework, teams of teachers would work with groups of children enrolled in a nongraded phase of schooling embracing three or four years of time—early schooling, intermediate, and so forth.

In the earliest phase, children would tend to stay together in multiage family groupings, since the important learnings at this stage are those acquired socially: learning to get along with peers and adults, exploring and sharing things together, examining all these relationships in a search for the meaning of selfhood within the context of a group. Later, children would begin to move out from the family group to develop special interests and talents in company with individuals from other school-family groups. But there would continue to be regular return to the base group for purposes of sharing and for finding personal meaning. A child should always be able to return to where he was before without fear or embarrassment. Later, more and more time would be spent with and without other students in alternative educational settings and workplaces. School would become, indeed, a concept but not simply a place.

There are many possible alternatives within the broad scenario laid out above. The essential concept is a thoroughly schooled society, with schooling extended to encompass a wide array of alternatives but with school as a place diminished in significance. Schooling and education become more nearly synonymous than is the case today.

Scenario Two: A Restricted Concept of School

Another scenario calls for a much more sharply limited school. Again, there could be many alternative versions. One involves a combination of school as a place and a completely open voucher system by means of which one spends educational voucher coupons as one wishes. Choices are in no way monitored by a school. Certain core learnings are the responsibility of a place called school. A small child might divide time between such a place, from which he and his cohorts venture out from time to time into the larger learning society, and some kind of home environment, as is the case today. Perhaps 10 percent of the young child's nonschool, nonhome educational experiences would be "purchased" in the educational marketplace. The vouchers for this purpose would be given to each child; those receiving the vouchers in payment for educational services would turn them in to the appropriate authorities for cash derived from state and federal taxes. By the age of twelve or so, a child might be deriving 50 percent of his education through the use of such vouchers. Presumably, too, he would have arrived at some sort of agreement with his parents as to what proportion of these were spent independently of parental wishes. In essence, vouchers distributed equitably to each person would serve as coin of the realm in determining the educational diet of the individual. A family might pool vouchers (adults would have them, too) to purchase an array of lessons, plays, musical performances or whatever, stored on tape by profit-making educational companies for replay at the convenience of users via television/computer terminals.

Although I am opposed to the use of voucher plans for the creation of entire schools (which would, in the words of a strong advocate "destroy the public school system as we know it"[21]), there are interesting possibilities in the modified plan proposed here. The school becomes responsible for only core learnings rather than the entire range of educational possibilities. Much career education might be done in work settings and a good deal of personal or vocational counseling by persons or institutions with less of a vested interest in schools.

With core learnings not left solely to the jurisdiction of the home nor scattered about among an array of specialized agencies, there remains ample opportunity for dispatching those traditional interests of the state in the common weal. One needs no great insight to realize that survival in the future will call for a general drawing back from the self-destructive course on which humankind is embarked. Enlightened self-interest must extend far beyond the limited boundaries of family or communal life. In time of stress, families tend to pull the wagons into a tight circle; understanding and compassion extend not far beyond. If self-interest is to extend beyond the family, it would be folly to leave responsibility for broadening it to that entity. But perhaps the state, in its most enlightened self-interest, will come to see the need to educate for a mankind perspective as part of our common learnings.[22]

Another virtue in the combined school and voucher plan described above is allocation of the vouchers to the individual who then exercises personal preferences. Such an arrangement recognizes that long-standing duality in educational aims expressed earlier: development of the individual and the needs of the larger society. It is recognized, of course, that parents will tend to serve as proxy for the young child, but they do so as one administers a trust; ownership cannot be revoked. In a learning society, educational vouchers might well replace money in helping to develop independence and a sense of potency in the young.

There are troublesome difficulties, admittedly, with any voucher scheme. However, this one avoids some of the most obvious: the regulation of entire schools eligible for voucher payments, the establishment of a bureaucracy to establish and administer standards, and the elimination of the humanizing role of the common school—that is, the process of humanizing the essential lore of the human race for popular consumption. Also, problems of discrimination and indoctrination are somewhat lessened but by no means eliminated. The problem of what enterprises are eligible still looms large.

We are left, of course, with the challenging question of determining core learnings for each successive phase of schooling. But this is no greater and is, indeed, a lesser problem than prevails today. Rather than having to provide within the narrow confines of school a range of offerings approximating human diversity (which is impossible), as well as some approximation of what should be common to all (a concept which ends up getting short shrift), we could confront only the latter. The problem is still a tough one, but it is clear and need not become fogged up by considerations of electives, majors, or minors.

Many readers will conjure up a vision of the three R's for the school-based core learnings, but I am not at all sure that these will be the most vital selections a few years from now. These can be learned more efficiently, individually, conveniently, and with less sex bias and emotional tension via machines than through the intervention of human teachers. However, because a child's freedom to use the larger environment without them is restricted, perhaps one phase of schooling will devote part of its time to assuring that these learnings occur. Nonetheless, the central core is more likely to involve the higher literacies defined by Chase as "the ability to use relevant processes for selection of goals and activities; the ability to select and use means appropriate to learning and other goals; the capacity and the disposition to apply aesthetic and ethical criteria to the manner in which activities are performed; the capacity to respond to an increasing range of phenomena and relationships with understanding, appreciation and appropriate overt action."[23] These learnings are enhanced by interaction with others and benefit from the guidance of an adult mentor.

The central function of school, then, will be to further the search for synthesis and integration. "The essential philosophical quest is for integration—which is to say, the need to bring together rational philosophy, spiritual belief, scientific knowledge, personal experience, and direct observation into an organic whole."[24] The search for how best to provide for this integration will be a continuing one requiring that the reconstruction of schooling be a never-ending process. The learning society cannot be a static one, with all the contingencies determined, refined, and in place.

The Deschooled Society

The foregoing scenarios, with their various alternative scenes and acts, are not improbable ones for the United States and many other countries. None of the elements is new or unenvisioned. The parts simply have not been put together—and certainly the necessary reconstruction of our cities and schools has not taken place. Progression into another scenario involving no places called school, even on a reduced-time basis, is not difficult to envision, either. In fact, 10 percent school and 90 percent on vouchers for an eighteen-year-old would come very close. There is really no need, then, to take up space with a detailed description, since conceptual extrapolation from what has been described is relatively easy, although the logistics would be somewhat complicated.

However, the successive scenarios for many other countries would be quite different, the problems being less ones of deschooling than of continuing to find better ways to provide what schools seek to do. If, for example, the goal is universal literacy quickly, the construction and staffing of schools may be one of the least effective alternatives available. Attaching some form of literacy training to the workplace may be both cheaper and more efficient. The educational futures of societies not yet schooled is a subject which, unfortunately, must be eschewed here.

Deschooling in the United States and other countries with comprehensive bureaucratized educational systems is less a matter of envisioning the possibilities than of determining the desirability and feasibility, at least within this century. Regarding feasibility, the problems of logistics appear less formidable than those of habit, attitude, and convenience. Rusch, for example, experienced goodwill and almost universal cooperation in seeking to use community resources for the busload of children constituting a kind of school.[25] But whether such cooperation would prevail were hordes of young people to be turned over to workers and workplaces for their education remains a question to be answered through audacious large-scale experiments. Interestingly, Rusch found that there was a need for quiet places to read and for spaces suited to discussion, which he found in libraries and YW- or YMCA buildings. If there were not enough such places in a deschooled society, we might find ourselves once more building them and be well on our way to schooling society once again. Perhaps school is one of those things we would invent if we did not already have it.

However, the desirability of deschooling everywhere is the more troublesome issue. It may be that the most educated and most affluent segments of humankind have about run the full course in their search for developing (and indulging in) individuality, at least until we put that larger setting called the world in much better order. What is required, I think, will not be found through escape to far-off exotic places because we already have made them part of the problem. Nor will it be found in backyard gardens, although many of us may find ourselves growing them. And it certainly will not be found in the backyard bomb shelter or its equivalent, carefully stocked to maintain one family until the air clears.

Many deschoolers assign the family a large but ill-defined educational role in a deschooled society (sometimes in a manner similar to the way the Constitution delegates educational responsibility to the states), at a time when the family is in considerable disarray. It is interesting to note that many of the proponents are well-educated liberals whose ability and willingness to provide education according to the most enlightened self-interest probably are considerable. But I am worried about those whose actions constitute the largest cause of children's deaths, injuries, and neglect. And I remain distrustful of the ability of most families to educate for the common weal in the times of stress ahead that will call for a combination of self-discipline and large-scale rational planning. We must be educated to understand that each of us is part of a world ecology and to develop a considerable awareness of the consequential character of individual behavior. None of us runs the course alone, no matter how much we value and seek our autonomy.

Movement must be toward the creation of more educational opportunities and easier access to them. I would resist placing the schools in charge of options in the larger society or as gatekeeper monitoring who and how one gets to them. I must opt, for the rest of this century at least, for a schooled nation, with schools to be reconstructed at the local level, each seeking a balance between education for responsible membership in the family, local, state, and world community and education for personal fulfillment. This prospect cannot be contemplated with unbridled optimism, but contemplating other alternatives provides little satisfaction.

Notes

[1]Philip H. Coombs, *The World Educational Crisis*, Oxford University Press, New York, 1968.

[2]Norman Cousins, "Watergate and Hiroshima," *World*, vol. 2, August 28, 1973, p. 12.

[3]John Holt, "A Letter from John Holt," *National Elementary Principal*, vol. 52, 1973, pp. 43–46.

[4]Robert M. Hutchins, *The Learning Society*, Praeger, New York, 1968, pp. 134–135.

[5]Stanford Research Institute, *Changing Images of Man*, The Institute, Menlo Park, California, 1973.

[6]Alvin Toffler, *Future Shock*, Random House, New York, 1970.

[7]William K. Frankena, "Moral Education, A Philosophical View of," *The Encyclopedia of Education*, vol. 6, Macmillan, New York, 1972, p. 396.

[8]Ibid., p. 395.

[9]John I. Goodlad (with Maurice N. Richter, Jr.), *The Development of a Conceptual System for Dealing with Problems of Curriculum and Instruction*, Cooperative Research Program, USOE, Project No. 454, 1966.

[10]Robert H. Anderson, *Opting for Openness*, National Association of Elementary School Principals, Washington, D.C. 1973.

[11]Seymour B. Sarason, *The Culture of the School and the Problem of Change*, Allyn and Bacon, Boston, 1971.

[12]Mary M. Bentzen and Kenneth A. Tye, "Effecting Change in Elementary Schools," in John I. Goodlad and Harold G. Shane (eds.), *The Elementary School in the United States*, Seventy-second Yearbook of the National Society for the Study of Education, Part II, University of Chicago Press, Chicago, 1973.

[13]John I. Goodlad, M. Frances Klein, and Associates, *Looking Behind the Classroom Door*, revised edition, Charles A. Jones, Worthingon, Ohio, 1974.

[14]Robert M. Hutchins, "The Great Anti-School Campaign," in *The Great Ideas Today, 1972*, Encyclopaedia Britannica, Inc., Chicago, 1972, pp. 210–211.

[15]J. McVicker Hunt, "How Children Develop Intellectually," *Children*, vol. 11, 1964, pp. 83–91.

[16]John I. Goodlad, M. Frances Klein, Jerrold M. Novotney, and Associates, *Early Schooling in the United States*, McGraw-Hill, New York, 1973.

[17]John I. Goodlad, "The Educational Program to 1980 and Beyond," in E. L. Morphet and C. O. Ryan (eds.), *Implications for Education of Prospective Changes in Society*, Designing Education for the Future, Denver, Colorado, 1967.

[18]Elliot W. Eisner, *English Primary Schools*, Stanford University, Stanford, California, 1973.

[19]Goodlad, Klein, Novotney, and Associates, op. cit.

[20]Goodlad, with Richter, op. cit.

[21]Christopher Jencks, "Is the Public School Obsolete?" *The Public Interest*, Winter 1965.

[22]John I. Goodlad, M. Frances Klein, Jerrold M. Novotney, Kenneth A. Tye, and Associates, *Toward a Mankind School: An Adventure in Humanistic Education*, McGraw-Hill, New York, 1974.

[23]Francis S. Chase, "School Change in Perspective," in John I. Goodlad (ed.), *The Changing American School*, Sixty-fifth Yearbook of the National Society for the Study of Education, Part II, University of Chicago Press, Chicago, 1966, pp. 290–291.

[24]Norman Cousins, *The Celebration of Life*, Harper, New York, 1974, p. 2.

[25]Charles W. Rusch, "MOBOC: A Mobile Learning Environment," in Gary J. Coates (ed.), *Alternative Learning Environments*, Dowden, Hutchinson and Ross, Inc., Strasburgh, Pa., 1974. See also Patricia Ward Biederman, "Mobile School Uses the City as a Classroom," *Summer Reporter*, vol. 8, 1972, pp. 1–2.

16

The School I'd Like to See

Most of the ideas presented in earlier chapters come together here to present a coherent view of Goodlad's educational vision. Though to some the picture may seem impossible to achieve, it will be, I hope, a call to action for many. [Editor]

What kind of school would I like to build? The first question I have to ask is: "What do I mean by school?" I hope I no longer mean a place where children spend from 9:00 to 3:00 in little boxes arranged side by side down an aisle, where they sit in rows all day and listen to a teacher expound or raise questions. For the future we have to think of school as a concept, not a place—not that physical plant, not those ten or twenty or thirty little boxes. We have to think of school as a concept of developing human potential for the sake of both the individual and society. It is a concept that leads to utilizing all possible resources—people or things, wherever they may be, in or out of school, at any time of day. It is a concept of guiding learning, not just from 9:00 to 3:00 but twenty-four hours a day.

What will be the prime goal of my school? If I had to sacrifice every single function or goal but one, my goal would be thinking.

SOURCE: John I. Goodlad, "The Child and His School in Transition," *National Elementary Principal*, vol. LII, no. 4, January 1973, pp. 28–34.

My school will be a thinking school. Humans are the time-binding, space-binding animal, so far as we know the only creature capable of linking themselves with all people, of all time, in all places. The basis of compassion, the basis of affect, is thought. When we treat another person unkindly, we are not thinking about his lot in life, his particular situation, his needs. Behind a great deal of our talk about affect and sensitivity is the realization that we have the ability to use our minds effectively and clearly in a whole range of situations involving our behavior toward others. Each individual must learn to deal in more rational, thinking ways with his fellow humans.

I want my school organized into phases—not grades—of three to four years each to permit family grouping. Perhaps this organization could be made to coincide with Erik Erikson's eight ages of man. One reason for multiage grouping is that every child should have the experience of being both the youngest and the oldest in a group. This is a very important developmental opportunity and one that we have ignored in our traditional graded schools. Into each phase of schooling would come 25 to 30 percent of the children each year, and 25 to 30 percent would move on to the next phase—not all at the same age, of course, but according to their development. My phases are organized around three to four-year groupings because it takes time to achieve any important function in life. It takes time to diagnose the individual's achievement, potentialities, problems, and to decide how we can help. In the usual September to June rat race, there simply is not time for this diagnosis.

Each of the phases in my school will be guided by a team, and not just a team of fully qualified teachers. There will be some fully qualified professionals, paid much more than any fully qualified professional today. And there will be paraprofessionals, aides, volunteers—maybe dentists, lawyers, artists, or folk singers—all part of the team, contributing bits and pieces of time. In the school I envision, everybody is a teacher—even the children.

Each of these phases of schooling will have its own unique function; that is, in addition to learning to think, which will be the prime focus of the entire school, some other major function will be stressed. For example, the early childhood phase (from three to six or four to seven) will be a period of self-transcendence. It will not be a time to learn to read or write (although most children will) but a time to transcend oneself, a time to come to grips with oneself as a person, to find out what kind of person one is. It will be a time to begin to move beyond the self—through fantasy, parallel play, and work with many different kinds of materials—to a true identification with other people. The literacy of learning to transcend the myopia of selfhood in developing an identification with other human beings I place much higher than the literacy of learning to read and write, and if that literacy is not attained early in life, I am not sure that it ever will be.

We will assure that during this period of three or four years every single child will develop a unique talent—some aspect of music, art, craft, sport, academic subject. It does not really matter what this talent may be, but the child must learn the rigor that goes with it. The process of nurturing a talent and developing the discipline that goes with it transfers to many other things. Show me a child who feels potent because he can do one thing well, and I will show you a child who is becoming equipped to deal with life's complexities.

How will the children in my school be grouped? Rather than trying to achieve homogeneity—we have spent most of this century trying to get homogeneous groups, and we have failed hopelessly— why don't we just turn the coin over and strive for heterogeneity? Let's put the children together because they are different. One kind of difference is expressed through multiage grouping, another through a wide religious, ethnic, and racial mix. One way to help achieve this mix is a transportation system that will get the young- sters to the educational opportunities that are right for them, in each case grouping children who will indeed learn to work together and understand each other. The future depends heavily on that under- standing.

How will the children be taught in my school? Mostly by peers. One of the problems in individualizing instruction is that we have not faced the possibility of how much youngsters can learn from one another. The older children can teach the younger ones, and the younger ones can teach the older ones. The younger child will see what subsequent periods of development are like by living daily with older children.

In my school children will be taught also by adult models, people who not only talk about a skill but also demonstrate it. There will be someone who can play the guitar or the flute, someone who can take a piece of clay and shape it, someone who can form sentences into an exciting story. These adults will not necessarily be certified; many of them will be volunteers, and they can be brought into the team as part of the instructional process. In many instances the children will go to planned educational laboratories where the teacher will be hard at work on a particular creative task and the children will join in and become part of it, learning from the adult model. Sports have proved to be a great model for young people in this country and a great means of upward mobility. But why only sports? Why not bring models of every phase of endeavor into the school? Why not take the children to the models so that they can see what they may want to do?

In my school the child will exercise a great deal of self-selection, but he will be accountable for his choices. If he encounters difficulties, he will be able to get help to keep him moving ahead rather than becoming discouraged and failing. And there will be much talk: "What would happen if we did so and so?" Reading and writing will emerge out of much of this talk, and ideas will be taught through every possible medium. We will think and dance about it, dance and think about it. We will think and construct, construct and think. Think and write, write and think. Look at it and think about it. We will use every conceivable way to develop a single concept, a single skill, a single idea.

How will the children in my school be classified and evaluated? Of course, there will be no grades or report cards, no external rewards of that kind. But there will be performance evaluation. Someone who can both perform and understand will sit down with the child and help him see his strengths and weaknesses and what areas need improvement. The standard will be the child's progress in relation to a criterion. If you are going to learn to play baseball, these are the skills one learns. If you are going to learn to play an instrument, these are the things one learns. How are you doing in relation to the performance criteria?

There also will be comprehensive assessments. Pupil, teacher, parents, and specialists will sit down together periodically to talk about how the child is doing in his total array of educational experiences. And there will be a different kind of educational voucher plan. At various times in a child's development, he will have a number of vouchers, not worth a dime in money but worth educational time—a voucher for art or a voucher for math with which the child "buys" the richest possible education from all the resources encompassed by the concept of school.

But my school is really only a transition to the school of 2001, a twenty-four-hour-a-day school that will reach out to all children and youth with all the educational resources and facilities available. In the school of 2001 there will be many roles for teachers, from counseling, to coordinating a team, to preparing materials, to preparing a televised lesson.

While we are spending the next few decades developing the school we would like to have, some other changes are going to be taking place in society. One of the most profound of these has to do with communication, especially public television. The time is only a short way off when we will be able to plug into forty or fifty channels of public television. Through a television network we can begin to talk about the strengths and the values in which we believe as a people. We can show the actions and institutions that support our beliefs and study the limitations of those that deny them.

Another change that will come about is a rejuvenation of the inner city so that the school no longer carries the burden currently carried by busing or other devices. The cities will be rejuvenated from the core outward. I see no alternative but elimination of the inner city as we know it now and the replacement of the slum with a cultural/educational center surrounding a central green space. The city will progress outward from there.

In the center there will be museums, art galleries, theatres, archives, libraries, and studios. There will be housing for managerial services, for artists, and for visitors—speakers, travelers, and entertainers who can enjoy the cultural life of the city while they are there. The inner cultural center will be common land, accessible to all for educational purposes and managed not by a superintendent of schools but by a commissioner of cultural affairs who is responsible for the whole. And into it will come the children, the middle-aged, and the elderly.

Private vehicles will be prohibited in the center of the city; moving belts and battery operated minibuses will move us about without cars. And there will be a free, nonpolluting rapid transit system, radiating like the spokes of a wheel into the outlying areas.

Residential communities and green belts will be scattered along the spokes of the transit wheel, and distributed along these transportation networks will be education facilities of all kinds. Children will move back and forth between home and educational and cultural facilities on fast-moving trains. In effect, everyone will be bused.

The educational districts will be cone or wedge shaped, starting from the center and fanning outward, so that the entire gamut of housing will be represented in the tax structure of each district. We will no longer have the problem of the cost of education increasing across the board while financial support for education increases unevenly because of different tax bases in different communities. Each district will contain a full array of educational services, provided by schools in the old sense and by industry, civil agencies, and the like, financed from both state and local resources. The cultural hub will be financed by the federal government.

The sophisticated transportation system will permit children from one school to "buy" with their vouchers the kind of educational enrichment, the kind of educational opportunities that simply cannot be provided through our present plans. Multisensory terminals will be available in various centers, certainly in every school. The terminal will do more than educate a child; it will print out all the cultural activities available at any time, any day, any week. Similar smaller devices will be used in the home, and once again the home will become a learning center.

And clearly, there will be a different kind of teaching staff; a core of highly prepared professionals and a whole array of others, some who do not plan on a teaching career, others moving up to fully professional status.

While we are putting together the ingredients of our new school, we cannot assume that the rest of the world will stay as it is today. Everything I have described here has been designed somewhere already, and some cities already are moving in these directions, though much too slowly.

The school we know today will evolve so as to be scarcely, if at all, recognizable. But this is not a process of deschooling. It is a process of making education out of our entire lives, of making a oneness out of all the modes of communication that impinge upon us. The process will require personal realization and fulfillment of an individual identity, the development of individuals who are able to participate in all the richness that could lie ahead. It also will require self-transcendence and the adaptation of selfhood to those practices of disciplined cooperation demanded by the fact that no person, no nation, is or can be an island unto itself.

We must transcend self and develop a mankind perspective, or there may be no twenty-first century man.

The power to create the kinds of schools we want in this country lies partially in the hands of those reading this book. How would you answer the questions I have raised? And what kind of school would you like to create?

Index